REVOLUTIONARY SUICIDE

HUEY P. NEWTON was born in Monroe, Louisiana, on February 17, 1942, to Walter and Armelia Newton. He is the cofounder of the revolutionary Marxist-Leninist organization the Black Panther Party, and was the Party's ranking leader and chief ideologue and strategist. In 1966, Newton enrolled in Merritt College in Oakland, where he became a member of the Phi Beta Sigma fraternity, led the effort to establish the first black history course, and met Bobby Seale. In October 1966, Newton and Seale founded what was then known as the Black Panther Party for Self-Defense. The Party urged members to challenge the status quo with armed patrols of the impoverished streets of black Oakland, and to form coalitions with organizations representing other oppressed groups. Internationally, Newton directed the Party to form coalitions with the Vietnamese, Chinese, and Cubans, as with, among others, African national liberation organizations like FRELIMO in Mozambique, ZANU in Zimbabwe, and the ANC in South Africa.

Within one year of the Party's founding, in October 1967, Newton was wounded and arrested by Oakland police and charged with the murder of a police officer, spawning the worldwide protest that came to be known as the "Free Huey Movement." Convicted of manslaughter, Newton was released in July 1970 for a new trial. He would be tried on this charge several times thereafter but never convicted. Upon his release, he led the Party's more than forty chapters to build up its community service programs, called Survival Programs, operating under the slogan "Survival Pending Revolution."

From the outset, the Party was a target for elimination by the U.S. government under the FBI's infamous COINTELPRO (counterintelligence) program, which openly stated that its agenda was to disrupt or destroy the Party. By 1981 the Party had been driven into its demise. In the aftermath, Newton earned a Ph.D. from the University of California, Santa Cruz, publishing his dissertation *War Against the Panthers: A Study of Repression in the United States*. Prior to that, Newton had authored *Revolutionary Suicide* and *To Die for the People*, in addition to numerous other treatises and articles, and was the coauthor with psychoanalyst Erik Erikson of the book *In Search of Common Ground*. On August 22, 1989, Newton was tragically shot to death on the blighted streets of West Oakland, leaving behind his widow, Fredrika Newton.

FREDRIKA NEWTON was raised in Berkeley, California, by her mother, Arlene Slaughter. She attended Wesleyan University, where she earned her B.A. Prior to that, in 1969, as a young teenager, Mrs. Newton joined the Black Panther Party, and in 1970 she met Huey P. Newton. In 1984, after the demise of the Party, they married. In the wake of Huey P. Newton's death in 1989, Fredrika Newton, along with former Black Panther leader David Hilliard, established the Dr. Huey P. Newton Foundation, a nonprofit educational corporation. She continues to serve as the foundation's president, and oversees its archive, materials publications, and other activities, including a number of community-based programs.

HUEY P. NEWTON

WITH THE ASSISTANCE OF

J. HERMAN BLAKE

Revolutionary Suicide

Introduction by FREDRIKA NEWTON

PENGUIN BOOKS

PENGUIN BOOKS

Published by the Penguin Group
Penguin Group (USA) Inc., 375 Hudson Street,
New York, New York 10014, U.S.A.
Penguin Group (Canada), 90 Eglinton Avenue East, Suite 700,
Toronto, Ontario, Canada M4P 2Y3 (a division of Pearson Penguin Canada Inc.)
Penguin Books Ltd, 80 Strand, London WC2R 0RL, England
Penguin Ireland, 25 St Stephen's Green, Dublin 2,
Ireland (a division of Penguin Books Ltd)
Penguin Group (Australia), 250 Camberwell Road,
Camberwell, Victoria 3124, Australia (a division of Pearson Australia Group Pty Ltd)
Penguin Books India Pvt Ltd, 11 Community Centre,
Panchsheel Park, New Delhi – 110 017, India
Penguin Group (NZ), 67 Apollo Drive, Rosedale, North Shore 0632,
New Zealand (a division of Pearson New Zealand Ltd)
Penguin Books (South Africa) (Pty) Ltd, 24 Sturdee Avenue,
Rosebank, Johannesburg 2196, South Africa

Penguin Books Ltd, Registered Offices:
80 Strand, London WC2R 0RL, England

First published in the United States of America by Harcourt Brace Jovanovich 1973
This edition with an introduction by Fredrika Newton published in Penguin Books 2009

3   5   7   9   10   8   6   4   2

Copyright © Dr. Huey P. Newton Foundation, 1973
Introduction copyright © Fredrika Newton, 2009
All rights reserved

LIBRARY OF CONGRESS CATALOGING-IN-PUBLICATION DATA
Newton, Huey P.
Revolutionary suicide / Huey P. Newton, with J. Herman Blake ; introduction by Fredrika Newton.
p.   cm. — (Penguin classics deluxe edition)
Originally published: New York : Harcourt Brace Jovanovich, 1973.
ISBN 978-0-14-310532-9
1. Newton, Huey P.   2. Black Panther Party—Biography.   3. Black power—United States.
4. African Americans—Biography.   I. Blake, J. Herman.   II. Title.
E185.97.N48A3 2009
322.4'2092—dc22
[B]   2009003017

Printed in the United States of America
Set in Sabon

*For my mother and father, who have given me strength
and made me unafraid of death and therefore unafraid of life*

Contents

Introduction

It has been twenty years since my late husband, Huey P. Newton, was shot and killed on the same streets of Oakland, California, that had witnessed his dramatic ascent as leader of the Black Panther Party two decades earlier. From 1966 when the Party was founded to its demise around 1980, Huey stood at the vanguard of the Black Liberation Movement. For most people then and now this legendary role is best personified in a photograph taken at the behest of Eldridge Cleaver, who sought to make a militant public statement about the Party and its leader. In the picture, Huey is seated in a tall wicker chair and looking defiantly at the camera, a rifle held in his right hand and a spear in his left. Eldridge's intended message was a symbolic bridging of the spear and the gun, or, put another way, the transference of the cultural nationalism of the past to a revolutionary culture in the future. This volatile image resonated deeply in an era marked by scores of riots and rebellions in black communities across the country. Later, when the photograph appeared on the cover of *Revolutionary Suicide,* the image of Huey as the intrepid African American freedom fighter was further cemented in the public's consciousness. As with all controversial figures, however, there were complicated and unseen dimensions beneath the famous public persona, which his autobiography makes abundantly clear.

When *Revolutionary Suicide* was first published in 1973, readers were offered a rare glimpse into the private life of the Party's founder. Not that people hadn't been reading and hearing all about Huey for years. He started making local headlines when he and Bobby Seale launched the Black Panther Party in

Oakland. Their armed self-defense patrols of the police caused an immediate stir in the press; so much so that a conservative state assemblyman introduced legislation the following year that proposed outlawing the Party's constitutional right to bear arms. One can imagine the alarm felt in Sacramento when a caravan of Black Panthers with rifles appeared on the steps of the State Capitol to protest the "Panther Bill." As with the police patrols, this demonstration was performed in full accordance with the law. Huey was a dedicated student of the California penal code and made certain the Party's actions were legal. People today often don't realize that walking down the street with a rifle was within the laws of the time. White racist militia groups like the Minutemen and the John Birch Society, for example, had in fact been driving through our communities with guns displayed for some time. Although these groups were better armed than the Black Panthers, the ruling establishment did not perceive whites with guns to be a threat to their interests and no attempt was made to curtail their activities. Once the Panther Bill was finally passed in the spring of 1967, Huey brought an end to the open display of firearms. Nevertheless, guns would continue to be closely associated with him— whether he chose them to be or not.

This association reached new heights that fall when Huey was charged with shooting and killing an Oakland police officer. He had been stopped in his car early one morning while looking for parking. Most local officers knew Huey by sight, making police harassment a routine procedure for him. Without asking for identification, the officer identified Huey by name, going so far as to ridicule him as the "great, *great* Huey P. Newton." He then ordered Huey from the car and proceeded to knock him to the ground with an unexpected blow to the face. Shots were fired and the officer dropped over dead. Huey maintained that he was innocent, insisting that an unknown gunman had fired the shots. To the city fathers this was an open-and-shut case of murder; the most famous black American revolutionary since Malcolm X had acted out his rage against the police. For the black masses and the white New Left, however, the charge became a cause célèbre. The movement to "Free Huey" coalesced overnight with hundreds of supporters taking to the streets to protest his innocence. Meanwhile, journalists from around the United States and abroad descended on Oakland to report on the sensational trial, providing the Black Panthers for the first time with not only a national but also an international stage. Millions of people who had been fed the establishment's slander against the Party since its inception were now given the opportunity to meet its well-spoken leader and listen to its platform laid out by him. This exposure led to a rapid period of growth for the Black Panthers over the next two years—so much so that when Huey was acquitted and released from prison in 1971, he barely recognized the Party or its members. What once had been a local phenomenon of a dozen comrades now counted more than forty chapters throughout the United States as well as those in Australia, Polynesia, England, India, Israel, and Algeria, where our International Section was headquartered.

Huey left prison a major celebrity, which was an identity he did not want or welcome. He understood that leaders of social protest movements had frequently been turned into celebrities by the media and the effectiveness of these individuals to lead was destroyed in the process. Besides, genuine social change didn't come from celebrities, Huey argued, but from the people themselves. He never lost sight of the fact that only the masses had the ability to transform society, and the Party's slogan "all power to the people" was a potent testament to this belief. Still, he couldn't fully escape the trappings of his iconic status. In spite of his resistance, Huey personified the Black Liberation Movement at a time when African Americans were in desperate need of leadership. The civil rights movement had wound down with some of its most prominent figureheads murdered and the movement splintered. The Black Panthers stepped into this historical gulf, and their rise marked a transition from civil rights agitation per se to a revolutionary cause demanding nothing less than a comprehensive restructuring of American life—everything from its institutions and laws to its basic economic system. What's more, the Party now had the numbers and influence to make demands of their country.

Needless to say the U.S. government was well aware of this turn of events, and the counterintelligence efforts that for years had been aimed at monitoring and creating friction among African American radicals intensified. Huey's celebrity served to further this scrutiny. The FBI, in its own words, sought to "expose, disrupt, misdirect, discredit, or otherwise neutralize the activities of the Black nationalists." Never mind that Huey hadn't been a Black Nationalist since college, nor was the Party a Black Nationalist group; FBI director J. Edgar Hoover was determined to prevent the rise of a black "messiah" by any means necessary. The full extent of the government's surveillance of the Party—to the extent that it can ever be known in full—was not revealed until the 1980s, long after *Revolutionary Suicide* was published. Huey therefore does not devote substantial attention to these activities. For a comprehensive discussion of the government's role in spying on and ultimately assisting in the destruction of the Party, readers should consult his final book, *War Against the Panthers: A Study of Repression in America*.

As for his first book, *Revolutionary Suicide* was published at the peak of Huey's fame. Yet for all the exposure he'd had in the media, the public still knew relatively little about his personal life, especially his childhood and his path to becoming a revolutionary. The courtroom prosecutors had strenuously sought to reduce him to a "cop killer," and the press frequently cooperated in these efforts with a decidedly conservative slant in their reporting. Huey's autobiography therefore would serve the function Malcolm X's autobiography had a decade before: the book would humanize the icon with highly personal and candid recollections of a troubled past along with accounts of the crucial birth of political consciousness that would redeem the author and allow him to make his mark on history. *Revolutionary Suicide* introduced readers to new and perhaps surprising elements of Huey's past, including such little-known facts as his being raised in a devoutly religious household by a minister father; growing up illiterate until he taught himself to read in order to prove that he was not stupid, as his teachers claimed; and that the Black Panther Party founders were not street hoodlums but college classmates who turned to a revolutionary platform of armed self-defense after traditional forms of non-violent protest proved ineffective and disappointing to them. But not everything Huey recalls is admirable, and he was not afraid to confess his participation in activities he later found shameful, like prostituting women and stealing from unlocked cars parked outside hospital emergency rooms. True to Huey's spirit, he took responsibility for his mistakes as well as his accomplishments.

Revolutionary Suicide was also written during a period of important transition in the Party. Most notably Eldridge Cleaver, the Minister of Information, "defected" from the Party in 1971. In spite of his influential leadership role, Eldridge and Huey had had uneasy relations from the start. The pair never agreed over what constituted serving the people. To Huey that meant meeting the needs of poor and working-class African Americans, while for Eldridge it was leading the masses in armed rebellion. Eldridge's "revolution now" rhetoric frightened and alienated black communities, who were more concerned about jobs, housing, and a decent education for their children. After his departure the Black Panthers sought to reconnect to the people by launching an ambitious series of free services called "survival programs." Through donations and volunteer support, the Party provided groceries, medical care, and legal counsel, among other essential services, to tens of thousands of African Americans nationwide. The photographs taken at these public gatherings speak to the excitement of those events. On the other hand, this was also a period of great sadness. A handful of the most respected Black Panther Party leaders were murdered in succession by government agents: Alprentice "Bunchy" Carter, Fred Hampton, John Huggins, George Jackson, and Bobby Hutton, to whom Huey dedicates *Revolutionary Suicide*. Their contributions were enormous, and I can assure you that the loss of any one of these beloved comrades was felt far more profoundly than the loss of Eldridge or that of the small band of former members who followed him in this so-called split.

It's fitting that Huey dedicated this book to Bobby Hutton, the first member to join the Party after Huey and Bobby Seale, and the first Black Panther to be killed: Bobby was just seventeen years old when, after a stand-off, police gunned down the unarmed youth as he surrendered. Huey was devastated by the murder but also clear-eyed enough to understand that a revolutionary is "a doomed man." In other words, every revolutionary fighter by definition struggles against the power imbalance of the establishment, and the cost of this struggle is often paid with one's own life. Huey coined the term "revolutionary suicide" to describe this phenomenon. Not to be confused with what he calls "reactionary suicide"—wherein a person kills himself in despair and helplessness—revolutionary suicide is infused with the possibility that one's death will further the revolutionary cause. As Huey explains, "[I]t is better to oppose the forces that would drive me to self-murder than to endure them. Although I risk the likelihood of death, there is at least the possibility, if not the probability, of changing intolerable conditions. . . . Revolutionary suicide does not mean that I and my comrades have a death wish; it means just the opposite. We have such a strong desire to live with hope and human dignity that existence without them is impossible. When reactionary forces crush us, we move against these forces, even at the risk of death." Bobby Hutton died a revolutionary suicide, and the publication of this new edition of Huey's autobiography will help ensure that readers for generations will remember him along with all the other fallen Black Panther Party comrades whose lives must not be forgotten.

After *Revolutionary Suicide* came out, the Party experienced a period of turmoil that lasted until its demise about seven years later. Intensified divisions within the organization were exacerbated by the infiltration of secret government agents who sought to bring down the Party from within. False reports of comrades turning traitors led Huey to distrust and expel key Party members, including Black Panther Chairman and co-founder Bobby Seale; his successor, Chairman Elaine Brown; and Chief of Staff and childhood friend David Hilliard. Compounding Huey's government-inspired paranoia was his drug addiction, and his actions under the influence confounded and worried his allies. Huey's personal troubles climaxed in 1974, when he was falsely charged with murdering an Oakland woman. Fearful that he would not receive a fair trial under California's Republican Governor, Huey fled to Cuba, where he lived in exile until a Democrat was elected governor in 1976. As with his previous murder trial, Huey was once again acquitted. Unlike the previous trial, however, he did not return to the streets a hero. Huey's behavior became more erratic as his addiction worsened, and the Party slowly began to unravel. I found it endlessly heartbreaking to witness Huey's downward spiral. I urged him toward recovery repeatedly, but in spite of his valiant attempts he never wanted a life without drugs more than he wanted the drug. His demons were too strong. In many respects Huey came to feel that he had lived too long, that he had somehow outlived himself.

I first met him at a brunch hosted by my mother in our Berkeley home in 1971. I was nineteen years old and, unlike my mother who was the Party's real-estate agent, not at all politically active. In fact I was intimidated by the Black Panthers and used to cross the street to avoid walking past their Berkeley office. Although Huey had never met me, I was certain he'd read between the lines and write me off as a bourgeois college girl. Instead I was surprised to discover him kind and patient with someone so obviously out of her element. He'd been acquitted of murdering the police officer and released from prison the previous summer, so I found the nerve to ask him how it felt to be incarcerated. He explained with great sensitivity that loneliness was the overwhelming emotion. I was so touched by his openness that my fears of Huey dropped away in that moment. No longer the world-famous figure in the wicker chair, here was a man with fears and emotions just like anyone. I immediately felt compassion and protectiveness toward him. He phoned later that day to invite me to his home, and we began our affair that night. I quickly joined the Party, first teaching in one of its schools, then as a cadre member working on the Black Panther newspaper at the Party's central headquarters. Our relationship along with my tenure with the Panthers was short-lived, however. Huey fled to Cuba, and I decided to return to college and complete my studies. When I returned home following graduation in 1976, I ran into Huey at a Santana concert and we resumed an on-again, off-again relationship that culminated in our marriage in 1984.

Although I'd known of or been involved with Huey for years, our decision to marry was sudden. He phoned me from out of the blue to propose, and one week later we were married in Reno. But the haste with which we wed largely characterized our relationship. There was an unspoken, ever prevailing sense between us that our life together was fleeting. Some of Huey's closest comrades in the Party had been gunned down, and the constant presence of an armed bodyguard in our lives was a daily reminder that Huey might meet the same fate. Of course we attempted to live our lives as if we were an ordinary family, flying kites with my son from a previous marriage and taking him on picnics and to the pumpkin patch for Halloween. But there was no denying the reality that Huey was and always would be a threat to the establishment. The government retaliated in a variety of ways: the IRS put a lien against our assets, our home was raided and ransacked by the police twice, and Huey was charged with and later acquitted of the illegal possession of a gun. In the process we lost our home and became homeless, living with friends and relatives wherever possible. Throughout this ordeal we nevertheless struggled to maintain some semblance of a happy family life.

Much has been written about Huey's final years and the demise of the Party. I would encourage anyone interested in these details to read David Hilliard's *This Side of Glory* and *Huey: Spirit of the Panther*. These books provide a candid insider's account of Huey's tragic freefall by a lifelong comrade who saved his own life by becoming a member of Alcoholics Anonymous. As it happens, much has also been written about these events by self-proclaimed "authorities": primarily journalists and professors who in order to call attention to their work stoop to portraying Huey and the Party in exclusively outlandish terms. J. Edgar Hoover himself could not perform a more thorough assassination of character, and I'm left to wonder what function these politically motivated attacks serve other than to advance the careers of these authors. As president of the Dr. Huey P. Newton Foundation, the nonprofit organization I helped establish to remember Huey and the Party, I welcome responsible historical reassessments and hope that this new edition of *Revolutionary Suicide* assists in that purpose.

Although this book was published more than twenty-five years ago, it remains the definitive account of Huey's life and Black Panther history. He never got around to writing a sequel, which would have included, among other highlights, the Ph.D. he earned from the University of Santa Cruz (selections from his academic writings along with a comprehensive collection of seminal essays written during his Black Panther tenure can be found in *The Huey P. Newton Reader*). Sadly, Huey did not live to see the publication of the *Reader* or the addition of *Revolutionary Suicide* into the distinguished Penguin Classics Library. He was murdered in 1989 by a drug dealer who claimed he killed the former Party leader in order to "get respect and become a shot caller" for the gang he belonged to. Still, Huey would have been thrilled to see this new edition of his autobiography. He understood that whether he lived or died, the crucial point was that his work would live on—that the people would carry on the fight in his absence. As Huey tells us, "I will fight until I die, however that may come. But whether I'm around or not to see it happen, I know that the transformation of society inevitably will manifest the true meaning of 'all power to the people.'" Although this transformation has yet to be realized these many years later, *Revolutionary Suicide* reminds us that one intrepid person can help promote the process that brings about revolutionary change.

FREDRIKA NEWTON
2009

Acknowledgments

For their generous support through good times and bad, which enabled me to complete this book, I am indebted to my brother Melvin Newton, my secretary Gwen V. Fountaine, my good friends and comrades Donald Freed, Bert Schneider, and David Horowitz, and my editors, Edwin Barber and Ethel Cunningham.

There are many others who have given generously of their time and efforts to make this book possible. Many friends of Herman Blake accompanied him on trips to the California Men's Colony in San Luis Obispo during the early phases of the book. Their help with driving during those arduous days made it possible for us to devote all our energies to the book. I am grateful to each one of them, even though it is not possible to list them by name.

I also wish to acknowledge the contributions of Diane Martin and Sabra Slaughter for doing some of the early research; Kathy Harris, Delois Burbie, Barbara Lee, Linda Cohee, Katherine Hall, and Joanne Sterricker for typing transcripts and manuscript. Careful proofreading of the book at various stages was done by Donna Healey, Mrs. Bessie Blake, and daughters Audrey, Lylace, and Vanessa. Juanita Jackson gave continuous support and encouragement, as well as some of the best gumbo I have ever tasted. Finally, Alex Haley provided valuable advice and encouragement in the early phases of this work. Each one has made an important contribution to this book.

A TRIBUTE TO LI'L BOBBY

Li'l Bobby was the beginning—the very first member of the Black Panther Party. He gave not only his finances; he gave himself. He placed himself in the service of his people and asked nothing in return, not even a needle or a piece of thread. He asked neither security nor high office, but he demanded those things that are the birthright of all men: dignity and freedom. He demanded this for himself and for his people.

Like a bright ray of light moving across the sky, Li'l Bobby came into our lives and showed us the beauty of our people. He was a living example of an infinite love for his people and for freedom. Now he has moved on, and the example he gave will serve as a beacon that lights our way and leads us on in the struggle for life, dignity, and freedom.

We salute Li'l Bobby and his family for what they have given us. He was the beginning of the Party. Let us make sure that his thinking, his desires for his people become a way of life.

Yours forever,

HUEY P. NEWTON
Minister of Defense
Black Panther Party
April 1968

REVOLUTIONARY SUICIDE

By having no family,
I inherited the family of humanity.
By having no possessions,
I have possessed all.
By rejecting the love of one,
I received the love of all.
By surrendering my life to the revolution,
I found eternal life.
Revolutionary Suicide.

HUEY P. NEWTON

Revolutionary Suicide

A MANIFESTO

Let a new earth rise. Let another world be born. Let a bloody peace be written in the sky. Let a second generation full of courage issue forth, let a people loving freedom come to growth, let a beauty full of healing and a strength of final clenching be the pulsing in our spirits and our blood. Let the martial songs be written, let the dirges disappear. Let a race of men now rise and take control!

MARGARET WALKER, "For My People"

Revolutionary Suicide: The Way of Liberation

For twenty-two months in the California Men's Colony at San Luis Obispo, after my first trial for the death of Patrolman John Frey, I was almost continually in solitary confinement. There, in a four-by-six cell, except for books and papers relating to my case, I was allowed no reading material. Despite the rigid enforcement of this rule, inmates sometimes slipped magazines under my door when the guards were not looking. One that reached me was the May, 1970, issue of *Ebony* magazine. It contained an article written by Lacy Banko summarizing the work of Dr. Herbert Hendin, who had done a comparative study on suicide among Black people in the major American cities. Dr. Hendin found that the suicide rate among Black men between the ages of nineteen and thirty-five had doubled in the past ten to fifteen years, surpassing the rate for whites in the same age range. The article had—and still has—a profound effect on me. I have thought long and hard about its implications.

The *Ebony* article brought to mind Durkheim's classic study *Suicide,* a book I had read earlier while studying sociology at Oakland City College. To Durkheim all types of suicide are related to social conditions. He maintains that the primary cause of suicide is not individual temperament but forces in the social environment. In other words, suicide is caused primarily by external factors, not internal ones. As I thought about the conditions of Black people and about Dr. Hendin's study, I began to develop Durkheim's analysis and apply it to the Black experience in the United States. This eventually led to the concept of "revolutionary suicide."

To understand revolutionary suicide it is first necessary to have an idea of reactionary suicide, for the two are very different. Dr. Hendin was describing reactionary suicide: the reaction of a man who takes his own life in response to social conditions that overwhelm him and condemn him to helplessness. The young Black men in his study had been deprived of human dignity, crushed by oppressive forces, and denied their right to live as proud and free human beings.

A section in Dostoevsky's *Crime and Punishment* provides a good analogy. One of the characters, Marmeladov, a very poor man, argues that poverty is not a vice. In poverty, he says, a man can attain the innate nobility of soul that is not possible in beggary; for while society may drive the poor man out with a stick, the beggar will be swept out with a broom. Why? Because the beggar is totally demeaned, his dignity lost. Finally, bereft of self-respect, immobilized by fear and despair, he sinks into self-murder. This is reactionary suicide.

Connected to reactionary suicide, although even more painful and degrading, is a spiritual death that has been the experience of millions of Black people in the United States. This death is found everywhere today in the Black community. Its victims have ceased to fight the forms of oppression that drink their blood. The common attitude has long been: What's the use? If a man rises up against a power as great as the United States, he will not survive. Believing this, many Blacks have been driven to a death of the spirit rather than of the flesh, lapsing into lives of quiet desperation. Yet all the while, in the heart of every

Black, there is the hope that life will somehow change in the future.

I do not think that life will change for the better without an assault on the Establishment,* which goes on exploiting the wretched of the earth. This belief lies at the heart of the concept of revolutionary suicide. Thus it is better to oppose the forces that would drive me to self-murder than to endure them. Although I risk the likelihood of death, there is at least the possibility, if not the probability, of changing intolerable conditions. This possibility is important, because much in human existence is based upon hope without any real understanding of the odds. Indeed, we are all—Black and white alike—ill in the same way, mortally ill. But before we die, how shall we live? I say with hope and dignity; and if premature death is the result, that death has a meaning reactionary suicide can never have. It is the price of self-respect.

Revolutionary suicide does not mean that I and my comrades have a death wish; it means just the opposite. We have such a strong desire to live with hope and human dignity that existence without them is impossible. When reactionary forces crush us, we must move against these forces, even at the risk of death. We will have to be driven out with a stick.

Che Guevara said that to a revolutionary death is the reality and victory the dream. Because the revolutionary lives so dangerously, his survival is a miracle. Bakunin, who spoke for the most militant wing of the First International, made a similar statement in his *Revolutionary Catechism*. To him, the first lesson a revolutionary must learn is that he is a doomed man. Unless he understands this, he does not grasp the essential meaning of his life.

When Fidel Castro and his small band were in Mexico preparing for the Cuban Revolution, many of the comrades had little understanding of Bakunin's rule. A few hours before they set sail, Fidel went from man to man asking who should be notified in case of death. Only then did the deadly seriousness of

*The power structure, based on the economic infrastructure, propped up and reinforced by the media and all the secondary educational and cultural institutions.

the revolution hit home. Their struggle was no longer romantic. The scene had been exciting and animated; but when the
simple, overwhelming question of death arose, everyone fell
silent.

Many so-called revolutionaries in this country, Black and
white, are not prepared to accept this reality. The Black Panthers
are not suicidal; neither do we romanticize the consequences of
revolution in our lifetime. Other so-called revolutionaries cling
to an illusion that they might have their revolution and die of
old age. That cannot be.

I do not expect to live through our revolution, and most serious comrades probably share my realism. Therefore, the expression "revolution in our lifetime" means something different to
me than it does to other people who use it. I think the revolution
will grow in my lifetime, but I do not expect to enjoy its fruits.
That would be a contradiction. The reality will be grimmer.

I have no doubt that the revolution will triumph. The people
of the world will prevail, seize power, seize the means of
production, wipe out racism, capitalism, reactionary inter-
communalism—reactionary suicide. The people will win a new
world. Yet when I think of individuals in the revolution, I cannot predict their survival. Revolutionaries must accept this fact,
especially the Black revolutionaries in America, whose lives are
in constant danger from the evils of a colonial society. Considering how we must live, it is not hard to accept the concept of
revolutionary suicide. In this we are different from white radicals. They are not faced with genocide.

The greater, more immediate problem is the survival of the
entire world. If the world does not change, all its people will be
threatened by the greed, exploitation, and violence of the power
structure in the American empire. The handwriting is on the
wall. The United States is jeopardizing its own existence and
the existence of all humanity. If Americans knew the disasters
that lay ahead, they would transform this society tomorrow for
their own preservation. The Black Panther Party is in the vanguard of the revolution that seeks to relieve this country of its
crushing burden of guilt. We are determined to establish true
equality and the means of creative work.

Some see our struggle as a symbol of the trend toward suicide among Blacks. Scholars and academics, in particular, have been quick to make this accusation. They fail to perceive differences. Jumping off a bridge is not the same as moving to wipe out the overwhelming force of an oppressive army. When scholars call our actions suicidal, they should be logically consistent and describe all historical revolutionary movements in the same way. Thus the American colonists, the French of the late eighteenth century, the Russians of 1917, the Jews of Warsaw, the Cubans, the NLF, the North Vietnamese—any people who struggle against a brutal and powerful force—are suicidal. Also, if the Black Panthers symbolize the suicidal trend among Blacks, then the whole Third World is suicidal, because the Third World fully intends to resist and overcome the ruling class of the United States. If scholars wish to carry their analysis further, they must come to terms with that four-fifths of the world which is bent on wiping out the power of the empire. In those terms the Third World would be transformed from suicidal to homicidal, although homicide is the unlawful taking of life, and the Third World is involved only in defense. Is the coin then turned? Is the government of the United States suicidal? I think so.

With this redefinition, the term "revolutionary suicide" is not as simplistic as it might seem initially. In coining the phrase, I took two knowns and combined them to make an unknown, a neoteric phrase in which the word "revolutionary" transforms the word "suicide" into an idea that has different dimensions and meanings, applicable to a new and complex situation.

My prison experience is a good example of revolutionary suicide in action, for prison is a microcosm of the outside world. From the beginning of my sentence I defied the authorities by refusing to cooperate; as a result, I was confined to "lock-up," a solitary cell. As the months passed and I remained steadfast, they came to regard my behavior as suicidal. I was told that I would crack and break under the strain. I did not break, nor did I retreat from my position. I grew strong.

If I had submitted to their exploitation and done their will, it would have killed my spirit and condemned me to a living death. To cooperate in prison meant reactionary suicide to me.

While solitary confinement can be physically and mentally destructive, my actions were taken with an understanding of the
risk. I had to suffer through a certain situation; by doing so, my
resistance told them that I rejected all they stood for. Even
though my struggle might have harmed my health, even killed
me, I looked upon it as a way of raising the consciousness of
the other inmates, as a contribution to the ongoing revolution.
Only resistance can destroy the pressures that cause reactionary suicide.

The concept of revolutionary suicide is not defeatist or fatal-
istic. On the contrary, it conveys an awareness of reality in
combination with the possibility of hope—reality because the
revolutionary must always be prepared to face death, and hope
because it symbolizes a resolute determination to bring about
change. Above all, it demands that the revolutionary see his
death and his life as one piece. Chairman Mao says that death
comes to all of us, but it varies in its significance: to die for the
reactionary is lighter than a feather; to die for the revolution is
heavier than Mount Tai.

PART ONE

During those long years in the Oakland public schools, I did not have one teacher who taught me anything relevant to my own life or experience.

I

Many migrants like us were driven and pursued, in the manner
of characters in a Greek play, down the paths of defeat; but
luck must have been with us, for we somehow survived....
                    RICHARD WRIGHT, Preface to *Black Metropolis*

Starting Out

Life does not always begin at birth. My life was forged in the
lives of my parents before I was born, and even earlier in the
history of all Black people. It is all of a piece.

I have little knowledge of my grandparents or those who
went before. Racism destroyed our family history. My father's
father was a white rapist.

Both of my parents were born in the Deep South, my father
in Alabama, my mother in Louisiana. In the mid-thirties, their
families migrated to Arkansas, where my parents met and married. They were very young, in their mid-teens—some said too
young to marry—but my father, Walter Newton, is a very good
talker, and when he decided he wanted Armelia Johnson for his
bride, she found him hard to resist. He has always known how
to be charming; even today I love to see his eyes light up with
that special glow when he gets ready to work his magic. They
were married in Parkdale, Arkansas, and lived there for seven
years before moving to Louisiana to take advantage of better
employment prospects.

My father was not typical of southern Black men in the thir-
ties and forties. Because of his strong belief in the family, my
mother never worked at an outside job, despite seven children
and considerable economic hardship. Walter Newton is rightly

proud of his role as family protector. To this day, my mother
has never left her home to earn money.

My father believed in work. He worked constantly, in a variety of jobs, usually holding several at one time to provide for
us. During those years in Louisiana he worked in a gravel pit,
a carbon plant, in sugar-cane mills, and sawmills. He eventually
became a railroad brakeman for the Union Saw Mill Company.
This pattern did not change when we moved to Oakland. As a
youngster, I well remember my father leaving one job in the afternoon, coming home for a while, then going to the other. In
spite of this, he always found time for his family. It was always
high-quality time when he was home.

In addition, my father was a minister. He pastored the Bethel
Baptist Church in Monroe, Louisiana, and later assisted in several of the Oakland churches. His preaching was powerful, if a
little unusual. The Reverend Newton planned his sermons in
advance and announced the topic a week early, but he never
seemed able to preach the sermon he had chosen. Eventually, he
adopted the practice of stepping right into the pulpit and letting
the spirit move him to deliver whatever message was appropriate. As a child I swelled up proud to see him up there leading
church services, moving the congregation with his messages.
All of us shared the dignity and respect he commanded. Walter
Newton is not a particularly tall man, but when he stepped into
that pulpit, he was the biggest man in the world to me.

My mother likes to say that she married young and finished
growing up with her children, and this is true. Only seventeen
years separate her from Lee Edward, the oldest child in the
family. When my older brothers and sisters were growing up in
Louisiana, Mother was one of their best playmates. She played
ball, jackrocks, and hide-and-go-seek. Sometimes my father
joined in, rolling tires and shooting marbles and keeping the
rules straight. This sense of family fun and participation has
helped to keep us close. My parents are more than the word
usually implies; they are also our friends and companions.

My mother's sense of humor affected all of us. It was pervasive, an attitude toward life that led us to insight, affection, humor, and understanding with each other. She helped us to see

the light side in even the most difficult situations. This lightness and balance have carried me through some difficult days. Often, when others expect to find me depressed by difficult circumstances, and especially by the extreme condition of prison, they see that I look at things in another way. Not that I am happy with the suffering; I simply refuse to be defeated by it.

I was born in Monroe, Louisiana, on February 17, 1942, the last of seven children. Like other Black people of that time and place, I was born at home. They tell me that my mother was quite sick while she carried me, but Mother says only that I was a fine and pretty baby. My brothers and sisters must have agreed because they often teased me when I was young, telling me I was too pretty to be a boy, that I should have been a girl. This baby-faced appearance dogged me for a long time, and it was one of the reasons I fought so often in school. I looked younger than I actually was, and soft, which encouraged schoolmates to test me. I had to show them. When I went to jail in 1968, I still had the baby face. Until then I rarely shaved.

My parents named me after Huey Pierce Long, the former Governor of Louisiana, assassinated seven years before I came along. Even though he could not vote, my father had a keen interest in politics and followed the campaigns carefully. Governor Long had impressed him by his ability to talk one philosophy while carrying out programs that moved Louisiana in exactly the opposite direction. My father says he was up front, "looking right into his mouth," when Huey P. Long made a speech about how Black men in the hospitals, "out of their minds and half naked," had to be cared for by white nurses. This was, of course, unacceptable to southern whites, and therefore a number of Black nurses were recruited to work in Louisiana hospitals. This was a major breakthrough in employment opportunities for Black professionals. Huey Long used this tactic to bring other beneficial programs to Blacks: free books in the schools, free commodities for the poor, public road- and bridge-construction projects that gave Blacks employment. While most whites were blinded by Long's outwardly racist philosophy, many Blacks found their lives significantly improved. My father believed that

Huey P. Long had been a great man, and he wanted to name a son after him.

In our family there was a tradition that each older child had particular responsibility for a younger one, looking after him at play, feeding him, taking him to school. This was called "giving" the newborn to an older brother or sister. The older child had the privilege of first taking the new baby outdoors. I was "given" to my brother Walter, Jr. A few days after I was born he took me outside, hauled me up onto the back of a horse, and circled the house while the rest of the family followed. This ritual is undoubtedly a surviving "Africanism" from the age-old matriarchal-communal tradition. I do not remember that or anything else of our life in Louisiana. Everything I know about that time I learned from the family. In 1945, we followed my father to Oakland when he came West to look for work in the wartime industries. I was three years old.

The great exodus of poor people out of the South during World War II sprang from the hope for a better life in the big cities of the North and West. In search of freedom, they left behind centuries of southern cruelty and repression. The futility of that search is now history. The Black communities of Bedford-Stuyvesant, Newark, Brownsville, Watts, Detroit, and many others stand as testament that racism is as oppressive in the North as in the South.

Oakland is no different. The Chamber of Commerce boasts about Oakland's busy seaport, its museum, professional baseball and football teams, and the beautiful sports coliseum. The politicians speak of an efficient city government and the well-administered poverty program. The poor know better, and they will tell you a different story.

Oakland has one of the highest unemployment rates in the country, and for the Black population it is even higher. This was not always the case. After World War I, there was a hectic period of industrial expansion, and again during World War II, when government recruiters went into the South and encourages thousands of Blacks to come to Oakland to work in the shipyards and wartime industries. They came—and stayed after the war, although there were few jobs and they were no longer wanted. Because of the lack of employment opportunities in Oakland today, the number of families on welfare is the second highest in California, even though the city is the fifth largest in the state. The police department has a long history of brutality and hatred of Blacks. Twenty-five years ago official crime became so bad that the California state legislature investigated the Oakland force and found corruption so pervasive that the police chief was forced to resign and one policeman was tried and sentenced to jail. The Oakland "system" has not changed since then. Police brutality continues and corruption persists. Not everyone in Oakland will admit this, particularly the power structure and the privileged white middle class. But, then, none of them actually lives in Oakland.

Oakland spreads from the northern border of Berkeley, dominated by the University of California with its liberal to radical life style, south to the Port of Oakland and Jack London Square, a complex of mediocre motels, novelty shops, and restaurants with second-rate food. To the west, eight miles across the bay, spanned by the San Francisco-Oakland Bay Bridge, is a metropolitan San Francisco; to the east is a lily-white bedroom city called San Leandro.

There are two very distinct geographic Oaklands, the "flatlands" and the hills. In the hills, and the rich area known as Piedmont, the upper-middle and upper class—the bosses of Oakland—live, among them former United States Senator William Knowland, the owner of the ultraconservative Oakland *Tribune,* Oakland's only newspaper. His neighbors include the mayor, the district attorney, and other wealthy white folks, who live in big houses surrounded by green trees and high fences.

The other Oakland—the flatlands—consists of substandard-income families that make up about 50 per cent of the population of nearly 450,000. They live in either rundown, crowded West Oakland or dilapidated East Oakland, hemmed in block after block, in ancient, decaying structures, now cut up into multiple dwellings. Here the majority of Blacks, Chicanos, and Chinese people struggle to survive. The landscape of East and West Oakland is depressing; it resembles a crumbling ghost town, but a ghost town with inhabitants, among them more than 200,000 Blacks, nearly half the city's population. There is a dreary, grey monotony about Oakland's flatlands, broken only by a few large and impressive buildings in the downtown section, among them (significantly) the Alameda County Court House (which includes a jail) and the Oakland police head-quarters building, a ten-story streamlined fortress for which no expense was spared in its construction. Oakland *is* a ghost town in the sense that many American cities are. Its white middle class has fled to the hills, and their indifference to the plight of the city's poor is everywhere evident.

Like countless other Black families in the forties and fifties, we fell victim to this indifference and corruption when we moved to Oakland. It was as difficult then as it is now to find decent homes for large families, and we moved around quite a bit in my early years in search of a house that would suit our needs. The first house I remember was on the corner of Fifth and Brush streets in a rundown section of Oakland. It was a two-bedroom basement apartment, and much too small to hold all of us comfortably. The floor was either dirt or cement, I cannot remember exactly; it did not seem to be the kind of floor that "regular" people had in their homes. My parents slept in one bedroom and my sisters, brothers, and I in the other. Later, when we moved to a two-room apartment at Castro and Eighteenth streets, there were fewer of us. Myrtle and Leola had married, and Walter had been drafted into the Army. On Castro Street, I slept in the kitchen. That memory returns often. Whenever I think of people crowded into a small living space, I always see a child sleeping in the kitchen and feeling upset about it; everybody knows that the kitchen is not supposed to be a bedroom. That is all we had, however. I still burn with the sense of unfairness I felt every night as I crawled into the cot near the icebox.

We were very poor, but I had no idea what that meant. They were happy times for me. Even though we were discriminated against and segregated into a poor community with substandard living conditions, I never felt deprived when I was small. I had a close, strong family and many playmates, including my brother Melvin, who was four years older than me; nothing else was needed. We just lived and played, enjoying everything to the fullest, particularly the glorious California weather, which is kind to the poor.

Unlike many others I knew, we never went hungry, although our food was the food of the poor. Cush was standard fare. Cush is made out of day-old corn bread mixed with other leftovers, such as gravy and onions, spiced very heavily and fried in a skillet. Sometimes we ate cush twice a day, because that was all we had. It was one of my favorite dishes, and I looked forward to it. Now I see that cush was not very nutritious and was downright bad for you if you ate it often; it is just bread—corn bread.

Life grew even sweeter when I was big enough—six or seven years old—to play outdoors with Melvin. Our games were filled with the joy and exuberance of innocent children, but even they reflected our economic circumstances. We rarely had store-bought toys. We improvised with the materials at hand. Rats were close at hand, and we hated rats because they infested our homes; one had almost bitten off my nephew's toe. Partly because of the hate and partly for the game of it, we caught rats and put them in a large can and poured coal oil into the can, then lighted it. The whole can would go up in flames while we watched the rats scoot around inside, trying to escape the fire, their tails sticking straight up like smoking grey toothpicks. Usually they died from the smoke before the flames consumed them.

We also despised cats, because we were told that cats killed little babies by sucking the breath out of them. We tested the tale about cats always landing on their feet. When we caught cats and took them to the top of the stairs and hurled them down, they would land on their feet—most of the time.

Dirt was a favorite toy. We used it to play at being builders. The roof of the house was our building site. We would climb up there and pull up the dirt-filled buckets behind us with rope, hand over hand, to the top of the house, and then dump the dirt down on the other side. There were no swimming pools near us, but when we got a little older we began to wander down to the bay with the other kids and go swimming off the pier in the dirty water. Dirt, rats, cats: these are the games and toys of the poor, as old and cruel as economic reality.

My parents insisted that we learn to get along with each other. When there was a dispute, my father never took sides. He was always an impartial judge, listening to both parties and getting to the bottom of things before making a decision. He was a fair and careful judge about all disputes, and later, when we had trouble in school, my father went every time to the teacher or the principal to learn what had happened. When we were right, he stood up for us, but he never tolerated wrongdoing.

We were not taught to fight by our parents, although my father insisted that we stand our ground when attacked. He told us never to start a fight, but once in it to stand fast until the end.

This was how we grew up—in a close family with a proud, strong, protective father and a loving, joyful mother. No wonder we came to feel that all our needs—from religion to friendship to entertainment—were met within the family circle. There was no felt need for outside friends; we were such good friends with each other.*

In this way the days of our childhood slipped past. We shared the dreams of other American children. In our innocence we planned to be doctors, lawyers, pilots, boxers, and builders. How could we know then that we were not going anywhere? Nothing in our experience had shown us yet that the American dream was not for us. We, too, had great expectations. And then we went to school.

---

*Even today my entire family lives in the San Francisco Bay area, close to our parents. Any disagreements among us are still taken to our parents for arbitration. When one member of the family entertains, most of the guests are other family members. Outsiders are rarely included in such gatherings.

2

The clash of cultures in the classroom is essentially a class war, a socio-economic and racial warfare being waged on the battleground of our schools, with middle-class aspiring teachers provided with a powerful arsenal of half-truths, prejudices, and rationalizations, arrayed against hopelessly outclassed working-class youngsters. This is an uneven balance, particularly since, like most battles, it comes under the guise of righteousness.

KENNETH CLARK, *Dark Ghetto*

Losing

Because we moved around a lot when I was growing up, I attended almost every grammar and junior high school in the city of Oakland and had wide experience with the kind of education Oakland offers its poor people.

At the time, I did not understand the size or seriousness of the school system's assault on Black people. I knew only that I constantly felt uncomfortable and ashamed of being Black. This feeling followed me everywhere, without letup. It was a result of the implicit understanding in the system that whites were "smart" and Blacks were "stupid." Anything presented as "good" was always white, even the stories teachers gave us to read in the early grades. *Little Black Sambo, Little Red Riding Hood,* and *Snow White and the Seven Dwarfs* told us what we were.

I remember my reaction to *Little Black Sambo.* Sambo was, first of all, a coward. When confronted by the tigers, he gave up the presents from his father without a struggle—first the umbrella, then the beautiful crimson, felt-lined shoes, everything, until he had nothing left. And afterward, Sambo wanted only to eat pancakes. He was totally unlike the courageous white knight who rescued Sleeping Beauty. The knight was our symbol of purity, while Sambo stood for humiliation and gluttony. Time after time, we heard the story of Little Black Sambo. We did not want to laugh, but finally we did, to hide our shame, accepting Sambo as a symbol of what Blackness was all about.

As I suffered through Sambo and the Black Tar Baby story in *Brer Rabbit* in the early grades, a great weight began to settle on me. It was the weight of ignorance and inferiority imposed by the system. I found myself wanting to identify with the white heroes in the primers and in the movies I saw, and in time I cringed at the mention of Black. This created a gulf of hostility between the teachers and me, a lot of it repressed, but still there, like the strange mixture of hate and admiration we Blacks felt toward whites generally.

We simply did not feel capable of learning what the white kids could learn. From the beginning, everyone—including us—judged smart Blacks in terms of how they compared with whites, whether they could read or do arithmetic as well as the white kids. Whites were the standard of comparison in all things, even personal attractiveness. Bushy African hair was bad; straight hair was good; light was better than dark. Our image of ourselves was defined for us by textbooks and teachers. We not only accepted ourselves as inferior; we accepted the inferiority as inevitable and inescapable.

By the third or fourth grade, when we began to do simple mathematics, I had learned to maneuver my way around the teachers. It was a simple matter to put pressure on the white kids to do my arithmetic and spelling assignments. The feeling that we could not learn this material was a general attitude among Black children in every public school I ever attended. Predictably, this sense of despair and futility led us into rebellious attitudes. Rebellion was the only way we knew to cope with the suffocating, repressive atmosphere that undermined our confidence.

Of all the unpleasant things that happened to me in elementary school, I remember two in particular. I had disciplinary problems from the beginning, plenty of them, but often they were not my fault. For instance, in the fifth grade at Lafayette Elementary School (I was eleven) I had an old white lady for a teacher. I have forgotten her name, but not her stern, disapproving face. Thinking once that I was not paying attention, she called me to the front of the room and pointedly told the class that I was misbehaving because I was stupid. She would show them just how stupid I was. Handing me a piece of chalk, she told me to write the word "business" on the blackboard. Now, I knew how to spell the word; I had written it many times before, and I knew I was not stupid. However, when I walked to the board and tried to write, I froze, unable to form even the first letter. Inside I knew she was wrong, but how could I prove it to her? I resolved the situation by walking out of the room without a word.

This happened to me time and again, growing worse with repetition. When I was asked to read aloud in class or spell a word, my mind went black and cold. Everybody thought I was dumb, I suppose, but I knew it was the lock inside my head. I had lost the key. Even now, when I read to a group of people, I am likely to stumble.

The other incident also happened at Lafayette. The school had a rule that you could dump the sand out of your shoes after recess, just before you sat down. One day I was sitting on the floor, dumping the sand from each shoe. I had quite a bit of sand, and dumping it took time, too much for the teacher, who came up behind me and slapped me across the ear with a book, accusing me of deliberately delaying the class. Without thinking, I threw the shoe at her. She headed for the door at a good clip and made it through just in front of my other one.

Of course I was sent to the principal, but I received a great deal of respect from the other children for that act; they backed me for resisting unjust authority. In our working- and lower-class community we valued the person who successfully bucked authority. Group prestige and acceptance were won through defiance and physical strength, and both of them led to racial and class conflict between the authorities and the students.

The only teacher with whom I never had trouble was Mrs. McLaren, who taught me sixth grade at Santa Fe Elementary School. She had also taught my brother Melvin several years earlier, and since he was a model student, Mrs. McLaren expected a lot of me. I felt, in turn, a responsibility to live up to Melvin's reputation. Mrs. McLaren never raised her voice. She was a tranquil person, at ease and peaceful, no matter what was happening. Nobody wanted to start a fight with her. She was the exception to the rule.

By then, however—even in the sixth grade—I had such a tough reputation in school there was no *need* to start fights with the instructors. They were waiting for me and often provoked trouble, thinking I would pull something anyway, even when I was going along with the program.

I went through a series of conversions and lapses. Each suspension brought a strong lecture from my parents, followed by a week or so of heavy soul searching and a decision to co-operate with the teachers and give my best effort. Mother and Father argued that the instructors had something I needed and that I could not expect to go into the class as an equal. I would return to school full of firm and good intentions; then, invariably, the instructors would provoke me, thinking I was there to continue the struggle. Sharp words, a fight, expulsion, and another semester down the drain. It often seemed that they simply wanted me out of the classroom.

During those long years in the Oakland public schools, I did not have one teacher who taught me anything relevant to my own life or experience. Not one instructor even awoke in me a desire to learn more or question or explore the worlds of literature, science, and history. All they did was try to rob me of the sense of my own uniqueness and worth, and in the process they nearly killed my urge to inquire.

3

Growing

Throughout my life all real learning has taken place outside school. I was educated by my family, my friends, and the street. Later, I learned to love books and I read a lot, but that had nothing to do with school. Long before, I was getting educated in unorthodox ways.

One of the first things any Black child must learn is how to fight well. My father taught us to play fair, and when I started school, I tried to follow his advice. His principles of justice did not prevail everywhere, however. Some games ended in fights, and at the time I did not like to fight. My first year of school, kindergarten, was tough. I developed a habit of feigning sickness so that I would not have to face some of the local bullies. When the sick excuse failed, I "lost" my clothes and took a long time to dress. My mother saw through these excuses, and when she learned why I was avoiding school, she had my brother Walter, Jr. (Sonny Man), take me. Eventually, I began to stand my ground when others wanted to fight, and the trouble stopped, because Walter taught me how to fight and fight well.

All of us at that time, around 1950, thought Joe Louis was a saint; he and Jersey Joe, Kid Gavilan, and Sugar Ray were our pantheon. I wanted to be a fighter, too, which seemed possible because I had the fastest hands on the block. Other boys assumed nicknames—Winchester, Duke, Count—but Huey was name enough for me. I beat up all the kids on the block, not to be a bully, but to protect my dignity and to survive. Many of these fights stemmed from my middle initial. The way they used to say it, Huey P. Newton became Huey "Pee" Newton, and when a rhyme came at me like "Huey P. goes wee, wee, wee," I started throwing hands until it stopped. It got so bad for a while that I wanted to simplify life by dropping the middle initial, but my mother would not let me.

On the streets we had our little boxing matches. We wrapped towels around our hands for gloves and went five rounds while the winos stood around betting nickels and urging us on. They loved the blood, and we gave it to them. We would be in there swinging, bleeding, and crying—really slugging each other. The winos called me "prize fighter." Because I thought a prize fighter received a prize when the battle was over, they sometimes bought me a ten-cent box of Cracker Jack, and I took the prize out of that—the only prize I ever knew. We could hardly eat the Cracker Jack our mouths were so bloody. I never thought of fighting in terms of money.

Later, I trained with Walter at the Campbell Street Center and had a few bouts at the Boys Club. My oldest brother, Lee Edward, had already left home by the time I began to grow up, but he often came by the house to see the family. He taught me a lot about fighting, too. Lee Edward had a big reputation in the community as a man who never lost a fight; any boy of that time would have been as proud as I was to have a brother known to defend himself in all circumstances. Even though he lived "on the block" and saw some rough times, he never stepped aside for anybody. More than anyone else, he taught me to persist in the face of bad odds, always to look an adversary straight in the eye, and to keep moving forward. Even if you were hurled back three or four times, he said, eventually you would prevail. He was right.

Fighting has always been a big part of my life, as it is in the lives of most poor people. Some find this hard to understand. I was too young to realize that we were really trying to affirm our masculinity and dignity, and using force in reaction to the social pressures exerted against us. For a proud and dignified people fighting was one way to resist dehumanization. You learn a lot about yourself when you fight.

Fighting is not just a means of survival; it is also a part of friendship. All the time I was growing up, fighting was an essential aspect of camaraderie on the block. It took many forms: you fought your friends, or with your friends you fought an outside aggressor. If the neighborhood boasted a good fighter, word got around. That was how I first heard of David Hilliard, now a member of the Black Panther Party. David was no bully; he never looked for trouble, but when attacked, he had great courage. He had won renown in our neighborhood as a brave adversary who never backed down. That is one of the qualities I have always admired most in him, and the bond that was formed then, eighteen years ago, has held.

I was thirteen years old and just out of elementary school the summer I met David. My family had just moved to North Oakland, where we were at last able to buy a house. David, who had come to Oakland from Alabama not long before, lived down the block from us. We soon became close friends. My parents were very fond of him, and eventually he became like one of the family. We have often wondered whether we may not be kin to one another, since my paternal grandmother was a Hilliard from Alabama.

David was the constant companion of my early teens, sharing with me all the usual activities of adolescents. Sometimes we spent whole days together, listening to records and rapping. Singing groups were very popular then. I could not sing, and still cannot, but David sings well, and he and some of his friends— Joe, Snake, and Early—had a group that practiced every day one summer, hoping to hit it big. Another interest we shared was girls. Some very pretty girls lived next door to David, which made the Hilliard house a popular gathering place.

The fall after we met, both of us started junior high school at Woodrow Wilson. Among our friends there was a pretty girl named Patricia Parks, whom I had known for some time. The truth is, I think I terrified her. When I came on the scene, she would disappear. But when I introduced her to David, they hit if off right away, and later were married. Patricia is not terrified of me any more.

David was part of my education. He still is. The steadfastness of our relationship cannot be put into words. Although we have been friends for eighteen years and have been in many fights together against others, we have never quarreled or had a serious disagreement. We are different in many ways, but we respect each other's differences.

Another good friend in junior high was James Crawford. He was a couple of years older than me, but behind in school. James and I used to fight each other a lot, falling out one day and coming together again the next. He could beat up most boys in the school, including me, and whenever we fought, I would lose, but I always came back with some kind of equalizer—a baseball bat or a short piece of rubber hose with a metal insert. He had to give me respect, because even when he beat me, I would come back to him. James and I stopped fighting each other in 1953, when we formed a gang called the Brotherhood, which eventually numbered thirty or forty regular members, all of them seventh- and eighth-grade Black boys. Another gang of ninth-graders were our allies. Crawford and I were the leaders. The Brotherhood (one of the few gangs in North Oakland) was a direct response to white aggression at school. At that time, Blacks were a small minority at Woodrow Wilson, and all the Blacks there viewed each other as blood relations. We called ourselves brothers or cousins and banded together to fight racist students, faculty, and administration. Back then, white staff people and students routinely called Blacks "niggers," and tension was high.

Black students stuck together on the playground, too. We had outgrown hide-and-go-seek, king-of-the-mountain, and ring-a-levio, but our games still reflected our poverty. We spent hours rolling dice and pitching and flipping pennies. Since none of us ever had enough money to buy lunch or even milk, we gambled for these things. We also played what some kids called "capping" or the "dozens." This is a game of verbal assault, in which kids insult each other by talking about sexual liberties they have taken with the opponent's mother. It is a very common game in the Black community. My contests would often end in fights because I was no good at putting people in the dozens. In the mornings David and I often talked about how to "cap" Crawford. But when we got to school, Crawford usually outcapped us. A typical dozens from Crawford might go like this: "Motorcycle, motorcycle, going so fast; your mother's got a pussy like a bulldog's ass." They were just words, and we were good friends in spite of it, really "tight partners."

My years in junior high were a repeat of elementary school. The teachers attempted to embarrass and humiliate me, and I countered defiantly to protect my dignity. While I did not see it at the time, fierce pride was at the bottom of my resistance. These struggles had the same result: I continued to be suspended from school. My parents, the principal, and the counselor lectured me for hours, and I would again make up my mind to knuckle under and go along. As soon as I hit the classroom, however, there would be another provocation, another visit with the principal, and back on the streets again. It was a kind of revolving door: each week things were the same.

The one class I took in junior high school that was not painful was a cooking class taught by the only Black teacher I had in all my years at school—Miss Cook. There was a reason for my taking this class. Most of the white kids had money to buy their lunch, but my family could not afford that. Since I was too proud to bring my lunch in a brown paper bag, and be ridiculed by my friends, I took cooking—and eating. It was either that, or gambling, or stealing from the white kids.

Crawford and I were in the same class, and we were always getting kicked out together. I remember clearly one of the teachers at Woodrow Wilson—Mrs. Gross. We had her three periods every day in what was called the dumb class; only Blacks were in it. We spent each day gambling and poking each other and generally raising hell. Crawford would shoot a rubber band at me, or I would slap him on the head, and then we would fight, and Mrs. Gross would kick us out. Sometimes she sent us to the principal's office, and sometimes she told us to stand in the hall. When you were booted from one of her classes, you were out for the whole day. It was a form of liberation—liberation from the dumb class.

Her class was particularly bad during reading sessions. We hated being there to begin with, because we were not interested in what Mrs. Gross was saying. When the reading-aloud sessions came, we were frantic to get out. We could not read, and we did not want the rest of the class to know it. The funny thing is that most of the others could not read, either. Still, you did not want them to know it.

At that time, and earlier, I associated reading with being an adult: when I became an adult, I would automatically be able to read, too. It was a skill that people naturally acquired in the process of maturation. Anyhow, why should I want to read when all they gave us were irrelevant and racist stories? Refusing to learn became a matter of defiance, a way of preserving whatever dignity I could hold onto in an oppressive system.

Therefore, when it was time for Crawford or me to read, we made a conscious effort to get kicked out of class, and were usually successful. Then we would sneak out of the school and steal a bottle of wine or ride our bikes to one of our partners' houses and while away the day playing cards. Later, after school let out in the afternoon, we often sneaked into the movies with other kids or went to David's house and listened to records and danced with the girls.

This is pretty much the way things went all during junior high. On the surface, my record was dismal. Yet those years were not significantly different from the adolescence of many Blacks. We went to school and got kicked out. We drifted into patterns of petty delinquency. We were not necessarily criminally inclined, but we were angry. We did not feel that stealing a bottle of wine or "cracking" parking meters was wrong. We were getting back at the people who made us feel small and insignificant at a time when we needed to feel important and hopeful. We struck out at those who trampled our dreams.

James Crawford had his dreams. He dreamed of becoming a great singer. There were days when Melvin and I sat listening for hours while James sang in his beautiful tenor voice. He was also a good cook and dreamed of opening a restaurant. James Crawford was talented, but the educational system and his psychological scars held him back. He never learned to read. To this day he cannot read. His fear of failure was reinforced rather than helped by those charged with his education, and his dreams slipped away. As he became more fearful and frustrated with each passing year, James was finally expelled from school as an "undesirable." Gradually, he sank into alcoholism and has been in and out of state mental hospitals since our school years. His face is scarred where the police beat him.

That is the story of my friend James Crawford; another dream blown to hell.

4

The glory of my boyhood years was my father . . . there was no hint of servility in my father's make-up. Just as in youth he had refused to remain a slave, so in all the years of his manhood he disdained to be an Uncle Tom. From him we learned, and never doubted it, that the Negro was in every way equal to the white man. And we fiercely resolved to prove it.

PAUL ROBESON, *Here I Stand*

Changing

Hope has always been a scarce commodity in the Black community. Claude Brown, who grew up in Harlem, has written of this in *Manchild in the Promised Land*. When he returned to Harlem after an absence of four years, he had a hard time finding many of the friends he had grown up with. "It seemed as though most of the cats that we'd come up with just hadn't made it," he says. "Almost everybody was dead or in jail." Many young Black men in our generation can say the same thing. Drugs, oppression, and despair take their toll. Survival is not a simple matter or something to be taken for granted.

When I look back on my early years, I see how lucky I was. Strong and positive influences in my life helped me escape the hopelessness that afflicts so many of my contemporaries. First, there was my father, who gave me a strong sense of pride and self-respect. Second, my brother Melvin awakened in me the desire to learn, and, third, because of him, I began to read. What I discovered in books led me to think, to question, to explore, and finally to redirect my life. Numerous other factors influenced me—my mother and the rest of my family, my experiences on the street, my friends, and even religion in a peculiar way. But these three—and most of all my father—helped me to develop and change.

When I say that my father was unusual, I mean that he had a dignity and pride seldom seen in southern Black men. Although many other Black men in the South had a similar strength, they never let it show around whites. To do so was to take your life in your hands. My father never kept his strength from anybody.

Traditionally, southern Black women have always had to be careful about how they bring up their sons. Through generations, Black mothers have tried to curb the natural masculine aggressiveness in their young male children, lest this quality bring swift reprisal, or even death, from the white community. My father was never subjected to this pressure, or, if he was, he chose to ignore it. He somehow managed to grow up with all his pride and dignity intact. As an adult he never let a white man humiliate him or any member of his family; he kept his wife at home, even though whites in Monroe, Louisiana, felt she should be working in their kitchens, and made that plain to him. He never yielded, always maintaining his stand as a strong protector, and he never hesitated to speak up to a white man. When we children were small, my father entertained us with stories of his encounters with whites. He has not been well for the past few years, but even now, as he tells these stories, the old strength surges through him again. None of us realized it then, but those old stories were more than simple entertainment; he was teaching us how to be men.

One time in Louisiana he got into an argument with a young white man for whom he was working. The disagreement had to do with some detail about the job, and the white man became angry when my father stood his ground. He told my father that when a colored man disputed his word, he whipped him. My father replied just as firmly that no man whipped him unless he was a better man, and he doubted that the white man qualified. This shocked the white man, and confused him, so that he backed down by calling my father crazy. The story spread quickly around town; my father became known as a "crazy man" because he would not give in to the harassment of whites. Strangely, this "crazy" reputation meant that whites were less likely to bother him. That is often the way of the oppressor. He cannot understand the simple fact that people want to be free. So, when a man resists oppression, they pass it off by calling him "crazy" or "insane." My father was called "crazy" for his refusal to let a white man call him "nigger" or to play the Uncle Tom or allow whites to bother his family. "Crazy" to them, he was a hero to us.

He even stood up to white men when they were armed. One evening, as he rode home from work with some other Black men, for some reason they stopped their car in front of a white man's house and began to talk and laugh. They did not see the white woman on the front porch, but pretty soon a white man came out of the house with an ax and yelled at them for laughing at his sister. The driver panicked and drove off. When they reached the corner, my father made him stop. He climbed out and walked back alone. The white man was advancing down the road with the ax. My father asked him why he had come out with that ax and what he had in mind to do with it. The white man passed off the incident lightly by saying something about "you know how these southern women can be," and how he had to make a show to satisfy his sister. My father realized that in the etiquette of southern race relations this was an apology. He accepted it, but not before he made it clear to the white man that he would not be threatened.

He never hesitated to make his view known to anyone who would listen. Once, when he felt cheated by a white man, he let all the town know what had happened. The man heard the stories and came to our house to see my father. This white man carried a gun in the glove compartment of his car. My father knew that, but he nevertheless went outside unarmed to talk. He maneuvered around to the right side of the car, and sat on the running board with the white man in front of him so that he could not get to the gun. Then he told the white man what he thought of him and said, "If you hit me a lick, the other folks will have to hunt me down because you'll be lying here in the road dead." The white man drove off, and my father heard no more about it.

Another time some whites invited him to go hunting. To this day I do not know why they asked him. They all took their shotguns. Knowing my father was a preacher, they tried to goad him into a discussion about the Bible and the origin of man. Adam and Eve were surely white, they said, so where did Black people come from? Their convenient interpretation was that Blacks must have sprung from the union of Adam and a gorilla. My father countered by saying that Adam must have been a low-life white man to have had sex with a gorilla. At this, the situation grew fairly tense, but nothing came of it.

His protection extended to every member of our family. At the age of fifteen, my oldest brother, Lee Edward, went to work with my father in a sugar-cane mill. The first step in the sugar-cane process was to feed stalks into a gasoline-powered grinder. The grinder never stopped, and it had to be kept full or it would burn out. This was Lee Edward's job. They had cut the engine down some in the hope that Lee Edward could run it, but he got tired his first day in the mill, and about eleven o'clock, after four hours on the job, he could not keep the machine full. It ran down and burned out. When the owner saw this, he began yelling at Lee Edward, but before he could say much, my father was right there. This white man was over six feet tall and weighed 200 pounds, but my father got right in the middle of it. He shut off the motor and told the owner it took a grownup to keep cane in the mill. My father took Lee Edward off the job after that. He wanted us to be good workers, just as he was, but he also wanted us to grow up proud.

I heard these stories and others like them over and over again until in a way his experiences became my own. Anyone who tried to bother us, Black or white, had to contend with my father. It made no difference that the South did not tolerate such behavior from Blacks. My father stood up to the white South until the day he left for California. He has never returned.

The fact that my father survived these encounters may go deeper than a simple white defense mechanism. His blood was, after all, half white, and that same blood flowed in the veins of other local people—in his father, his cousins, aunts, and uncles. While local whites were willing enough to shed the blood of Black people, it may be that they were afraid of being haunted by the murder of another "white." Statistics bear this out. The history of lynching in the South shows that Blacks of mixed blood had a much higher chance of surviving racial oppression than their all-Black brothers.

In any case, my father's pride meant that the threat of death was always there; yet it did not destroy his desire to be a man, to be free. Now I understand that because he was a man he was also free, and he was able to pass this freedom on to his children. No matter how much society tried to steal our self-esteem, we survived on what we got from him. It was the greatest possible gift. All else stems from that.

This strong sense of self-worth created a closeness among us and a sense of responsibility for each other. Since I was the youngest in the family, all the other children had a deep influence on me, but particularly my three brothers. Of the three, it was Melvin who opened up most decisively the possibilities for intellectual growth and a special kind of self-realization.

Melvin is only four years older than I am, and during childhood we were constant playmates. Melvin planned to become a doctor, and I dreamed of being a dentist so that we could open an office together in the community. Somewhere along the way these desires were lost, probably in school, where my scholarly ambitions died early. Although Melvin did not go to medical school, he was always a good student. Now he teaches sociology at Merritt College in Oakland.

I always admired Melvin's intellectual activities; it was he who helped me to overcome my reading difficulties. When he began college, I used to follow him around and listen to him discuss books and courses with his friends. I think this later influenced me to go to college, even though I had not learned anything in high school. Melvin also taught me poetry by playing recordings of poems or reading to me. He was studying literature in school, and I suppose teaching me poems was a way of learning them himself. We often discussed their meanings.

Sometimes Melvin explained the poems to me, but after a while I found that I could understand them alone, and I began to explain them to him.

I seem to remember poetry without effort, and by the time I entered high school, my memory held a lot of poetry I had heard read aloud. As Melvin studied for his literature class at Oakland City College, I learned Edgar Allan Poe's "The Bells" and "The Raven," "The Love Song of J. Alfred Prufrock" by T. S. Eliot, Shelley's "Ozymandias" and "Adonais." I also liked Shakespeare, particularly Macbeth's despairing speech that begins "Tomorrow, and tomorrow, and tomorrow / Creeps in this petty pace from day to day. . . ." Shakespeare was speaking of the human condition. He was also speaking to me, for my life sometimes crept aimlessly from day to day. I was often like the player fretting and strutting my brief hour upon the stage. Soon, like a brief candle, my life would go out. I was learning a lesson, however, that contradicted Macbeth's despair. While life will always be filled with sound and fury, it can be more than a tale signifying nothing.

"Adonais," too, had a special impact on me. The poem tells the story of a man whose friend dies or is killed. One of the best things in the poem is the sense that with the passing of years the poet's feelings alter and he begins to see things differently. He tells how he feels, how his attitude toward his friend changes as time goes on. This was an experience I began to have near the end of high school as my friends drifted into the service, or got married, or tried to become part of the very system that had humiliated us all the way through school. As time passed, I began to see the futility of the lives toward which they were headed. Marriage, family, and debt; in a sense, another kind of slavery.

"Ozymandias" impressed me because I felt there were different levels of meaning in it. It is a rich and complex poem:

> I met a traveller from an antique land
> Who said: Two vast and trunkless legs of stone
> Stand in the desert. Near them, on the sand,
> Half sunk, a shattered visage lies, whose frown,

And wrinkled lip, and sneer of cold command,
Tell that its sculptor well those passions read
Which yet survive, stamped on these lifeless things,
The hand that mocked them and the heart that fed:
And on the pedestal these words appear:
"My name is Ozymandias, king of kings:
Look on my works, ye Mighty, and despair!"
Nothing beside remains. Round the decay
Of that colossal wreck, boundless and bare
The lone and level sands stretch far away.

The poem could mean that a man's life is like the myth of Sisyphus. Each time you push the rock up the mountain, it rolls back down on you. Men build mighty works, and yet they are all destroyed. This king foolishly thought that his works would last forever, but not even works of stone survive. The king's great monument was destroyed, victim of the inevitable changes that come with time. On the other hand, it could be that the king was so wise that he wanted people to take their minds off their achievements and look with despair because they, too, would reach that edge of time, where everything around will be leveled.

Often it is impossible to understand at any specific period in your life just what is happening to you, since changes take place in imperceptible ways. This was true of my own adolescence. My admiration for Melvin led to a love of poetry and later to my interest in literature and philosophy. When my brother and I analyzed and interpreted poetry, we were dealing in concepts. Even though I could not read, I was becoming familiar with conceptual abstractions and the analysis of ideas and beginning to develop the questioning attitude that later allowed me to analyze my experiences. That led in turn to the desire to read, and the books I read eventually changed my life profoundly.

5

It's about a kid like you were who believed. He was born be-
lieving but as he grew, everything around him, beginning with
his parents and sisters and teachers, everybody seemed to say
that what he believed wasn't so. Sure, they said they believed
and they prayed and cried to God and Jesus Christ Almighty
but that was a few moments out of a couple of hours in church
each week. So somehow he became two personalities, one as
sincere as the other, and then three, because he could stand off
and watch the other two. The reason was that he suspected
maybe the people who didn't believe might be right, that there
was nothing to believe in. But if he accepted this and put down
the beautiful honest good things he'd lose out on all he could
have gained if he'd never lost his belief in believing.

CHARLES MINGUS, *Beneath the Underdog*

Choosing

During my adolescence, often without realizing it, I was making important choices. Some influences in our early years are so
clear that their effect cannot be denied. We also may uncon-
sciously reject other influences as we go along. It is hard to say
at any point how things will turn out. All the time I was going
to junior high school and getting into trouble, fighting on the
block, listening to poetry, and talking with Melvin, other strong
forces were at work. Often they were contradictory in nature
and pulled me in different directions. This caused confusion
and conflict later, until I learned to sort them out and understand what they meant.

One of the most long-lasting influences on my life was religion. Both my parents are deeply religious, and when Melvin and I were small, my father often read to us from the Bible. My favorite was the Samson story, followed closely by David and Goliath. I must have heard those stories a thousand times. Samson's strength was impressive, as well as his wisdom and his ability to solve the riddles put to him. Strength and wisdom—I still link the hero with my father in those terms. I liked David and Goliath because, despite Goliath's strength and power, David was able to use strategy and eventually gain the victory. Even then, the story of David seemed directed to me and to my people.

When we were growing up, we went to church every day, or so it seemed. Back then, the Antioch Baptist Church was only a little storefront, where the faithful gathered. I belonged to the Baptist Young People's Union, the Young Deacons, the junior choir, and I attended Sunday school and worship services weekly. My father was the associate pastor for a long time. He liked to preach the sermon about the prodigal son, and as he preached he really moved around in the pulpit, waving his arms and beating the stand. He terrified me with tales of fire and brimstone and how sinners and the unrepentant would end up in a lake of fire. He was a real "burner."

The whole family was involved in church one way or another, holding offices, singing in the choir, serving on the usher board or other committees. I was very active as a junior deacon, and every third Sunday the regular deacons gave us their chairs below the pulpit. We sat in their places and administered certain parts of the services—taking up the collection and leading the congregation in prayer, everything except delivering the sermon. I did it all. I even read the sick list and special messages, although I had difficulty with reading. None of the other junior deacons did any better, however; we were all pretty illiterate.

If we were weak in reading, however, other activities compensated. I loved to act in plays because I had acquired a certain eloquence reciting the poetry that Melvin taught me. It was easy for me to remember a part after I heard it once or twice. My activities in church led to music. My parents were so impressed with everything I was doing that they decided to have me study the piano, mainly as a good way for me to take a more active role in the religious services. I studied piano for seven years with some excellent music theorists and classical pianists.

Looking back, I see that my friends and I were all in the same boat—heading for hell on earth and trying to reach heaven in church. Nevertheless, taking part in church activities and leading the services gave us a feeling of importance unequaled anywhere else in our lives.

For years our pastor, Reverend Thomas, had a sign on the pulpit: PRAYER CHANGES THINGS. The congregation was encouraged to see prayer as the only way to salvation. If we had problems—sickness, accidents, financial difficulties—prayer was the answer. Everybody in the church prayed with you, sharing a common purpose that relieved tension and had a cathartic effect. No other institution in the community provided such an outlet. At the time the church was the only stable force in the Black community, and while some people do not think it was very effective, it did offer a kind of permanence and stability to our lives. The church was always there, providing solace and hope.

For me the church was a source of inspiration that offered a countermeasure against the fear and humiliation I experienced in school. Even though I did not want to spend my life there, I enjoyed a good sermon and shouting session. I even experienced sensations of holiness, of security, and of deliverance. They were strange feelings, hard to describe, but involving a tremendous emotional release. Though I never shouted, the emotion of others was contagious. One person stimulated another, and together we shared an ecstasy and believed our problems would be solved, although we never knew how. James Baldwin has described this religious experience very well in *The Fire Next Time*. He writes about the excitement and ecstasy that can fill a church during the service. "There is no music," he says, "like that music, no drama like that drama of the saints rejoicing, the sinners moaning, the tambourines racing, and all those voices coming together crying holy unto the Lord. . . . Their

pain and their joy were mine, and mine were theirs—they surrendered their pain and joy to me, I surrendered mine to them."
Once you experience this feeling, it never leaves you.

For a while I thought of becoming a minister, but I gave it up
when I studied philosophy in college. I began asking questions
about the concept of religion and the existence of God. In trying to find God and understand Him as a philosophical existen-
tial Being, I began to question not only the Christian definition
of God, but also the very foundation of my religion. I saw that
it was based on belief alone, the soundness of which was never
questioned.

Because I eventually found it necessary to question and examine every idea and every belief that touched my life, I reached
a kind of impasse with religion. Yet its impact on me continues
in different ways. To this day, for example, I rarely use profanity. People who have come to know me often ask why. I can
only say that profanity was never used in our home. If I had
been caught using it, my father would have punished me. My
mother and father always lived as Christians, and this extended
to the way they spoke.

When I think back on the meetings in that storefront, it
seems to me that religion made an impression in a more important, yet less direct, way. It has nothing to do with a personal
system of belief, but rather an awareness of what religious action can or ought to be. Something remarkable was taking
place during every prayer service. When people in the congregation prayed for each other, a feeling of community took over;
they were involved in each other's problems and trying to help
solve them. Even though it was entirely directed to God and
did not go beyond the meeting, it suggested how powerful and
moving it can be to have a shared sense of purpose. People
really related to each other. Here was a microcosm of what
ought to have been going on outside in the community. I had
the first glimmer of what it means to have a unified goal that
involves the whole community and calls forth the strengths of
the people to make things better. I am sure that is part of why I
was drawn to religion and why it offered so much to me then.

At the same time I was growing aware of a wholly different style of life that had nothing to do with religion. One of the reasons so many people found comfort and solace in church was that it provided—even though briefly—an escape from the burdens and troubles of everyday life. There was another way of life, however, that did not seem to find this relief necessary. From what I could see, this other life also had none of the worries and problems that beset ordinary working-class people.

In our community some people had achieved a special kind of status. They drove big cars, wore beautiful clothes, and owned many of the most desirable things life has to offer. Almost without trying, they seemed to have gotten the things for which the rest of the people were working so hard. Moreover, they were having fun in the process. They were not forced to compromise by imitating white boys and going on in school. They succeeded in spite of the humiliations of the school system. As a matter of fact, they often won success at the expense of the very people who caused our troubles. They opposed all authority and made no peace with the Establishment. In doing so, they became big men in the lower-class community.

This was the world of Walter, Jr., my second-oldest brother, who was always called "Sonny Man" in our family. When I was small, he often took care of me, and I looked up to him. By the time I was a teen-ager, Sonny Man was a hustler, with a reputation as a ladies' man. (To this day he has never married.) To be a hustler means to be a survivor. The brothers on the block respected him and called him a hipster, even in those days. When people asked me what I wanted to be when I grew up, I said I wanted to be like him. To me, Sonny Man was much freer than the rest of us. Compared with my father's struggle, the way Sonny Man lived offered much to my hungry eyes.

My father's constant preoccupation with bills is the most profound and persistent memory of my childhood. We were always in debt, always trying to catch up. From an early age "the bills" meant I could not have any of the extra things I wanted. I hated the word so much it made me cringe inside, just the way I felt listening to *Little Black Sambo* and the Tar Baby stories.

For me, no words on the street were as profane as "the bills." It killed me a little each time they were mentioned, because I could see the never-ending struggle and agony my father went through trying to cope with them. It is a situation familiar to most people in the Black community. In one of his letters to his father, George Jackson spoke for me: "How do you think I felt when I saw you come home each day a little more depressed than the day before? How do you think I felt when I looked in your face and saw the clouds forming, when I saw you look around and see your best efforts go for nothing—nothing." I know exactly what he meant.

My father always paid his bills on time. He might complain about them, particularly about the interest, but he paid. As I grew older, I would sometimes examine the bills he received, and I saw that in most cases the greater portion of the money was going to pay interest. If we bought something like a refrigerator, we wound up paying double the original cost. Sometimes the bills exceeded his whole paycheck.

My father never mailed his payments. Melvin and I took them to the stores because he wanted the receipts stamped. He felt that if he mailed the payments, they might make a mistake, not send the receipt, and charge him more. This had happened in the past. Every two weeks, or once a month, depending on when the payment was due, he would make out a list for us and arrange the money in separate envelopes, one for each store, with the receipts inside. Then, when we returned, he would carefully check the receipts. For years Melvin and I made the rounds of Oakland stores, paying bills for our father. I was still doing this when I was arrested in 1967.

When I became aware of the effect of the bills on my family, I wanted to be free of them. It was more than the bills that disturbed me, however. We were in an impoverished state, and I found it hard to understand how my father could work so hard yet have so little. He was a jack-of-all-trades—carpenter, brick mason, plumber—no job was beyond him. He worked at two and sometimes three jobs at once, and yet we never got ahead. After finishing one of his various jobs, he would hurry home and work around the house or in the garden, and then go off to another job. We could not understand how he did it—never a day to rest or relax—and never a complaint. I think the years of hard work are partially responsible for his poor health now. He was always a strong person and never sick until his later years.

When I was older and had a chance to see how people in better circumstances lived, I saw that our difficulty resulted from the large number of people in our family. For years all nine of us lived in three or four rooms, with little opportunity for privacy. Until I was eleven or twelve, I had to sleep with Melvin in the kitchen, and sometimes before that, in bed with my sisters. It never occurred to me that I could have a room of my own. Fortunately, there was a great deal of affection and humor among us all, but still it was hard. I see now that in those years the idea took root in my mind that we were suffering such hardship through our own fault. I equated the idea of the family with being trapped and plagued by bills. At an early age I made up my mind never to have bills when I grew up. I could not know then that this determination would extend eventually to the point of not being married or having a family of my own.

My fear of being hounded by debt led me down Sonny Man's road for a while. When I saw how much he was respected on the block, I began to spend most of my time there, at first in the little gangs we had in school, and at parties, but later in the pool hall and bars. For a long time I was attracted to this way of life, until I discovered it was not what it seemed. That came later.

Even though I was attempting to be like Sonny Man, I nonetheless admired Melvin and his educational achievements. Both avenues seemed to offer a way, but I could not know which road was best. I had seen Blacks take the education road and get nowhere. Many of them returned to the block, scorning their years in school, and cursing the white man for holding them back. Other Blacks had apparently made it on the block but ended up broken men, in prison or dead. There was no clear pattern to follow; it was hard to know what to do.

This dilemma faces almost all young Black men struggling to achieve a sense of identity in a society that denies them their basic rights. The Black teen-ager, in his most impressionable and vulnerable years, looks around and sees a contradiction between society's expressed values and reality—the way things actually are. The "Sonny Men" of the community who defy authority and "break the law" seem to enjoy the good life and have everything in the way of material possessions. On the other hand, people who work hard and struggle and suffer much are the victims of greed and indifference, losers. This insane reversal of values presses heavily on the Black community. The causes originate from outside and are imposed by a system that ruthlessly seeks its own rewards, no matter what the cost in wrecked human lives.

This can be profoundly disorienting to a teen-ager trying to understand and define himself. Like adolescents everywhere, he wants an image to model himself after, and he becomes confused because there is such disparity between what he is taught and what he sees. Most adolescents in Black communities expect no justice from school authorities or the police. The painful reality of their lives from childhood on reveals that the inequities they encounter are not confined to a few institutions. The effects of injustice and discrimination can be seen in the lives of nearly everyone around them. A brutal system permeates every aspect of life; it is in the air they breathe.

In attempting to cope, the teen-ager seeks some kind of protection for himself in order to survive, some way of dealing with the contradictions that surround him. This usually takes the form of resistance to all authority. For many adolescents it is the only weapon they have. Most of the time, their rebellion is directed against authority outside the home; but if there is no strong family support, it can disrupt their relationships at home. Even the closest families crumble because outside pressures are so relentless.

To a certain extent this was true for me when I was in junior high school. My rebellion was minor and never became a serious problem, though it caused friction for a while. Looking back, I see that it was a reflection of the confusion and sense of fragmentation I was going through, part of the process of finding out who I was. It was also the beginning of my independence.

Everyone in our home shared the household chores. Mine were the usual ones: taking out the garbage and, after my sisters left home, washing the dishes and cleaning the stove. I also had to trim the hedges around the house. My father supervised the outside, while my mother's domain was inside the house. I hated chores and always tried to escape them, pedaling away on my bike and leaving everything to Melvin. I often stayed away from home until late at night, even though I knew my parents would punish me when I returned. Sometimes I made up fancy stories to tell them, but nothing could save me from punishment. I preferred my mother's whippings—she was more gentle—but most of the time my father did it. Another responsibility I failed to carry out was a paper route I had for a time. I spent all the money I collected and could not pay the bill. When the people who had paid money did not receive their papers, I had to give it up.

This kind of resistance was due in large part to the need to assert myself as a separate person, apart from my parents. I was beginning to want to make my own decisions. Often this independence took the form of avoiding responsibilities; at other times it was more constructive.

Ever since I can remember, I have hated to see anyone do without the things he needs. This attitude probably came from my father's influence and the ideas he expressed in church. Once, when I was about fifteen, I met a kid who had no food at home. This was one of those nights when I was staying out late, and I brought him home and woke up my parents rummaging through the kitchen cabinets. When I told them the boy and his family needed food and that we could share ours, they did not object, although they were angry about my staying out late. Another time, when Melvin was going to San Jose State College, he needed a car but had no money. I had a small savings account, about $300, and I gave him all of it. My parents teased me about giving away all my money, but at bottom, they were proud of this example of family closeness.

Other times, though, I showed my sense of closeness in ways they did not approve of. Whenever my sister Myrtle got stranded at a party or somewhere else, she always called and asked me to pick her up. I would wait until my parents were asleep and then swipe the car keys. I did this every time she asked me, and every time I got into trouble for taking the car because I was not old enough to drive.

My parents never spared the rod when I was young. As I grew older, they punished me in other ways, but I knew they did it because they cared about me and wanted me to develop a sense of responsibility. I think, too, they admired my independence, even though it sometimes worried them. They must have known I was at a difficult stage of development. Most Black parents are very aware of the conflicting and bewildering influences that surround their children, and they experience a deep anxiety over whether they will get into trouble with the law or at school. They understand only too well how the system works. The loving discipline exerted in our home was not lost on me, and when the time came, it stood me in good stead.

6

We love our country, dearly love her, but she does not love us—she despises us.

MARTIN DELANY, 1852

High School

Throughout high school I constantly did battle with the instructors. The clashes I had steadily intensified and finally led to my transfer out of the Oakland system for a while. In the tenth grade I was attending Oakland Technical High School on Broadway and Forty-first. One day the teacher sent me to the principal's office for a minor offense I had committed the day before. The principal and teacher agreed that I could come back if I said nothing in class for the rest of the semester. I had already decided that I wanted out of school entirely, but I tried to sit mutely in class and not violate any of the rules, such as chewing gum, or eating sunflower seeds. One day I forgot the agreement and raised my hand to ask a question. The teacher blew up. "Put your hand down," he said. "I don't want to hear any more from you this whole term!" I stood up and told him it was impossible to learn anything if I was forbidden to ask questions. Then I walked out of the class.

Leaving school then meant I was short of classes and would be unable to go on to the eleventh grade and graduate. So I went to live in Berkeley with my oldest sister, Myrtle, and transferred to Berkeley High School.

Although Oakland was known in the East Bay Area as a rough community, it was not until I transferred to Berkeley High School that real trouble started with the police. One Sunday, while walking over to a girl's house, I met four or five girls I knew. They asked me to go with them to a party. Although I did not take up their offer, we walked along together, since we were going the same way. Pretty soon a car pulled up carrying a guy named Mervin Carter (he's dead now) and some others. They jumped out and began hassling me about messing around with their girl friends. I recognized Merv Carter; in fact, I had hung around Berkeley High with him and a couple of his friends. Like everybody else, they were turf-conscious and hated to see an outsider making time with their girls. I reminded him that we knew each other, that I was not interfering with the girls, and was on my way somewhere else. "Anyway," I said, "we hang around together in school." He told me we were friends inside school but not outside. I could not understand why he said that, whether he meant it or was just trying to impress his buddies.

By that time they had dropped a half circle on me. I realized they were going to jump me, so I hit Merv in the mouth, and then they all came at me. They beat me up pretty badly, but I refused to fall down. The girls were yelling at me to run, but I would not. No matter how many guys Merv had with him, I meant to stand my ground. As long as I could, I was going to look them in the eye and keep going forward.

Somebody called the police, but by the time they arrived Carter and the others had gone, and I was there alone, bleeding, and missing several teeth. Although the police tried to find out who did it, I would not tell them anything. I did not want to be an informer because this was a problem between the brothers; the outside racist authorities had nothing to do with it. I have always believed that to inform on someone to the teacher, to the principal, or to the police is wrong. These people represent another world, another racial group. To be white is to have power and authority, and for a Black to say anything to them is a betrayal. So I did not inform, and they escaped the police; but they could not escape me.

The next day I went to school carrying a carpenter's hammer and an old pistol I had swiped from my father. The pistol did not work—it lacked a firing pin—but I had no intention of

shooting anybody anyway. At lunchtime I "cold-trailed" Merv
and about six of his buddies downtown. Catching up with
them finally, I started to swing on him with the hammer. I hit
him several times, wanting to hurt him, but he rolled with most
of the blows and was not hurt too badly. Meanwhile, I forgot
I had the gun. When the others began picking up rocks and
sticks, I remembered the gun and used it to keep them at bay.
This was the only way I could defend myself, because I had no
friends at Berkeley High School to help me. I could not let them
get away with what they had done, particularly since they had
falsely accused me of messing with their girl friends. Somebody
called the police again, and when I heard the sirens, I ran farther downtown, where I was arrested. I was only about fourteen then, so they took me to Juvenile Hall, where I stayed for
a month while they investigated my family background. Then I
was released to the custody of my parents.

This was my first time into anything that could be called
"criminal," even though I had raided fruit trees, cracked parking meters, and helped myself to stuff in the neighborhood
stores. I never looked upon that as stealing or doing anything
illegal, however. To me, that was not taking things that did not
belong to us but getting something really ours, something owed
us. *That* "stealing" was merely retribution.

When I was released from Juvenile Hall, Berkeley High
School refused to admit me again because my parents lived in
Oakland. I went back to Oakland Tech. My friends there and
others who knew me praised what I had done in Berkeley. What
I had done was an accepted action under the circumstances. If
I had not retaliated, I would have been less respected.

Things went along well at Oakland Tech for a change. I was
able to handle my differences with the teachers a little better
because of my satisfaction with life outside the classroom. My
reputation as a fighter kept the wolves away. I was also known
as a hipster like my brother Sonny Man, and I liked that, too.
Some of the kids even called me "crazy," but that never bothered me because they used to call my father that. To me "crazy"
was a positive identity.

When I got my first car, it did a lot to help my "crazy" reputation. My father gave me one that had a lot of spots on it from primer paint. Melvin named it the "Gray Roach." We would pile into it and go riding, looking for girls or some action. My friends did not like the way I drove, which led to any number of arguments and fights. Since there were so few cars available to joyride in, they had little choice. Sometimes I backed up as fast as I could, down a whole block, and when we reached the corner, I would jam on the brakes. The guys would fall out of the car, yelling. Sometimes fights started right there. At railroad crossings, when the guard rail was down to signal an approaching train, I kept right on driving around the guard rail and over the tracks. I had several near misses, and as soon as we crossed the tracks, everyone would pile out of the car again, arguing and fighting. When the fights were over, our friendships were stronger than ever. They respected me, even though they thought I was crazy. I thought I could outmaneuver anybody, anything, and never passed up a chance to try. Since I always won, I soon believed that I could always defeat the invincible and the powerful, the way David defeated Goliath. Eventually, in my pride, I believed that I could outmaneuver death.

I have never feared death. The escape from finitude was an idea that came to me after I saw the movie *Black Orpheus*. I loved that film, and saw it many times, although I thought the outcome would have been different had it been my life. Whereas Orpheus flirted with death and died, I had been in lots of conflicts, near death on many occasions, but had always come out alive. Since I had not been killed, I guess I concluded that I could not be killed. Orpheus, too, attempts to outmaneuver death, even though the history of mankind proves that death always wins. In spite of this, the only way that Orpheus can maintain his dignity is to be unafraid and attempt to outmaneuver his oppressor. This seems characteristic of human existence, for although all of us are sentenced to death each day, we try desperately to get away from it. If we cannot, we try to put it off by acting in a manner that discredits death and eliminates our fear of it. This is our victory.

Black Orpheus demonstrates an even more profound truth: it is possible to circumvent death through the heritage that one generation passes on to another. At the end of the film the little girl is dancing while the little boy plays Orpheus's guitar. Though Orpheus and his woman are dead, her dance is a victory over death. The new generation survives, and the sun still rises. The world does not stop because death has crushed a beautiful and significant part of it. Orpheus had passed on his guitar to the little boy. This means of sustaining life raises the sun again.

I held on to the idea that I was immune to death for a long time. I still do not fear the end, but I no longer believe that I cannot be killed. Life has taught me that it is an ever-present possibility; too many of my comrades have died in the past few years to let me feel that my last day will never come. Even so, I tell the comrades you can only die once, so do not die a thousand times worrying about it.

Around this time some people got the notion that I had mystical powers. I began to put various friends and acquaintances into hypnotic trances, mostly at parties or in some of the rap sessions with brothers on the block. I learned the technique first from Melvin, who had been taught by Solomon Hill, a fellow student at Oakland City College. Later, I studied hypnosis techniques on my own and became pretty good at it. It is easy to learn, but dangerous. Just learning the technique does not teach you all you should know when you are dealing with a person's mind. You can easily hurt someone.

I guess I have put over two hundred people into trances at various times. I gave them posthypnotic suggestions—to eat grass, bark like a dog, or crawl over the floor like a baby—and sometimes I stuck pins and needles into their flesh. Once I used autohypnosis and put myself into a trance. When Melvin put a red-hot cigarette on my arm, I did not move or feel any pain, although he burned me pretty badly. This incident impressed a lot of people, but Melvin was pretty upset about it. Far from using hypnosis in a destructive way, I used it for "styling" in the community. As my reputation grew, the novelty wore off, and finally I stopped, because it was no longer interesting.

When I was not putting people into trances or racing around in the Gray Roach and drinking wine with the brothers, I was standing in a crowd of people at parties reciting poetry. My problem was that I could not dance, and when the music began, I felt self-conscious. If I did not leave when the dancing started, I would begin discussions or recite poetry. By the time I reached high school I was really very good at remembering the poetry I had heard read aloud. Much of it was poetry that Melvin had taught me. David's favorite was the *Rubaiyat of Omar Khayyam*. Whenever I recited at parties or got people into deep conversations, everyone would stop dancing and gather around. Some of them would ask me to recite things I had memorized. The host or hostess usually became angry when people stopped dancing, and often I would be asked to sit down and shut up, or split. This usually signaled the beginning of a fight.

Somehow I managed to stay in Oakland Tech until I graduated, despite my continued defiance of the authorities. They tried to down me for many years, but I knew inside that I was a good person, and the only way I could hold on to any self-esteem was to resist and defy them.

Everything they opposed I supported. That was how I first became a supporter of Fidel Castro and the Cuban Revolution. Earlier, when I heard teachers criticizing Paul Robeson, I defended him and believed in him, even though I knew very little about his life. When they started putting down Castro and the revolution of the Cuban people, I knew it must be good, too. I became an advocate of the Cuban Revolution.

My high school diploma was a farce. When my friends and I graduated, we were ill-equipped to function in society, except at the bottom, even though the system said we were educated. Maybe they knew what they were doing, preparing us for the trash heap of society, where we would have to work long hours for low wages. They never realized how much they had actually educated me by teaching the necessity of resistance and the dignity of defiance. I was on my way to becoming a revolutionary.

PART TWO

I began to question what I had always taken for granted.

7

*I knew right there in prison that reading had changed forever
the course of my life. As I see it today, the ability to read awoke
inside me some long dormant craving to be mentally alive. . . .
My homemade education gave me, with every additional book
I read, a little bit more sensitivity to the deafness, dumbness,
and blindness that was affecting the black race in America.*

The Autobiography of Malcolm X

Reading

By the time I had reached my last year of high school, I was a
functional illiterate. Melvin was in college and doing very well.
I felt that I could do it, too, but when I talked to a counselor
about it, he made the mistake of telling me I was not college
material. I set out to prove them wrong. First, I had to learn to
read. The school authorities told me not only that I was not
college material because of my performance in school, but also
that I was not intelligent enough to do college work. According
to the Stanford-Binet test, I had an I.Q. of 74. They felt justified
in discouraging me. I knew I could do anything I wanted to do;
that was how I maintained my self-respect. I wanted to go to
college, so my defiance of their opinion, as well as my admiration for Melvin, were incentives for me to learn to read.

I knew I would have to read well in order to make it in college. I also knew that it would be difficult to find someone to
teach me because I was embarrassed. I decided to teach myself.
My key was the poetry I had learned to recite. I knew plenty of
words but could not yet recognize them in print. Using Melvin's

poetry books, I began to study the poems I knew, associating the sounds in my head with the words on the page.

Then I picked up Melvin's copy of Plato's *Republic,* bought a dictionary, and started learning to read things I did not already know. The *Republic* seemed a logical choice; I wanted to join Melvin and his friends in their intellectual conversations. It was a long and painful process, but I was determined. Lee Edward had taught me to look them in the eye and keep advancing. They said I was not college material, so I was advancing on them.

I spent long hours every day at home going through the *Republic* and pronouncing the words I knew. If I did not know a word, I would look it up in the dictionary, learn how to sound it out if I could, and then learn the meaning. Proper names and Greek words were difficult, and I soon began to ignore them. Day after day, for eight or nine hours at a time, I worked on that book, going over it page by page, word by word. I had no help from anyone because I did not want it. Embarrassment overwhelmed me. My mother loved reading and devoured books. Here I was, an adult who could not read, as my father, my mother, and Melvin could. I felt so low I stayed in my room where nobody could see what I was doing, poring over the words, using the dictionary on every single line, and memorizing the sounds and the meanings.

Once or twice I asked Melvin to pronounce a word for me or explain it. He was shocked that I could not recognize some of them and at first, I think, disgusted. That hurt. His disgust could not compare with my own. He said that not knowing how to read was a very bad thing, but I knew that by then, and his disapproval made it even more difficult to learn. My sense of shame had kept me from seeking help earlier; now it became impossible for me to ask. I had to do it by myself.

It seems to me that nothing is more painful than a sense of shame that overwhelms you and afflicts the soul. This pain may not even be your fault, but it can still be very acute. It hurts more when you know that there is no natural process, as in the body, whereby the pain will go away. You have to relieve it with your own strength of will, your own discipline, and determination. I had been hurt many times in fights, but nothing equaled the pain I felt at not being able to read. The pain from fighting went away in time. The shame I felt would not go away.

I do not know how long it took me to go through Plato the first time, probably several months. When I finally finished, I started over again. I was not trying to deal with the ideas or concepts, just learning to recognize the words. I went through the book about eight or nine times before I felt I had mastered the material. Later on, I studied the *Republic* in college. By then I was prepared for it.

When I began to read, a whole new world opened to me. I became interested in books. I still could not read very well, but each new book made it easier. I did not mind spending many hours, because reading was enjoyment, rather than work. When I reached this point, I accumulated books and read one after another. I did this all through my senior year in high school and the summer following. By the time I really knew my way through a book, I had graduated from high school.

8

*All my life I had been looking for something, and everywhere
I turned someone tried to tell me what it was. I accepted their
answers too, though they were often in contradiction and even
self-contradictory. I was naïve. I was looking for myself and
asking everyone except myself questions which I, and only I,
could answer. It took me a long time and much painful boo-
meranging of my expectations to achieve a realization everyone
else appears to have been born with: That I am nobody but
myself.*

RALPH ELLISON, *The Invisible Man*

Moving On

About two years before I completed high school, my inner life
was plunged into a sea of confusion and turmoil that lasted until Bobby Seale and I organized the Black Panther Party. For
four years I went through the kind of pain that comes when
you are letting go of old beliefs and certainties and have nothing to take their place. This distress had begun earlier and was
a result of contrasting and varying elements in my life. As I ma-
tured physically, the problems seemed more insoluble, the
strain became greater; I felt adrift. I began to question everything about my life. There seemed no haven of security in anything I was doing or hoping to do.

I questioned my religious activities and my search for God. I
questioned whether school was worth the effort. Most of all,
I questioned what was happening in my own family and in the
community around me. My father's struggle with bills was com-

mon in many of the families of my comrades. He had worked hard all his life only to sink more deeply in debt. It seemed that no matter how hard he worked and sacrificed for his family, it led to more work. Things never became easier. I began to ask why this had happened to us and to everybody around us. Why could my father never get out of debt? If hard work brought success, why did we not see more success in the community? The people were certainly working hard. It seemed we were predestined to endless toil. We poor people never reached the point of having time to pursue the things we wanted. We had neither leisure time nor material goods. Not only did I want to know why this was so; I wanted to avoid a similar fate.

While I was looking for answers to the questions of family and religion, I was also thinking of joining a monastery, not so much out of religious conviction as for the isolation and time to examine these questions in peace. I felt the need to have a place where I could examine things without interference. Isolation would shield me from the troubles that were suffocating my father and my family. But I did not entertain the idea very seriously and soon gave it up. I began to think that Melvin's approach through books was one way to examine these questions. His life required a certain amount of detachment from the community, and that was attractive to me.

On the other hand, there was my brother Sonny Man. For a long time I had believed that he had the freedom I was seeking. He had possessions galore, no bills, and was defying the authorities and getting away with it. Even so, I came to the conclusion that he had not so much defied the authorities as compromised with them. All the hipsters with cars, clothes, and money had rejected the family relationship that I valued so highly. They had achieved a level of freedom at great personal cost. To me this was not freedom but another form of subjugation to the oppressor. Even if Sonny Man had escaped their control, his life did not answer my questions. It did not help me understand why most Blacks never gained the freedom he seemed to have. I finally decided that Sonny Man and his comrades did not have the power to determine their destiny. They operated through someone else's power—the oppressor's—and they were not free as long as they had to reject some part of themselves.

The religious beliefs acquired in childhood also troubled me. After struggling through some of Socrates' works, as well as those of Aristotle, Hume, and Descartes, I began to question what I had always taken for granted. The ideas in the philosophical works that Melvin was studying spilled over into my confused mind. All the while, I felt damned. To question religion was a profane, heretical act that went against every moral tenet I had known at home. I identified very strongly with Stephen Dedalus in James Joyce's *Portrait of the Artist as a Young Man* because he went through a similar experience. He felt great guilt when he first questioned Catholicism, believing that he would be consumed by the fires of hell for his doubt. In a way, that is what happened to me.

The struggle with religious faith is a difficult experience to describe because it involves many things that are either repressed earlier in life or not understood. In the process, the fears that are not related to religious beliefs are released. By then you no longer have any protection from your religion, and you have to start dealing with your dread. The real world closes in on you, cutting off traditional comforts like a simple prayer. Eventually, you, and you alone, have to deal with troubling questions. This always leads to anxiety. There is nothing, so you are free—and terrified.

In a way, the turmoil and conflict I was experiencing were a kind of madness, with no way out. The patterns that appealed to me as answers to my questions were closed to me. Sonny Man represented an attractive way of life, but it did not provide the answers I was seeking. Melvin was into another appealing pattern, but I had never been able to handle school effectively. I was confused. Sonny Man had an illusion of freedom; Melvin had an approach, but I could not read. Nobody had any answers for me. Sometimes I went one way, sometimes another.

I never expressed these feelings to my parents. I had such respect and admiration for my father, who had done so much for us, that I could not openly question his life. He would not have understood what I was going through. I was grateful, I was appreciative, and I loved and admired him, but I had questions not easily answered.

When my high school years came to an end, these doubts and troubles were at a high pitch; they were still with me when I started Oakland City College in the fall of 1959 and were reflected in the new way of life I was beginning. My life style alarmed my parents. They must have sensed my inner turmoil because they began to object strenuously to certain things I was doing. It was the beatnik era in the Bay Area, and I grew a beard. To my parents, a beard meant a bohemian, and my father insisted that I shave it off. I refused. Because he was accustomed to wielding total authority in our family, my refusal was a serious family violation. My father pressed me again to shave; I continued to resist. The climax came abruptly one night when he confronted me with an ultimatum to shave right then and there. I told him I would not do it. He struck me, and I ran to him, grabbing him with a bear hug to restrain his arms, and then pushing him away. He chased me out of the house, but I could run much faster. I also knew that I was strong enough to overpower him, but I would never have done that. I just fled. My love for my father had clashed with a need for independence, symbolized by the beard. Knowing I could not return without shaving, I decided to move out. While my father was at work the next day, I packed my things and moved in with a friend, Richard Thorne. For years, a room was kept for me in my father's house, and periodically I returned home for short periods of time. Our differences mellowed and eventually disappeared. My room in my parents' house was not considered given up until 1968, when I was sentenced to prison.

9

Black is not only beautiful; it's bad, too. It's fast, classy, name-taking and ass-kicking, too.

MELVIN VAN PEEBLES, *Ain't Supposed to Die a Natural Death*

College and the
Afro-American Association

In 1959, when I started at Oakland City College (now Merritt College), it was a junior college located in North Oakland, surrounded by the Black community. Many local Black people attended it at that time, and I joined the crowd. College for me was more than books and lectures and classes, although they were important. For one thing, I never really left my neighborhood, and I still ran with the brothers on the block. Any money I had came from petty crime, an old pattern with me. This, however, became a time for making new friends and joining organizations that started me in new directions.

One of my first friends at Oakland City College was Richard Thorne. Richard was a very tall, very black fellow who even then, prior to the "Black cultural revolution," wore his hair in a natural. His appearance caused awe in some people and frightened others. He knew how to excite these feelings and how to exert an influence over those around him.

I stayed with Richard for about a month after I left home, before I moved into Poor Boys Hall. Poor Boys Hall was behind a bookstore across from the college. The owners had converted a big storage warehouse into a dormitory with rooms—not really rooms but stalls—with thin plywood dividers. A stall rented for $15 a month. I loved being around Poor Boys Hall because most of my friends among the "roomers" were young fellows just beginning to "get their thing together." Like me, they were searching. Some of them have gone on to become a part of the system, while others have been further victimized. I kept up close contact with Richard Thorne, too, and we spent a lot of time together at his apartment. Richard usually had several girls around and was always talking about the two or three books he intended to write. I was more interested in the girls.

Richard had a theory about intimate human relations. He saw nonpossessive love as pure love, the only love, and possessive love as a mockery of pure love. Nonpossessive love did not enslave or constrain the love object. Richard was critical of what he called "bourgeois love relationships," of the marriage system and the requirements of the marriage partners to each other (*i.e.*, sex with one partner, jealousy, limits upon mobility, well-defined roles based upon sex). He felt that people should not be like cars or houses. No man should *own* a wife, nor should a wife *own* a husband, because ownership is predicated upon control, fences, barriers, constraints, and psychological tyranny. Nonpossessive love is based upon shared experiences and friendship; it is the kind of love we have for our bodies, for our thumb or foot. We love ourselves, our bodies, but we do not want to enslave any part of ourselves.

Richard and I engaged in some deep discussions. Sometimes we stayed at his house for days talking about the general situation, cursing the white man for everything, and drinking wine. When I tired of these sessions, I made it down to the block to be with the righteous street brothers.

I was an angry young man at this time, drinking wine and fighting on the block, burglarizing homes in the Berkeley Hills, and going to school at Oakland City College. I was moving away from family and church, which had offered me so much comfort in earlier days, and was looking for something new. The questions I asked during this period were so disturbing that I acted outrageously to drive them away. I was looking for something more tangible with which to identify. I saw all my turmoil in terms of racism and exploitation and the obvious discrepancies between the haves and have-nots. I was trying to figure out how to avoid being crushed and losing respect for myself, how to keep from embracing the oppressor that had already maimed my family and community.

In the discussions at Phi Beta Sigma, a social fraternity I joined for a while, I expressed my anger about society and white racism. The others told me that I sounded like a guy named Donald Warden who was preaching Blackness at the Berkeley campus of the University of California. He was the head of an organization called the Afro-American Association.

I went to Berkeley to find Warden and hear what he was saying. The first member I met, though, was Maurice Dawson, one of Warden's tight partners. He turned me off with his arrogance. I had come searching for something, and he scorned me because I did not already know what I was seeking. I could not understand what he was saying about "Afro-Americans." The term was new to me. Dawson really put me down.

"You know what an Afro-Cuban is?"

"Yes."

"You know what an Afro-Brazilian is?"

"Yes."

"Then why don't you know what an Afro-American is?"

It may have been apparent to him, but not to me. But I was still interested.

Maurice taught me a lesson that I try to apply to the Black Panther Party today. I dissuade Party members from putting down people who do not understand. Even people who are unenlightened and seemingly bourgeois should be answered in a polite way. Things should be explained to them as fully as possible. I was turned off by a person who did not want to talk to me because I was not important enough. Maurice just wanted to preach to the converted, who already agreed with him. I try to be cordial, because that way you win people over. You cannot win them over by drawing the line of demarcation, saying you are on this side and I am on the other; that shows a lack of consciousness. After the Black Panther Party was formed, I nearly fell into this error. I could not understand why people were blind to what I saw so clearly. Then I realized that their understanding had to be developed.

I started going to meetings of the Afro-American Association, whose purpose was mainly to develop a sense of pride among Black people for their heritage, their history, and their contributions to culture and society. Donald Warden, a lawyer from the University of California at Berkeley, had started it. Most of the meetings were book-discussion groups, which I enjoyed, because by then I was relating to books more and more. I began reading books about Black people, and every Friday we sat up half the night discussing them. We read *The Souls of Black Folk* by W. E. B. Du Bois, Ralph Ellison's *Invisible Man, Up from Slavery* by Booker T. Washington, and *The Fire Next Time* by James Baldwin.

I was one of the first ten to join the organization. On Saturday afternoons we would go into the Black community in Oakland or San Francisco and speak on the street corners, running down the racist system. People came to listen because they were bored and wanted some entertainment, not because Warden's words were relevant to their lives.

I started to bring more of the poor, uneducated brothers off the block into the Association. Most of the people in the Association were college students and very bourgeois, but my people were off the block; some of them could not even read, but they were angry and looking for a way to channel their feelings. Warden was glad to have the lumpen brothers along. He needed some strong-arm men who would just follow instructions without question. Some brothers and I formed a bodyguard for him. Sometimes our street meetings on Saturdays ended in fights, because white boys came around looking for trouble. That was when I began to see through Warden.

My family thought that Warden was up to no good, and they were quite unhappy when I joined him. They said that he was interested only in building up his law practice. But I had to find out for myself.

My disillusionment began when I realized he would not stand his ground in a fight. Once, in a San Francisco meeting, some white guys yelled at us from a window and then came down to fight. I was throwing hands, trying to protect Warden, and when I looked up, he had run off, leaving us there by ourselves.

My real decision to quit the group came after I observed Warden in a debating situation, where his training and skill should have put him in a superior position. The Oakland *Tribune* ran an article reporting how the City Council had made derogatory remarks about the Association. Warden wrote and asked to be placed on the agenda of their next meeting. About twenty of us went down to City Hall expecting Warden to take them to task. We were eighth on the agenda, and when our turn came, Mayor John Houlihan (who later went to jail for embezzlement) said that we could not speak then because some important people were there from Piedmont, an all-white, upper-class area within the city limits of Oakland. Houlihan told us to wait until last, even though it was our turn on the agenda. I thought Warden would object, but no, he just bowed his head, and I thought I saw him shuffle a little.

After the Piedmont merchants made their presentation, Houlihan declared the agenda closed because there was time to consider only ten items. He told us to write the City Council and say our piece. One of the councilmen insisted we be heard, however, since we had written to them in accordance with the rules and had been properly placed on the agenda. Don still had not taken a position. When he rose to speak, he started by saying we were there because the *Tribune* had reported some derogatory remarks made about us at the council's last meeting. He denied that the Afro-American Association wanted trouble. The Association, he said, wanted an end to the lethargy of Black people, to get them off welfare, make them clean themselves up, and sweep their streets in a big self-help effort. He said he wanted Black people to stop lying around collecting unemployment checks.

That was when I decided that my parents were right about him. Afterward, the whole City Council, including Mayor Houlihan, patted Warden on the back. He ate it up.

In our own meetings—with no white people around—he really took them apart. But he had little interest in Black people.

He was interested in getting Barry Goldwater's daughter to contribute money to his sister's little sewing shop, which he claimed was a clothing factory. Goldwater's daughter became an honorary member of the Afro-American Association.

I was really sick when I saw what went down before the City Council. Warden talked about Black folks as if we were a lazy bunch of people who hated ourselves and had no will to better our own situation. He said nothing about causes, although in that City Council room he was speaking to some of the major causes of Black people's suffering in the city of Oakland.

Disillusioned, I left the organization, but not before I had gotten a lot out of it. For one thing, I had begun to learn about the Black past, but I could not accept Warden's refusal to deal with the Black present. He was obviously interested in building his law practice and routinely began street meetings by saying that he did not have to be there, that he was Phi Beta Kappa and a lawyer. A lot of people who went to him for legal services found him out. They thought he would charge less money, being one of them, but he charged high fees. I went to him once, and he charged more than double the usual fee. Another attorney asked $250, but Warden wanted $750 before he even stepped into the courtroom.

He offered the community solutions that solved nothing. I could have accepted this if he had been ignorant, but I believe he knew what he was doing. At least he knew what the popular position was. That is why I tell the Black Panther Party that we must never take a stand just because it is popular. We must analyze the situation objectively and take the logically correct position, even though it may be unpopular. If we are right in the dialectics of the situation, our position will prevail.

Warden was just the opposite. He rode the tide, even if it went against the community. He talked of a mass exodus to Africa, and never believed in it. He maintained that capitalism in general, and Black capitalism in particular, was the best economic system. The only thing wrong with it, he said, was the racism in the system. He never spoke of the link between capitalist exploitation and racism. Wanting whites to believe that Blacks were behind him, Warden talked up Black power and

Black history, using the people to gain their support. Downtown, he looked for whites to support him out of their fear of organized Blacks. Warden gathered the people around him to lead them like sheep. That is what he did at the City Council.

He is the only Black man I know with two weekly radio programs and one on television. The mass media, the oppressors, give him public exposure for only one reason: he will lead the people away from the truth of their situation.

Others also drifted away from the Afro-American Association. Richard Thorne was in it for a while, but he left to found the Sexual Freedom League. Later, he organized a spiritual cult called Om Eternal and changed his name to Om. He is now that cult's unquestioned high priest (God). Another member of the Afro-American Association at that time was a skinny, bright, and articulate fellow called Ron Everett. He went from the Association to Watts in Los Angeles, where he established his own cultural nationalist group, US, which eventually became a cult. He called himself Karenga—"the original." Later, the Black Panthers had some bitter confrontations with US, and they killed two of our finest comrades.*

---

*The Black Panther Party believes that Karenga's organization and the Los Angeles police conspired against our Los Angeles Party organizers, John Huggins and Alprentice "Bunchy" Carter, and assassinated them. The police wanted to stop the Black Panthers' organizing efforts, and Karenga's organization wanted to curtail a competitive group and buy the friendship of the police.

My soul has grown deep like the rivers.
LANGSTON HUGHES, "The Negro Speaks of Rivers"

Learning

Life was opening up for me. I was trying to relate to Donald Warden and his program, trying to stay close with my righteous partners on the block, and also attending Oakland City College on a "come-and-go" basis. My motivation had been to prove to my high school teachers that they were wrong about me. To my surprise I found myself enjoying the learning process and tremendously stimulated by ideas I encountered. Since I had studied classical piano for almost seven years, I took music appreciation, music history, music theory, and also art appreciation and art history.

Most semesters I started out with a regular load, but if something came up in class that excited my imagination, I sometimes skipped classes, gathered as many books and materials as I could find on the subject, and stayed in the library or at home in my apartment reading.

While studying psychology, for example, I became fascinated with the principle of stimulus response and the biological behaviorism of John B. Watson. I read a number of books on the subject, works by B. F. Skinner and Pavlov, and read about their studies and theories of personality and human development. By the time I was satiated with stimulus response, or whatever, the class had moved on to another unit that was of no interest to me.

Philosophy was another favorite subject. I still remember

some of the issues raised in logic class thirteen years ago. Such points as the difference between lexical and stipulative definitions I use in discussions today. Even now I find it difficult to enter into a dialogue on philosophy or Black Panther ideology until there is agreement on basic definitions. This presents problems when I speak on college campuses. I try to lead an audience into rational and logical discussions, but many students are looking for rhetoric and phrasemongering. They either do not want to learn or they do not believe that I can think.

I was also impressed with A. J. Ayer's logical positivism, particularly his distinction between three kinds of statements—the analytical statement, the synthetic statement, and statements of assumption. These ideas have helped me to develop my own thinking and ideology. Ayer once stated, "Nothing can be real if it cannot be conceptualized, articulated, and shared." That notion stuck with me and became very important when I began to use the ideological method of dialectical materialism as a world view. The ideology of the Black Panthers stands on that premise and proceeds on that basis, to conceptualize, articulate, and share. Some key aspects of Black Panther ideology and rhetoric, like "All Power to the People" and the concept "pig," developed out of that. They were not haphazardly introduced into our thinking or vocabulary.

While studying philosophy, I realized that I had been moving for some time toward existentialism. I read Camus, Sartre, and Kierkegaard and saw that their teachings were similar to lessons I had learned from the Book of Ecclesiastes in the Bible. Actually the "Preacher" was the first existentialist:

All things come alike to all: there is one event to the righteous, and to the wicked; to the good and to the clean, and to the unclean; to him that sacrificeth, and to him that sacrificeth not: as is the good, so is the sinner; and he that sweareth, as he that feareth an oath.

This is an evil among all things that are done under the sun, that there is one event unto all: yea, also the heart of the sons of men is full of evil, and madness is in their heart while they live, and after that they go to the dead.

For to him that is joined to all the living there is hope: for a living dog is better than a dead lion. . . .

I returned, and saw under the sun, that the race is not to the swift, nor the battle to the strong, neither yet bread to the wise, nor yet riches to men of understanding, nor yet favour to men of skill; but time and chance happeneth to them all.

From then on, I began to engage friends in existentialist discussions. If a brother was hungry, I would say that it is all the same whether you are hungry or full, whether you are cold or warm. It is all the same. They *really* thought I was crazy. Then I began living like an existentialist, hitchhiking to Los Angeles and back, walking into the class dirty, without shoes, and sometimes soaked to the skin from the rain. It was all the same to me. One way or another I kept my reputation going. All the time I was on the streets I read Ecclesiastes at least once a month, until I was sentenced to the penitentiary, where they refused me all reading material.

I was still questioning. Although college work did not give me answers as such, I was beginning to comprehend human beings and the universe, to feel I could develop answers that suited my own experience and my knowledge of the world. Then, too, I was convincing myself that they had been wrong about me in public schools. When that teacher told me to write "business" on the board, she wanted to show the class that I was stupid; when they discouraged me from going to college, it was because they thought I was stupid. As a matter of fact, some of my college teachers thought I was stupid, too, because I never did well on those silly little tests they gave us. One psychology teacher told me that I scored at the level of a "dull normal" on an I.Q. test. Since I really liked this teacher, that hurt me badly. Then he gave another test, which he said "indicated" that I was intelligent. Only *I* knew what was happening inside of me; only I knew what was happening between me and those books up in my apartment. I was learning, and learning well. I could think, I could read, and I could retain the most difficult ideas. For over twelve years, they had tried to knock me down, but I kept getting up, and now I was advancing on them.

What I learned from Sonny Man also helped me to acquire an education. I was free to pursue my education in my own style, because I could support myself with activities on the block. Most important, I did not have to work. I ran gambling sessions at my apartment, serving as the "houseman." This meant that I set up the games—cards or craps—for everybody else to participate in, and then took a cut of the winnings.

It was my studying and reading in college that led me to become a socialist. The transformation from a nationalist to a socialist was a slow one, although I was around a lot of Marxists. I even attended a few meetings of the Progressive Labor Party, but nothing was happening there, just a lot of talk and dogmatism, unrelated to the world I knew. I supported Castro all the way. I even accepted an invitation to visit Cuba and recruited others for the trip, but I never made it. When I presented my solutions to the problems of Black people, or when I expressed my philosophy, people said, "Well, isn't that socialism?" Some of them were using the socialist label to put me down, but I figured that if this was socialism, then socialism must be a correct view. So I read more of the works of the socialists and began to see a strong similarity between my beliefs and theirs. My conversion was complete when I read the four volumes of Mao Tse-tung to learn more about the Chinese Revolution. It was my life plus independent reading that made me a socialist—nothing else.

I became convinced of the benefits of collectivism and a collectivist ideology. I also saw the link between racism and the economics of capitalism, although, despite the link, I recognized that it was necessary to separate the concepts in analyzing the general situation. In psychological terms, racism could continue to exist even after the economic problems that had created racism had been resolved. Never convinced that destroying capitalism would automatically destroy racism, I felt, however, that we could not destroy racism without wiping out its economic foundation. It was necessary to think much more creatively and independently about these complex interconnections.

Even though I liked my lectures and the discussions, I did not identify with the life style on campus. As soon as I finished my classes, I would go down to the block—sometimes to Sacramento Street in Berkeley or over into West or East Oakland—and drink wine, gamble, and fight. More than once I came from the block to class dead drunk. I never minded being drunk in class because the ideas were more intoxicating; but I had instructors who hated having anyone go to the bathroom while they were lecturing. It disturbed them. But when you are full of wine, you just cannot hold your urine.

College was enjoyable, largely because I was not forced to go; this made it different from high school. I could go to school or stay in my apartment and read. Some days I went to a movie or stayed on the block. I started each semester setting my own pace, which often included a trip to Mexico, or to jail, or dropping out, and all along I learned a great deal.

In spite of the learning, I was still searching for answers to other questions. The Afro-American Association had been a deep disappointment. I had often felt that it was nothing more than a training ground for the Muslims; Warden seemed to have adopted a lot of their styles and rhetoric. I began to investigate them more closely. I had read C. Eric Lincoln's book *Black Muslims in America,* but what attracted me most was Minister Malcolm X.

I first heard Malcolm X speak at McClymonds High School in Oakland, when he attended a conference sponsored by the Afro-American Association on "The Mind of the Ghetto." Muhammad Ali (then Cassius Clay) was with Malcolm, and he told about his conversion to Islam. He was not yet the heavyweight champion. Malcolm X impressed me with his logic and with his disciplined and dedicated mind. Here was a man who combined the world of the streets and the world of the scholar, a man so widely read he could give better lectures and cite more evidence than many college professors. He was also practical. Dressed in the loose-fitting style of a strong prison man, he knew what the street brothers were like, and he knew what had to be done to reach them. Malcolm had a program: armed defense when attacked, and reaching the people with ideas and programs that speak to their condition. At the same time, he identified the causes of their condition instead of blaming the people.

I started going to the Muslim mosques in both Oakland and San Francisco, although not regularly. However, I knew a number of Muslims and talked to them fairly often. I did read their paper regularly to follow the speeches and ideas of Malcolm. I would have joined them, but I could not deal with their religion. By this time, I had had enough of religion and could not bring myself to adopt another one. I needed a more concrete understanding of social conditions. References to God or Allah did not satisfy my stubborn questioning.

Back at the college, Kenny Freeman along with Isaac Moore, Doug Allen, Ernie Allen, Alex Papillon, and some others had begun to organize the West Coast branch of RAM, the Revolutionary Action Movement. They claimed to function as an underground movement, but instead of revolutionary action, they indulged in a lot of revolutionary talk, none of it underground. They were all college students, with bourgeois skills, who wrote a lot. Eventually, they became so infiltrated with agents that when an arrest was made, the police spent all their time showing each other their badges.

Bobby Seale tried to get me into the RAM chapter, but the members refused to accept me. They said I lived in the Oakland hills and was too bourgeois, which was an absolute lie. All my life I have lived in the flatlands. Actually, I think I threatened them, because I could use my head but could also "get down" like the street brothers. They claimed to be dedicated to the armed overthrow of the government, when, in reality, most of them were headed for professional occupations within the system. Freeman and the other RAM members eventually excluded Bobby because he lacked bourgeois skills.

RAM formed a front group on campus, the Soul Students Advisory Council, and Kenny Freeman stacked it with his boys. I became very active in it, joining the main thrust to get a course in Negro history into the curriculum. We held street meetings outside the college and met with the administrators, who offered foolish reasons about why Negro history should not be offered; most of them came down to the belief that Black people had no history to teach. We eventually brought about a few changes, not many, and for a short while RAM seemed very engaging to me. I considered it the answer to many things I was searching for and felt fulfilled when I talked with others about the African past and what we had contributed to the world (all the groups I went through had that in common). Everyone— from Warden and the Afro-American Association to Malcolm X and the Muslims to all the other groups active in the Bay Area at that time—believed strongly that the failure to include Black history in the college curriculum was a scandal. We all set out to do something about it.

The Soul Students Advisory Council lacked any real depth, and when we succeeded in getting the Black history class on campus, we had nothing else to do. There were the usual parties and other social activities, but these had no real meaning for me and provided no satisfaction.

As for the future, the young streetcorner man has a fairly good picture of it. . . . It is a future in which everything is uncertain except the ultimate destruction of his hopes and the eventual realization of his fears. The most he can reasonably look forward to is that these things do not come too soon.

ELLIOT LIEBOW, *Tally's Corner*

The Brothers on the Block

Nothing we had done on the campus related to the conditions of the brothers on the block. Nothing helped them to gain a better understanding of those conditions. As I saw so many of my friends on their way to becoming dropouts from the human family, I wanted to see something good happen to them. They were getting married and beginning to have babies. Ahead of them were the rounds of jobs and bills my father had gone through. It was almost like being on an urban plantation, a kind of modern-day sharecropping. You worked hard, brought in your crop, and you were always in debt to the landholder. The Oakland brothers worked hard and brought in a salary, but they were still in perpetual debt to the stores that provided them with the necessities of life. The Soul Students Advisory Council, RAM, the Muslims, and the Afro-American Association were not offering these brothers and sisters anything concrete, much less a program to help them move against the system. It was agonizing to watch the brother move down those dead-end streets.

The street brothers were important to me, and I could not turn away from the life I shared with them. There was in them an intransigent hostility toward all those sources of authority that had such a dehumanizing effect on the community. In school the "system" was the teacher, but on the block the system was everything that was not a positive part of the community. My comrades on the block continued to resist that authority, and I felt that I could not let college pull me away, no matter how attractive education was. These brothers had the sense of harmony and communion I needed to maintain that part of myself not totally crushed by the schools and other authorities.

At Oakland City College many of the Blacks were working as hard as they could to become a part of the system; I could not relate to their goals. These brothers still believed in making it in the world. They talked about it loud and long, expressing the desire for families, houses, cars, and so forth. Even at that time I did not want those things. I wanted freedom, and possessions meant nonfreedom to me.

It was a complex scene. Sonny Man was involved only with the brothers who did not go to college. His friends who had gone to college were estranged from him. Some of his closest "running partners" in high school moved away from him after they went to college and he stayed on the block. Now that I was also in college, I did not want to move away from the street brothers, as Walter's friends had done. That is why when I was not studying or in class, I was down on the block with the righteous brothers.

I think one of the reasons why I, in particular, had so many fights was because I weighed only about 130 pounds. You got a lot of prestige from being able to fight the hefty guys, who first gained their reputation by downing lightweights like me. There were not many others as small as I was, who looked the big ones in the eye. I had an added disadvantage: all the way through school my baby face made people think I was younger than I was. I resented being treated like a baby, and to show them I was as "bad" as they were, I would fight at the drop of a hat. As soon as I saw a dude rearing up, I struck him before he struck me, but only when there was going to be a fight anyway. I struck first, because a fight usually did not last very long, and nine times out of ten the winner was the one who got in the first lick.

Sonny Man was very good with his hands, and he taught me how to hit hard in spite of my light weight. Most of the other guys really did not know how to hit, so I always fired first and knocked them out, or at least knocked out a tooth or closed up an eye. Finally, I got a reputation as a bad dude, and I did not have to fight as much. Every once in a while, however, one of the "tush hogs"—our name for a bad, tough street fighter on the block—would challenge me. After the fight we usually became really good friends, because he would realize that my features were deceiving.

Sometimes I got into teaching on the block, reciting poetry or starting dialogues about philosophical ideas. I talked to the brothers about things that Hume, Pierce, Locke, or William James had said, and in that way I retained ideas and sometimes resolved problems in my own mind.

These thinkers had used the scientific method by applying their ideas to particular formulas. They excluded those things that did not fit into the formulas. I explained this to the brothers, and we talked about such questions as the existence of God, self-determination, and free will. I would ask them, "Do you have free will?"

"Yes."

"Do you believe in God?"

"Yes."

"Is your God all-powerful?"

"Yes."

"Is he omniscient?"

"Yes."

Therefore, I told them, their all-powerful God knew everything before it happened. If so, I would ask, "How can you say that you have free will when he knows what you are going to do before you do it? You are predestined to do what you do. If not, then your God has lied or He has made a mistake, and you have already said that your God cannot lie or make a mistake." These dilemmas led to arguments that lasted all day, over a fifth of wine; they cleared my thinking, even though I sometimes went to school drunk.

Some of the brothers thought I was a pedant, putting them down. Fights started occasionally over an imaginary insult, especially with newcomers to the group, who did not know me or my relationship to the brothers. I liked talking about ideas, and street brothers were the only ones I wanted to be with at the time, because I liked the things we were doing—standing on the corner, meeting people, watching the women, and relating to those who struggled for survival on the block.

Rap sessions like this took place all over, in cars parked in front of the liquor store on Sacramento Street near Ashby in Berkeley, outside places where parties were being held, and sometimes inside.

I told them about the allegory of the cave from Plato's *Republic,* and they enjoyed it. We called it the story of the cave prisoners. In the cave allegory Plato describes the plight of the prisoners in a cave who receive their impression of the outside world from shadows projected on the wall by the fire at the mouth of the cave. One of the prisoners is freed and gets a view of the outside world—objective reality. He returns to the cave to tell the others that the scenes they observe on the wall are not reality but only a distorted reflection of it. The prisoners tell the liberated man he is crazy, and he cannot convince them. He tried to take one of them outside, but the prisoner is terrified at the thought of facing something new. When he is dragged outside the cave anyway, he sees the sun and is blinded by it. The allegory seemed very appropriate to our own situation in society. We, too, were in prison and needed to be liberated in order to distinguish between truth and the falsehoods imposed on us.

The dudes on the block still thought I was "out of sight" and sometimes just plain crazy. One of the reasons for the "crazy" label was because I always did the unexpected, a valuable practice in keeping your adversary off balance. If I knew that some guys wanted to jump on me, I would go where they hung out— just show up by myself and challenge them right on the spot. Many times they were too shocked to do much about it.

This street philosophy also crept into my academic work. The brothers were hostile toward the police because they were always brutalizing and intimidating us. So I began to study police science in school to learn more about the thinking of police and how to outmaneuver them. I learned how they conducted investigations. I also began to study law. My mother had always urged me to do this, even in high school, because I was good at arguing points, and she thought I would be a good lawyer. I studied law, first at City College and later at San Francisco Law School in San Francisco, not so much to become a lawyer but to be able to deal with the police. I was doing the unexpected.

One day, in 1965, as I was walking across Grove Street to the college, I saw a white man sideswipe a brother's car. A motorcycle cop came up, and the two drivers entered into an argument over who was wrong. The cop was about to write a ticket for the brother. I had been standing there with the other people watching this incident, and I waked over to the white man and told him that he was wrong. Angry at this, the cop told me to be quiet because I was not involved. I came back at him and told him that I *was* involved because I knew how he treated people on the block. The fact that he had a gun, I said, did not give him the right to intimidate me. The gun did not mean anything, because the people were going to get guns of their own and take away the guns of the police. I ran these things down to him in front of all the people. That was the first time I stood a policeman down.

12

What is property? Property is theft.

PIERRE-JOSEPH PROUDHON, 1840

The brigand . . . is the true and only revolutionary.

BAKUNIN, 1870

Scoring

I first studied law to become a better burglar. Figuring I might get busted at any time and wanting to be ready when it happened, I bought some books on criminal law and burglary and felony and looked up as much as possible. I tried to find out what kind of evidence they needed, what things were actually considered violations of the law, what the loopholes were, and what you could do to avoid being charged at all. They had a law for everything. I studied the California penal code and books like *California Criminal Evidence* and *California Criminal Law* by Fricke and Alarcon, concentrating on those areas that were somewhat vague. The California penal code says that any law which is vague to the ordinary citizen—the average reasonable man who lives in California and who is exposed to the state's rules, regulations, and culture—does not qualify as a statute.

Later on, law enforcement courses helped me to know how to deal with the police. Before I took Criminal Evidence in school, I had no idea what my rights really were. I did not know, for instance, that police can be arrested. My studying helped, because every time I got arrested I was released with no charge. Until I went to prison for something I was innocent of,

I had no convictions against me; yet I had done a little of every-thing. The court would convict you if it could, but if you knew the law and were articulate, then the judges figured you were not too bad because your very manner of speaking indicated that you had been "indoctrinated" into their way of thinking.

I was doing a lot of things that were technically unlawful. Sometimes my friends and I received stolen blank checks from a company, which we would then make out for $150 to $200, never more than an amount consistent with a weekly paycheck. Sometimes we stole the checks ourselves; other times we bought them from guys who had stolen them. You had to do this fast, before the companies distributed check numbers to banks and stores.

We burglarized homes in the Oakland and Berkeley hills in broad daylight. Sometimes we borrowed a pickup truck and put a lawn mower or garden tools in it. Then we drove up to a house that appeared empty and rang the bell. If no one an-swered, we rolled the lawn mower around to the back, as if we planned to cut the grass and trim the hedges. Then, swiftly, we broke into the house and took what we wanted.

Often I went car prowling by myself. I would walk the streets until I saw a good prospect, then break into the car and take what was on the seat or in the glove compartment. Many people left their cars unlocked, which made it easier.

We scored best, however, with the credit game or short-change games. We stole or bought stolen credit cards and then purchased as much as possible with them before their numbers were dis-tributed. You could either sell the booty or use it yourself.

A very profitable credit game went like this: we would pay $20 or $30 to someone who owned a small business to say that we had worked for him five years or so. This established a work record good enough for credit in one of the big stores. Then we would charge about $150 worth of merchandise and pay $20 down. Of course, we used an assumed name and a phony address, but we let them check the address, because we gave them a location and telephone number where one of our friends lived. We made payments for a couple of months. Then we would charge over the $150 limit. If you were making payments, they raised your credit. We would buy a big order, and then stop making payments. If they called our "place of work," they were told we had just quit. If they called our alleged address, they learned we had "moved over a month ago." The store was left hanging. They did not really lose, because they were actually robbing the community blind. They just wrote off the amount and continued their robbing. The lesson: you can survive through petty crime and hurt those who hurt you.

Once into petty crime, I stopped fighting. I had transferred the conflict, the aggression, and hostility from the brothers in the community to the Establishment.

The most successful game I ran was the short-change game. Short-changing was an art I developed so well that I could make $50 to $60 a day. I ran it everywhere, in small and large stores, and even on bank tellers. In the short-change game I would go into a store with five one-dollar bills, ask the clerk for change, and walk out with a ten-dollar bill. This was the $5-to-$10 short-change. You could also do a $10-to-$20 short-change by walking into the store with ten one-dollar bills and coming out with a twenty-dollar bill.

The $5-to-$10 short-change worked this way: you folded up four of the bills into a small tight wad. Then you bought something like candy or gum with the other bill so that the clerk had to open the cash register to give you change. I always stood a little distance from the register so that the clerk had to come to me to give me the change. You have to get the cash register open and get the clerk to move away from it so that his mind is taken off what he has in the register.

When he brought my change from the candy, I handed him the wad of four one-dollar bills and said, "Here are *five* singles. Will you give me a five-dollar bill for them?" He would then hand me the five-dollar bill before he realized that there were only four singles in the wad. He has the register open, and I am prepared for him to discover the error. When he did, I would then hand him another single, but also the five-dollar bill he had given me and say, "Well, here's six more; give me a ten." He would do it, and I would take the $10 and be gone before he realized what had happened. Most of the time they never understood. It happened so fast they would simply go on to another customer. By the time things began to click in their minds, they could never be sure that something had in fact gone wrong until the end of the day when they tallied up the register. By that time I was just a vague memory. Of course, if the clerk was quick and sensed that something was not right, then I pretended to be confused and would say I had made a mistake and give him the right amount. It was a pretty safe game, and it worked for me many times.

The brother who introduced me to short-changing eventually became a Muslim, but before that he taught me to burglarize cars parked by the emergency entrances of hospitals. People would come to the hospital in a rush and leave their cars unlocked, with valuables in the open. I never scored on Blacks under any condition, but scoring on whites was a strike against injustice.

Whenever I had liberated enough cash to give me a stretch of free time, I stayed home reading, books like Dostoevsky's *Crime and Punishment, The Devils,* and *The House of the Dead, The Trial* by Franz Kafka, and Thomas Wolfe's *Look Homeward, Angel.* I read and reread *Les Misérables* by Victor Hugo, the story of Jean Valjean, a Frenchman who spent thirty years in prison for stealing a loaf of bread to feed his hungry family. This really reached me, because I identified with Valjean, and I often thought of my father being in a kind of social prison because he wanted to feed his family. Albert Camus's *The Stranger* and *The Myth of Sisyphus* made me feel even more justified in my pattern of liberating property from the oppressor as an antidote to social suicide.

I felt that white people were criminals because they plundered the world. It was more, however, than a simple antiwhite feeling, because I never wanted to hurt poor whites, even though I had met some in school who called me "nigger" and other names. I fought them, but I never took their lunches or money because I knew that they had nothing to start with. With those who had money it was a different story. I still equated having money with whiteness, and to take what was

mine and what the white criminals called theirs gave me a feeling of real freedom.

I even bragged to my friends how good I felt about the whole
matter. When they were at my apartment during times when
there wasn't any food to eat, I told them that even though I
starved, my time was my own and I could do anything I wanted
with it. I didn't have a car then, because most of my money was
spent on the apartment, food, and clothes. When friends asked
me why I did not get a car, I told them it was because I did not
want bills and that a car was not my main goal or desire. My
purpose was to have as much leisure time as possible. I could
have pulled bigger jobs and gotten more, but I did not want
any status symbols. I wanted most of all to be free from the life
of a servant forced to take those low-paying jobs and looked at
with scorn by white bosses.

Eventually, I got caught, and more than once, but by then I
had developed a fairly good working knowledge of the law,
and I decided to defend myself. Although no skilled legal tech-
nician, I could make a good defense. If you are an existentialist,
defending yourself is another manifestation of freedom. When
you are brought into the courts of the Establishment, you can
show your contempt for them. Most defendants want to get
high-priced counsel or use the state to speak for them through
the Public Defender. If you speak for yourself, you can say exactly what you want, or at least not say what you do not want
to. Or you can laugh at them. As Elaine Brown, a member of
the Black Panther Party, says in her song, "The End of Silence,"
"You laugh at laws passed by a silly lot that tell you to give
thanks for what you've already got." The laws exist to defend
those who possess property. They protect the possessors who
should share but who do not. By defending myself, I showed
my contempt for that structure.

It gave me real pleasure to defend myself. I never thought in
terms of conviction or acquittal, although it was an added treat
to escape their net. But even a conviction would not have dis-
mayed me, because at least I had the opportunity to laugh at
them and show my contempt. They would see that I was not in-

timidated enough to raise the money to get counsel—money
that I did not have in the first place—or to accept a Public
Defender.

I especially liked traffic violations. For a while, I paid a lot of
traffic tickets. When I became my own defender, I never paid
another one. Of the three major cases in which I defended myself, the only one I lost was the one in which I was innocent.

Once, I was indicted on sixteen counts of burglary through
trickery as a result of the short-change game, and I beat the
cases during the pretrial period because the police could not establish the *corpus delicti* or the elements of the case. Each law
had a body of elements, and each element has to be violated in
order for a crime to have been committed. That's what they call
the *corpus delicti*. People think that term means the physical
body, but it really means the body of elements. For example,
according to California law, in order to commit armed robbery
you have to be armed, and you must expropriate through fear
or force related to weapons; you can have armed robbery without any bullets in the gun. The elements of the case relate to
fear and force in connection with weapons.

In the short-change or "bunko" case I was accused of running my game in sixteen stores. However, they could get only a
few people to say they were short in their registers. I was really
saved from being convicted because the police tried to get a
young woman teller from a bank to say that I had short-changed
her. A lot of people will not admit they have been short-changed.
In the pretrial, in which they were trying to get a federal case,
they asked me whether I had gone into the bank. I refused to
admit it. I knew that the young woman whom they wanted to
testify against me had not shown up at court. When I bailed
out, I went to her bank and asked her if the police had been
there. She said they had and that they were trying to persuade
her that I had short-changed her. She said she would not testify
because she knew it had not happened. I invited her to court to
testify on my behalf. She came and explained to the judge that
the police had tried to persuade her to testify, but she would
not comply.

My argument was that the police had invented the short-change rap against me. I pointed out that clerks who were short-changed would have missed the money either when I was in the store or at the end of the day. None of these people had notified the police. The police had sought them out and by suggesting that they had been short-changed were really offering the clerks a chance to make five or ten extra dollars—a sort of pay-off for testifying. Most people, I said, are not as honest as the young girl bank teller.

Another argument I put forth in my defense was that if someone else had gotten change after I had been in the store before inventory of the register, it was quite possible, even probable, that the money had been lost at some other time. I got a dismissal on the grounds of insufficient evidence.

In the second major case, I was accused of having stolen some books from a store near the school and of having burglarized the car of another student and taken his books. He reported to the bookstore that his books had been stolen. They were on the lookout for books with the marking he had described. I had not stolen the books, even though they were in my possession. I was doing a lot of gambling at the time, and some students who owed me money gave me the books instead. We used books for money, because if a book was required in a course, we could sell it to the bookstore. Even though I did not know where the books came from, I suspected that they were stolen.

I figured there was about $60 worth of books in the stack. When I needed money, I sent my cousin to the bookstore to cash them in. The bookstore took them away from her, claiming that they were stolen. They would not give her any money, nor would they return the books. I went down to the store and told them they could not confiscate my books without due process of law. They knew I was a student at the college and that they could call the police on me any time they wanted. I told them that either they return the books right then or I would take as many books as I thought would equal the amount they had stolen from me. They gave me the books, and I went on to class.

Apparently the bookstore notified the Dean of Students, who

called the police. While I was in class, the Oakland police came and escorted me with the books to the campus police, who took me to the Dean's office. No one could arrest me, because there was no warrant. The bookstore wanted to wait until the man who had reported the books stolen returned from the Army to identify them. So they took me to the Dean's office, and the Dean said he would give me a receipt, keeping the books until the owner came back. I told him that he would not give me a receipt, because they were my books and he could not confiscate my property without due process of law; to do so would be a violation of my constitutional rights. I added, "Furthermore, if you try to confiscate my property, I will ask the police over there to have you arrested." The police stood looking stupid, not knowing what to do. The Dean said the man would not be back for about a week, but he wanted the books. I took the books off his desk and said, "I'm enrolled here, and when you want to talk to me, I'll be around." Then I walked out of the office. They did not know how to deal with a poor oppressed Black man who knew their law and had dignity.

When I was charged and brought to trial, I defended myself again. The case revolved around identifying the books. The man knew that his books had been stolen; the bookstore knew they had lost some books. Identification had not been made, but I was charged with a theft. I had stashed the books away so that nobody could locate them, and when I came to court, I left them behind. They brought me to trial without any factual evidence against me, and I beat the case with the defense I conducted, particularly my cross-examination.

The woman who owned the bookstore took the stand. The previous year, on Christmas Eve, she had invited me to her home, and I had seen her off and on after that. When I was unwilling to continue a relationship with her, she became angry. I wanted to bring this out, but when I began this line of questioning, the judge was outraged and stopped it. By this time, however, she had broken down in tears on the stand, and it was apparent to the jury by the questions I asked and her reaction to them that she had personal reasons for testifying against me.

When the Dean testified, I really went to work. Although no books were entered into evidence, he said that I had in my possession some books identical to those on the list the day the police brought me to his office. I asked him, "Well, if the police were right there, why didn't you put me under arrest?" He said, "I wasn't sure of my rights." This was the opening I needed. I said, "You mean to say that I attend your school, and you're teaching me my rights without even knowing your own? You're giving me knowledge, and you don't know your basic civil rights?" Then I turned to the jury and argued that this was strange indeed. The judge was furious and almost cited me for contempt of court. I was in contempt, all right, and not only of the court. I was contemptuous of the whole system of exploitation, which I was coming to understand better and better.

I knew what the jury was thinking, and when the Dean said that he did not know his rights, I used his ignorance to my advantage. People automatically think, "You mean you're a college professor and you don't know something that basic and simple?" Once I planted this idea in the minds of the jurors, it completely negated the Dean's testimony.

I told the jury that I collected books, which I did, traded and sold them, and that I had some volumes similar to those named in the indictment—same names, authors, and so forth. When they wanted to view the books, I asked the judge if I could go home and get them. The judge said that he could not stop a trial in the middle (it was a misdemeanor case) to let me go home. My strategy worked, however, and I ended up with a hung jury.

Then came the second trial. This time I had the books in court, but nobody could identify them. I had acquired some different books—same authors and same names—and put some similar markings in them. The man who claimed his car had been burglarized, the Dean, and the owner of the bookstore could not positively identify them. They kept saying that the books were either similar or the same, but they were not sure.

I emphasized this uncertainty, saying that all I knew was I had purchased the books from another person. I told the jury that I had not in fact stolen the books and that by bringing them to court I was trying to find out if they belonged to those who had brought the charges. I got another hung jury.

They tried me a third time, with the same result. When they brought the case up a fourth time, the judge dismissed it. Off and on, with continuances and mistrials, the case dragged over a perid of nine months. It was simple harassment, as far as I was concerned, because I had not stolen the books. They might also have been trying to test new prosecutors; I had a different one every time, every chump in Alameda County, and still they got nowhere. I looked them straight in the eye and advanced.

The third case came out of a party I attended with Melvin at the home of a probation officer who had gone to San Jose State College with him. Melvin had known some of the people at the party quite a while, and most of them were related to each other in some way, either by blood or by marriage. Melvin and I were outsiders. As usual, I started a discussion. A party was good or bad for me depending on whether I could start a rap session. I taught that way for the Afro-American Association and recruited a lot of the lumpens.

Some of these sessions ended in fights. It was almost like the dozens again, although here, ideas, not mothers, were at issue. The guy who could ask the most penetrating questions and give the smartest answers "capped," or topped, all the others. Sometimes after a guy was defeated, or "shot down," if he wanted to fight, I would accommodate him. It was all the same. If I could get into a good rap and a good fight, too, the night was complete.

At the party, while we were talking, someone called Odell Lee came up and entered the conversation. I did not know him, had only seen him dancing earlier in the evening, but I had gone to school with his wife, Margo, who was there. Odell Lee walked up and said, "You must be an Afro-American." I replied, "I don't know what you mean. Are you asking me if I am of African descent, or are you asking me if I'm a member of Donald Warden's Afro-American Association? If the latter, then I am not. But if you're asking me if I'm of African ancestry, then I am an Afro-American, just as you are." He said some words in Chinese and I came back in Swahili. Then he asked me,

"Well, how do you know that I'm an Afro-American?" I replied, "Well, I have twenty-twenty vision, and I can see your hair is just as kinky as mine, and your face just as black, so I conclude that you must be exactly what I am, an Afro-American."

Saying that, I turned my back and began to cut my steak. I was the only one in the room with a steak knife. All the others had plastic utensils, but since the steak was kind of tough, I had gone into the kitchen for a regular steak knife. Having made my point, my move, so to speak, I turned my back on Lee in a kind of put-down. To him it was a provocative act.

Odell had a scar on his face from about the ear to just below his chin. This was a very significant point, because on the block you run into plenty of guys with scars like that, which usually means that the person has seen a lot of action with knives. This is not always the case, but when you are trying to survive on the block, you learn to be hip to the cues.

So I turned my back and began cutting steak with the knife I had in my right hand. He grabbed my left arm with his right and turned me around abruptly. When he did, my knife was pointed right at him in ready position. Lee said, "Don't turn your back on me when I'm talking to you." I pushed his hand off my arm. "Don't you ever put your hands on me again," I said, and turned around once more to my steak.

Ordinarily I would not have turned my back a second time, because he had all the signs of a tush hog. But somehow the conditions did not add up. Most people there were professionals— or training to become professionals—and this man with the scar did not seem to fit. We were not on the block, so I thought perhaps the scar meant nothing. All of a sudden, however, he was acting like a bully, and now he wanted everyone to know he was not finished with me. When I turned my back on him a second time, this would have ended the whole argument for the Black bourgeoisie, but the tush hog responded in his way.

He turned me around again, and the tempo picked up. "You must not know who you're talking to," he said, moving his left hand to his left hip pocket. I figured I had better hurry up. Since the best defense is a good offense, my steak knife was again in a ready position, instinctively. I said to him, "Don't draw a knife on me," and I thrust my knife forward, stabbing him several times before he could come up with his left hand. He held on to me with his right hand and tried to advance, but I pushed him away. I still do not know what he was doing with his left, but I was expecting to be hurt any time and determined to beat him to the punch.

Melvin grabbed Lee's right arm and pushed him into a corner, where he fell, bleeding heavily. He got up and charged me again, and I continued to hold my knife ready. Then Melvin jumped between us, and Lee fainted in his arms. As Melvin took the knife from me, we turned to the rest of the people, and somebody asked, "Why did you cut him?" Melvin said, "He cut him because he should have cut him," and we backed out of the room. Melvin wanted me to press charges against the man, but I would never go to the police.

About two weeks later, Odell Lee swore out charges against me. I don't know why he delayed so long, perhaps because he was in the hospital for a few days. Maybe he was hesitant. He had been talking about getting me, I know, but I also heard that his wife had urged him to press charges instead. To me, he was not the kind of character who would go to the police. I saw him as a guy who would rather look for me himself and deal right there. When he sent word that he was after me, I started packing a gun. Instead, I was arrested at my house on a warrant and indicted for assault with a deadly weapon. After I pleaded not guilty, it went to a jury trial. I defended myself again.

I was found guilty as charged, but only because I lacked a jury of my peers. My defense was based on the grounds that I was not guilty, either by white law or by the culture of the Black community. I did not deny that I stabbed Odell Lee— I admitted it—but the law says that when one sees or feels he is in imminent danger of great bodily harm or death, he may use whatever force necessary to defend himself. If he kills his assailant, the homicide is justified. This section of the California penal code is almost impossible for a man to defend himself under unless he is a part of the oppressor class. The oppressed have no chance, for people who sit on juries always think you could have picked another means of defense. They cannot see or understand the danger.

A jury of my peers would have understood the situation and exonerated me. But the jurors in Alameda County come out of big houses in the hills to pass judgment on the people whom they feel threaten their "peace." When these people see a scar on the face of a man on the block, they have no understanding of its symbolism. Odell Lee got on the stand and said that his scar resulted from an automobile accident. It may well have. But taking everything in context—his behavior at the party, the move toward his left hip, and his scar—my peers would never have convicted me.

Bobby Seale explains it brilliantly in *Seize the Time:* you may go to a party and step on someone's shoes and apologize, and if the person accepts the apology, then nothing happens. If you hear something like "An apology won't shine my shoes," then you know he is really saying, "I'm going to fight you." So you defend yourself, and in that case striking first would be a defensive act, not an offensive one. You are trying to get an advantage over an opponent who has already declared war.

It is all a matter of life styles that spills over into the problem of getting a jury of one's peers. If a truck driver is the defendant, should there be only truck drivers on the jury, or all white racists on the jury if a white racist is on trial? I say no. There is, nevertheless, an internal contradiction in a jury system that totally divides the accused and his jury. Different cultures and life styles in America use the same words with different shades of meaning. All belong to one society yet live in different worlds.

I was found guilty of a felony, assault with a deadly weapon, and faced a long jail sentence for the first time. Before and during the trial, I had been out on bail for several months. I came to court each time I was supposed to, but when I was convicted, the judge decided to revoke my bail immediately and place me in the custody of the bailiff while he considered what sentence to impose. Wanting none of this, I demanded to be sentenced right then. The judge said that if he sentenced me then, I would be sent to the state penitentiary. I told him to send me there immediately so that I could start serving my time. He refused, asking me, "Do you realize what you're saying?" I said, "I know what I'm saying, that you found me guilty. But I am not guilty, and now I don't want to wait around a month serving dead time while you think about it." No time was dead to me. It was all live time, life. I felt that if the judge wanted to think about it for thirty days, he should let me stay out on bail while he did so. But he would not. He had me confined to the Alameda County Jail, a place I would get to know well—very well.

While I was waiting, my family hired a lawyer to represent me at the sentencing. The judge was a man named Leonard Dieden, who did not give lawyers, much less defendants, any respect. He has sent so many people to the penitentiary that a section of San Quentin is called "Dieden's Row." I was against my family hiring a lawyer because I felt it was useless. Nevertheless, they did, and he charged them $1,500 to go to court one time. When I arrived for sentencing, he was there, and he worked his "white magic": the judge sentenced me to six months in the county jail. Even though I had been convicted of a felony, the time they gave me was for a misdemeanor. This was to become a critical issue in my later capital trial, because the law says you can reduce a felony to a misdemeanor by serving less time. The penalty for a felony is no less than a year in the state penitentiary and no more than a life sentence or death. For a misdemeanor the maximum is one year in the county jail.

13

. . . all women, even the very phenomenal, want at least a promise of brighter days, bright tomorrows. I have no tomorrows at all.

GEORGE JACKSON, *Soledad Brother*

Loving

My relationships with women could be described as complex or strange, depending on how you look at them. Varying influences helped to form my attitude—the influence of my parents, of Christianity, of my older brothers, and, later, my reading and the theories of Richard Thorne. Because these influences were often contradictory, they led to certain conflicts in my feelings and involvements with women, conflicts that were not to be resolved until the communal life of the Black Panther Party displaced problematical individual relationships.

When I was very young, I accepted the institution of marriage. As I grew older and saw my father struggling to take care of a wife and seven children, having to work at three jobs at once, I began to see that the bourgeois family can be an imprisoning, enslaving, and suffocating experience. Even though my mother and father loved each other deeply and were happy together, I felt that I could not survive this kind of binding commitment with all its worries and material insecurity. Among the poor, social conditions and economic hardship frequently change marriage into a troubled and fragile relationship. A strong love between husband and wife can survive outside pressures, but that is rare. Marriage usually becomes one more imprisoning experience within the general prison of society.

My doubts about marriage were reinforced when I met Richard Thorne. His theory of nonpossessiveness in the love relationship was appealing to me. The idea that one person possesses the other, as in bourgeois marriage, where "she's my woman and he's my man," was unacceptable. It was too restrictive, too binding, and ultimately destructive to the union itself. Often it absorbed all of a man's energies and did not leave him free to develop potential talents, to be creative, or make a contribution in other areas of life. This argument—that a family is a burden to a man—is developed in Bertrand Russell's critique of marriage and the family. His observations impressed me and strengthened my convictions about the drawbacks of conventional marriage.

As a result of thinking and reading, I decided to remain unmarried. This is a decision I do not regret, although it has caused me pain and conflict from time to time and brought unhappiness to me and some of the women whom I have loved.

After I moved out of Poor Boys Hall and had my own apartment, I was involved with several beautiful young women, who loved me very much. I loved them just as much. For a while, I accepted money and favors from them, but only after I had explained that our relationship probably would not work because I was unprepared to follow the old road. If they wanted to be with me, I told them, they would have to do certain things. I never forced or persuaded them. As a matter of fact, I said that in their place, I would not do it at all. I also explained my principle of nonpossessiveness. I believed that if I was free, so were they, free to be involved with other men. I told them they could have any kind of relationship they wanted with someone else, but that we had a special relationship that could not be duplicated with any other person, no matter how many people we might be involved with at the same time. This meant freedom for me, because I could have three or four relationships at the same time without having to keep one secret from the other.

I was living alone, and we would all be together at my house at the same time. Richard would bring his friends over, too. Together we became almost a cult. We spread our ideas around Oakland City College and Berkeley before group living and communalism became popular. I might even say that this was the origin of the Sexual Freedom League, since Thorne went on from this to start that organization. The girls found our experiments unusual and romantic and thought we were very exciting. The main foundation of our relationship was mutual honesty and the elimination of jealousy. Within a given period, Richard and I would sleep with more than one woman to see if they could deal with this without regressing to their old values, which we, in our wisdom, considered outdated and bourgeois, as well as mentally unhealthy.

Although much of this involved a new philosophy about the family, another part of it was exploitative. I was serious about our attempt to question matters through practice, but I also felt that we were taking advantage of the women for practical reasons. Women paid my rent, cooked my food, and did other things for me, while any money I came by was mine to keep.

Around this time I was pulling small-time armed robberies with some of my "crime partners." We hid in the parking lots of expensive white clubs, and when the people came out, we took their fur wraps, wallets, rings, and watches. I never wanted to do these things on a large scale. What I wanted was leisure time to read and make love. My idea was to be involved with a number of women—and I was. I look back on this time as a kind of "God experience," when I was "free" to do anything I wanted.

There was conflict, however, because, while I was exploiting women, I was also fighting some internal values that would not let me alone. Perhaps these arose from the Christian principles that had been instilled in me from birth, perhaps from traditional mores. Still more likely, the conflict arose out of my desire not to treat another human being as an object. The fact that I found it necessary to explain to women that they were at a disadvantage in their relationship with me indicated that I needed some kind of defense mechanism against the guilt I felt. Still, women made my freedom possible by sacrificing their traditional ideas of husband and family.

While I loved many women, only twice did I feel an impulse to marry. Even then, after serious consideration, I could not go through with it. Every time I felt close to a woman, I knew it was time for the relationship to end. No matter how deeply I felt, I could not share her goals if they led to a compromise with society.

For a time I tried the pimping life, but this caused altogether too much inner turmoil. Whenever I pimped a Black sister, my mind would be filled with flashes of the slave experience—the racist dogs raping Black women. I began to feel that if my conscience would not allow me to pimp Black women, perhaps I should pimp white women—the "enemy." But when I "turned out" a white woman and found there was still a crisis of conscience, I realized that I could never pimp for a living. With Black women the feeling was shame, because I was selling my sister's body. With white women the feeling was not shame but guilt, because I was now in the role of the oppressor. I had a "weakness" for women. Therefore, I could never be harsh with them; I always identified with them and fell in love. I flirted with pimping for only about nine months.

It was during this period that I met Dolores. She and I were together for five years, until I went to jail after the Odell Lee case. Slowly, imperceptibly, I fell more deeply in love with her than I ever had before. She had certain qualities that set her apart from all the others; she was special, unique. Dolores was a beautiful Afro-Filipino free-spirit child-woman, who lived with a passionate intensity. Life with her was spontaneous, unpredictable, and filled with surprises, for she had the unselfconsciousness of an impulsive and mischievous child. Sometimes, if I was reading or absorbed, she would steal up behind me and jump on my back. She loved fighting games and played aggressively, often Melvin and I had to retreat from a barrage of small stones that came flying at us, accompanied by triumphant laughter and taunts.

Yet there was a deeper, more complex side to her nature, for she was a creature of great contrasts. Dolores had an unusual gift for language and a sensitivity to the nuances and subtleties of words. She composed small poems that to me seemed remarkable. They revealed an awareness of the tenuousness of all human involvements, and the sense of despair that hovers constantly at the lover's threshold of consciousness. Here is one she wrote for me:

> The two of us are multitude;
> Without you I am dead.
> I'd rather not be
> Than to be deceived
> By the one who keeps me alive.

In our relationship there was an intense contradiction. I could live with her but not in the context of conventional family life. During our five years together we broke up from time to time, but never for more than three months; some intense need always drove us back to each other. In spite of her childlike qualities, Dolores was mature in many ways. She was a hard worker and willing to support us; she really understood and accepted my problem.

I was in conflict, wanting to do the things that are expected of a man in our society, even trying a couple of times, without success. I worked on a construction job once and at a cannery for a couple of seasons, but I could not deal with work on a permanent basis. Often I considered marrying Dolores, but to do so meant accepting the conditions necessary to marriage in an oppressive situation. If two people are together as a unit, rather than in some haphazard way, a certain amount of security must exist. In the event of children they must sacrifice their time to have that security. I was afraid of that.

Many of my contemporaries were getting married in the hope of securing a good job and raising a family. But their marriages soon broke up because it cost so much to live and their jobs were so treacherously menial that all their time was spent grubbing for basic necessities. Their dreams were crushed by the realities of their lives. When I saw myself heading in that direction, I balked. By rejecting marriage and a family I held on to my "freedom," but I lost the intimacy and companionship of a woman—an experience that is probably as great as, perhaps greater than, the freedom I wanted.

My inability to make a total commitment led Dolores to disaster. Our years together, and our closeness, had created a deep dependence in her, although I tried to maintain my own freedom in various ways. One of these was to see other women. One night I brought another woman to my parents' home; while we were there, Dolores unexpectedly came over. The other woman and I went out, leaving Dolores there. Finally, about two in the morning, I left my companion and returned to our apartment. Dolores was gone. After some frantic calls, I made one to my cousin, who lived nearby. She told me Dolores had taken forty sleeping pills. I rushed over and found Dolores unconscious. An ambulance came and took her to the hospital. No one knew if help had arrived in time. I rushed to the hospital. She was alive.

I should have seen the danger. Some of her poems had foreshadowed the self-destructive impulse. One of them, in particular, had a somber, despairing quality:

> The pigeons of my conscience
> Make shadows on the wall.
> The cannibal that lives within my mind
> Leaves no room for the imagination.
> I regret just this.

My experience with Dolores reinforced, in the end, my conviction that the demands two people make upon each other can be crippling and destructive. No matter how much they love each other, the values of our society conspire to add intolerable pressures to a binding relationship. The contradictions inherent in marriage make it all but impossible to survive.

These contradictions have been solved by the values of the Black Panther Party and by the Party's communal life. The closeness of the group and the shared sense of purpose transform us into a harmonious, functioning body, working for the destruction of those conditions that make people suffer. Our unity has transformed us to the point where we have not compromised with the system; we have the closeness and love of family life, the will to live in spite of cruel conditions. Consciousness is the first step toward control of a situation. We feel free as a group; we know what troubles us, and we act.

Bourgeois values define the family situation in America, give it certain goals. Oppressed and poor people who try to reach these goals fail because of the very conditions that the bourgeoisie has established. There is the dilemma. We need a family, because every man and woman deserves the kind of spiritual support and unity a family provides. Black people try to reach the goals set by the dominant culture and fail without knowing why.

How do you solve the situation? By staying outside the system, living alone? I found that to be an outsider is to be alienated and unhappy. In the Party we have formed a family, a fighting family that is a vital unit in itself. We have no romantic and fictional notions about getting married and living happily ever after behind a white picket fence. We choose to live together for a common purpose, and together we fight for our existence and our goals. Today we have the closeness, the harmony and freedom that we sought so long.

PART THREE

We believe that Black people will not be free until we are able to determine our destiny.

14

Locked in jail, within a jail, my mind is still free. . . . What if a person was so oriented that the loss of no material thing could cause him mental disorganization? This is the free agent.
GEORGE JACKSON, Soledad Brother

Freedom

Jail is an odd place to find freedom, but that was the place I first found mine: in the Alameda County Jail in Oakland in 1964. This jail is located on the tenth floor of the Alameda County Court House, the huge, white building we call "Moby Dick." When I was falsely convicted of the assault against Odell Lee, Judge Dieden sent me there to await sentencing. Shortly after I arrived, I was made a trusty, which gave me an opportunity to move about freely. Conditions were not good; in fact, the place blew up a few weeks later, when the inmates refused to go on eating starches and split-pea soup at almost every meal, and went on a food strike. I joined them. When we were brought our split-pea soup, we hurled it back through the bars, all over the walls, and refused to lock up in our cells.

I was the only trusty who took part in the strike, and because I could move between cell blocks, they charged me with organizing it. True, I had carried a few messages back and forth, but I was not an organizer then, not that it mattered to the jail administration. Trusties were supposed to go along with the Establishment in everything, and since I could not do that, I was slapped with the organizing label and put in the "hole"—what Black prisoners call the "soul breaker."

I was twenty-two years old, and I had been in jail before on various beefs, mostly burglary and petty larceny. My parents were pretty sick of me in my late teens and the years following, so I had to depend on Sonny Man to come up from Los Angeles, or wherever he was, to bail me out. Since I had been "given" to him, he came whenever he could. But sometimes I could not find him. At any rate, I was no stranger to jail by 1964, although I had never been in extreme solitary confinement.

Within jail, there are four levels of confinement: the main line, segregation, isolation, and solitary—the "soul breaker." You can be in jail in jail, but the soul breaker is your "last" end of the world. In 1964, there were two of these deprivation cells at the Alameda County Court House; each was four and a half feet wide, by six feet long, by ten feet high. The floor was dark red rubber tile, and the walls were black. If the guards wanted to, they could turn on a light in the ceiling, but I was always kept in the dark, and nude. That is part of the deprivation, why the soul breaker is called a strip cell. Sometimes the prisoner in the other cell would get a blanket, but they never gave me one. He sometimes got toilet paper, too—the limit was two squares— and when he begged for more, he was told no, that is part of the punishment. There was no bunk, no washbasin, no toilet, nothing but bare floors, bare walls, a solid steel door, and a round hole four inches in diameter and six inches deep in the middle of the floor. The prisoner was supposed to urinate and defecate in this hole.

A half-gallon milk carton filled with water was my liquid for the week. Twice a day and always at night the guards brought a little cup of cold split-pea soup, right out of the can. Sometimes during the day they brought "fruit loaf," a patty of cooked vegetables mashed together into a little ball. When I first went in there, I wanted to eat and stay healthy, but soon I realized that there was another trick, because when I ate I had to defecate. At night no light came in under the door. I could not even find the hole if I had wanted to. If I was desperate, I had to search with my hand; when I found it, the hole was always slimy with the filth that had gone in before. I was just like a mole looking for the sun; I hated finding it when I did. After a few days the

hole filled up and overflowed, so that I could not lie down
without wallowing in my own waste. Once every week or two
the guards ran a hose into the cell and washed out the urine
and defecation. This cleared the air for a while and made it all
right to take a deep breath. I had been told I would break before the fifteen days were up. Most men did. After two or three
days they would begin to scream and beg for someone to come
and take them out, and the captain would pay a visit and say,
"We don't want to treat you this way. Just come out now and
abide by the rules and don't be so arrogant. We'll treat you
fairly. The doors here are large." To tell the truth, after two or
three days I *was* in bad shape. Why I did not break I do not
know. Stubbornness, probably. I did not want to beg. Certainly
my resistance was not connected to any kind of ideology or
program. That came later. Anyway, I did not scream and beg; I
learned the secrets of survival.

One secret was the same that Mahatma Gandhi learned—to
take little sips of nourishment, just enough to keep up one's
strength, but never enough to have to defecate until the fifteen
days were up. That way I kept the air somewhat clean and did
not have the overflow. I did the same with water, taking little
sips every few hours. My body absorbed all of it, and I did not
have to urinate.

There was another, more important secret, one that took
longer to learn. During the day a little light showed in the two-
inch crack at the bottom of the steel door. At night, as the sun
went down and the lights clicked off one by one, I heard all the
cells closing, and all the locks. I held my hands up in front of
my face, and soon I could not see them. For me, that was the testing time, the time when I had to save myself or break.

Outside jail, the brain is always being bombarded by external stimuli. These ordinary sights and sounds of life help keep
our mental processes in order, rational. In deprivation, you
have to somehow replace the stimuli, provide an interior environment for yourself. Ever since I was a little boy I have been
able to overcome stress by calling up pleasant thoughts. So very
soon I began to reflect on the most soothing parts of my past,

not to keep out any evil thoughts, but to reinforce myself in some kind of rewarding experience. Here I learned something. This was different.

When I had a pleasant memory, what was I to do with it? Should I throw it out and get another or try to keep it to entertain myself as long as possible? If you are not disciplined, a strange thing happens. The pleasant thought comes, and then another and another, like quick cuts flashing vividly across a movie screen. At first they are organized. Then they start to pick up speed, pushing in on top of one another, going faster, faster, faster, faster. The pleasant thoughts are not so pleasant now; they are horrible and grotesque caricatures, whirling around in your head. Stop! I heard myself say, stop, stop, stop. I did not scream. I was able to stop them. Now what do I do?

I started to exercise, especially when I heard the jangle of keys as the guards came with the split-pea soup and fruit loaf. I *would not* scream; I *would not* apologize, even though they came every day, saying they would let me out if I gave in. When they were coming, I would get up and start my calisthenics, and when they went away, I would start the pleasant thoughts again. If I was too tired to stand, I would lie down and find myself on my back. Later, I learned that my position, with my back arched and only my shoulders and tight buttocks touching the floor, was a Zen Buddhist posture. I did not know it then, of course; I just found myself on my back. When the thoughts started coming again, to entertain me, and when the same thing happened with the speed-up, faster, faster, I would say, stop! and start again.

Over a span of time—I do not know how long it took— I mastered my thoughts. I could start them and stop them; I could slow them down and speed them up. It was a very conscious exercise. For a while, I feared I would lose control. I could not think; I could not stop thinking. Only later did I learn through practice to go at the speed I wanted. I call them film clips, but they are really thought patterns, the most vivid pictures of my family, girls, good times. Soon I could lie with my back arched for hours on end, and I placed no importance on the passage of time. Control. I learned to control my food, my body, and my mind through a deliberate act of will.

After fifteen days the guards pulled me out and sent me back to a regular cell for twenty-four hours, where I took a shower and saw a medical doctor and a psychiatrist. They were worried that prisoners would become mentally disorganized in such deprivation. Then, because I had not repented, they sent me back to the hole. By then it held no fears for me. I had won my freedom.

Soul breakers exist because the authorities know that such conditions would drive *them* to the breaking point, but when I resolved that they would not conquer my will, I became stronger than they were. I understood them better than they understood me. No longer dependent on the things of the world, I felt really free for the first time in my life. In the past I had been like my jailers; I had pursued the goals of capitalistic America. Now I had a higher freedom.

Most people who know me do not realize that I have been in and out of jail for the past twelve years. They know only of my eleven months in solitary in 1967, waiting for the murder trial to begin, and the twenty-two months at the Penal Colony after that. But 1967 would not have been possible without 1964. I could not have handled the Penal Colony solitary without the soul breaker behind me. Therefore, I cannot tell inexperienced young comrades to go into jail and into solitary, that that is the way to defy the authorities and exercise their freedom. I know what solitary can do to a man.

The strip cell has been outlawed throughout the United States. Prisoners I talk to in California tell me it is no longer in use on the West Coast. That was the work of Charles Garry, the lawyer who defended me in 1968, when he fought the case of Warren Wells, a Black Panther accused of shooting a policeman. The Superior Court of California said it was an outrage to human decency to put any man through such extreme deprivation. Of course, prisons have their ways, and out there right now, somewhere, prisoners without lawyers are probably lying in their own filth in the soul breaker.

I was in the hole for a month. My sentence, when it came, was for six months on the county farm at Santa Rita, about fifty miles south of Oakland. This is an honor camp with no walls, and the inmates are not locked up. There is a barbed-wire fence, but anyone can easily walk off during the daytime. The inmates work at tending livestock, harvesting crops, and doing other farm work.

I was not in the honor camp long. A few days after I arrived, I had a fight with a fat Black inmate named Bojack, who served in the mess hall. Bojack was a diligent enforcer of small helpings, and I was a "dipper." Whenever Bojack turned away, I would dip for more with my spoon. One day he tried to prevent me from dipping, and I called him for protecting the oppressor's interests and smashed him with a steel tray. When they pulled me off him, I was hustled next door to Graystone, the maximum security prison at Santa Rita.

Here, prisoners are locked up all day inside a stone building. Not only that. I was put in solitary confinement for the remaining months of my sentence. Because of my experience in the hold, I could survive. Still, I did not submit willingly. The food was as bad in Graystone as it had been in Alameda, and I constantly protested about that and the lack of heat in my cell. Half the time we had no heat at all.

Wherever you go in prison there are disturbed inmates. One on my block at Santa Rita screamed night and day as loudly as he could; his vocal cords seemed made of iron. From time to time, the guards came into his cell and threw buckets of cold water on him. Gradually, as the inmate wore down, the scream became a croak and then a squeak and then a whisper. Long after he gave out, the sound lingered in my head.

The Santa Rita administration finally got disgusted with my continual complaints and protests and shipped me back to the jail in Oakland, where I spent the rest of my time in solitary. By then I was used to the cold. Even now, I do not like any heat at all wherever I stay, no matter what the outside temperature. Even so, the way I was treated told me a lot about those who devised such punishment. I know them well.

15

*Seale is the heir to the early organizing efforts of young blacks
and whites in the rural South. He inherits ... the demands of
the early sixties students that fundamental constitutional guar-
antees and promises—so long violated by illegitimate white
power—be immediately honored, while reserving the right to
attack the system itself.*

JULIAN BOND, *A Time to Speak, A Time to Act*

Bobby Seale

Out of jail and back on the street in 1965, I again took up with
Bobby Seale. We had a lot to talk about; I had not seen him in
more than a year.

Bobby and I had not always agreed. In fact, we disagreed the
first time we met, during the Cuban missile crisis several years
before. That was the time President Kennedy was about to
blow humanity off the face of the earth because Russian ships
were on their way to liberated territory with arms for the people
of Cuba. The Progressive Labor Party was holding a really outside Oakland City College to encourage support for Fidel Castro, and I was there because I agreed with their views. There
were a number of speakers and one of them, Donald Warden,
launched into a lengthy praise of Fidel. He did this in his usual
opportunistic way, tooting his own horn. Warden was about
halfway through his routine, criticizing civil rights organizations and asking why we put our money into that kind of thing,
when Bobby challenged him, expressing opposition to Warden
and strong support for the position of the National Association
for the Advancement of Colored People. He felt that the NAACP

was the hope of Black people and because of this, he supported the government and its moves against Cuba. I explained to him afterward that he was wrong to support the government and the civil rights organizations. Too much money had already been put into legal actions. There were enough laws on the books to permit Black people to deal with all their problems, but the laws were not enforced. Therefore, trying to get more laws was only a meaningless diversion from the real issues. This was an argument I had heard in the Afro-American Association and in Oakland by Malcolm X, who made the point over and over again. Bobby began to think about this and later came over to my point of view.

Whatever our early disagreements, Bobby and I were close by 1965. Later, I recruited him into the Afro-American Association, but when I left it, he continued to stick with Warden. At that time I was still going through my identity crisis, looking for some understanding of myself in relation to society. While I took a back seat in the Association and refused to make a stand on any position, Bobby threw all his energy into it, even after I left.

Still, we did not establish close contact until I got out of the hole in 1965. At that point, Bobby was planning to get married, and he needed a bed for his new apartment. I was breaking up with my girl friend and had a bed I no longer wanted. I sold it to him, and we hauled it to his home. That afternoon we began to talk; he told me that he also had left the Afro-American Association to hook up with Ken Freeman and his group, the Revolutionary Action Movement (RAM). Most of the brothers in this group attended Oakland City College, but the organization was a sort of underground, off-campus operation. They also had a front group called Soul Students Advisory Council, which was a recognized campus organization. The RAM group was more intellectual than active. They did a lot of talking about the revolution and also some writing. Writing was almost a requirement for membership, in fact, but Bobby was no writer. At the time I got out of jail, Bobby had been involved in an argument with the members and had been suspended for a time. Still angry about this, he told me he intended to break with them. Like me, like thousands of us, Bobby was looking for something and not finding it.

Bobby and I entered into a period of intense exploration, trying to solve some of the ideological problems of the Black movement; partly, we needed to explain to our own satisfaction why no Black political organization had succeeded. The only one we thought had promised long-term success was the Organization of Afro-American Unity started by Malcolm X, but Malcolm had died too soon to pull his program together. Malcolm's slogan had been "Freedom by any means necessary," but nothing we saw was taking us there. We still had only a vague conception of what freedom ought to mean to Black people, except in abstract terms borrowed from politicians, and that did not help the people on the block at all. Those lofty words were meant for intellectuals and the bourgeoisie, who were already fairly comfortable.

Much of our conversation revolved around groups in the San Francisco, Oakland, and Berkeley areas. Knowing the people who belonged to them, we could evaluate both positive and negative aspects of their characters and the nature of their organizations. While we respected many of the moves these brothers had made, we felt that the negative aspects of their movements overshadowed the positive ones.

We started throwing around ideas. None of the groups were able to recruit and involve the very people they professed to represent—the poor people in the community who never went to college, probably were not even able to finish high school. Yet these were our people; they were the vast majority of the Black population in the area. Any group talking about Blacks was in fact talking about those low on the ladder in terms of well-being, self-respect, and the amount of concern the government had for them. All of us were talking, and nobody was reaching them.

Bobby had a talent that could help us. He was beginning to make a name for himself in local productions as an actor and comedian. I had seen him act in several plays written by brothers, and he was terrific. I had never liked comedians, and I would not go out of my way to hear one. If a person presents his material in a serious way and uses humor to get his points across, he will have me laughing with all the rest, but stand-up, wisecracking comedians leave me cold. Still, I recognized Bobby's talent and I thought he could use it to relate to people and persuade them in an incisive way. Often, when we were rapping about our frustrations with particular people or groups, Bobby would act out their madness. He could do expert imitations of President Kennedy, Martin Luther King, James Cagney, Humphrey Bogart, and Chester of "Gunsmoke." He could also imitate down to the last detail some of the brothers around us. I would crack my sides laughing, not only because his imitations were so good, but because he could convey certain attitudes and characteristics so sharply. He caught all their shortcomings, the way their ideas failed to meet the needs of the people.

We planned to work through the Soul Students Advisory Council. Although SSAC was just a front for RAM, it had one large advantage—it was not an intellectual organization, and for that reason it would appeal to many lower-class brothers at City College. If these brothers belonged to a group that gave them feelings of strength and respect, they could become effective participants. It was important to give them something relevant to do, something not degrading. Soul Students was normally an ineffective and transitory group without a real program. Only if something big was happening did their meetings attract a lot of people. In the quiet times only two or three would show up.

Just then, however, Soul Students had a hot issue—the establishment of a program of Afro-American history and culture in the college's regular curriculum. Although it was a relevant program, the authorities were resisting it tooth and nail. Every time we proposed a new course, they countered with reasons why it could not be; at the same time, ironically, they encouraged us to be "concerned." This was simple trickery; they were dragging their feet.

Bobby and I saw this as an opportunity to move Soul Students a step further by adopting a program of armed self-defense. We approached, them, proposing a rally in front of the college in support of the Afro-American history program. We pointed out that this would be a different kind of rally—the Soul Students members would strap on guns and march on the sidewalk in front of the school. Partly, the rally would express our opposition to police brutality, but it would also intimidate the authorities at City College who were resisting our program. We were looking for a way to emphasize both college and community, to draw them in together. The police and the school authorities needed a strong jolt from Blacks, and we knew this kind of action would make them realize that the brothers meant business. Carrying guns for self-defense was perfectly legal at the time.

We explained all this to Soul Students and showed them that we did not intend to break any laws but were concerned that the organization start dealing with reality rather than sit around intellectualizing and writing essays about the white man. We wanted them to dedicate themselves to armed self-defense with the full understanding that this was defense for the survival of Black people in general and in particular for the cultural program we were trying to establish. As we saw it, Blacks were getting ripped off everywhere. The police had given us no choice but to defend ourselves against their brutality. On the campus we were being miseducated; we had no courses dealing with our real needs and problems, courses that taught us how to survive. Our program was designed to lead the brothers into self-defense before we were completely wiped out physically and mentally.

The weapons were a recruiting device. I felt we could recruit Oakland City College students from the grass roots, people who did not relate to campus organizations that were all too intellectual and offered no effective program of action. Street people would relate to Soul Students if they followed our plan; if the Black community has learned to respect anything, it has learned to respect the gun.

We underestimated the difficulty of bringing the brothers around. Soul Students completely rejected our program. Those brothers had been so intimidated by police firepower they would not give any serious consideration to strapping on a gun, legal or not. After that setback we went to the Revolutionary Action Movement. They did not have many members, just a few guys from the college campus who talked a lot. We explained that by wearing and displaying weapons the street brothers would relate to RAM's example of leadership. We also talked about a new idea, patrolling the police, since the police were the main perpetrators of violence against the community. We went no further than those two tactics: armed self-defense and police patrol. A more complete program was sure to get bogged down on minor points. I just wanted them to adopt a program of self-defense, and after that was worked out, we could then develop it more fully. We were not aiming then at party organization; there were too many organizations already. Our job was to make one of them relevant; that would be contribution enough. However, we were having a lot of trouble breaking through. RAM rejected the plan, too. They thought it was "suicidal," that we could not survive a single day patrolling the police.

This left us where we had been all along: nowhere.

16

As a sapling bent low stores energy for a violent backswing, blacks bent double by oppression have stored energy which will be released in the form of rage—black rage, apocalyptic and final.

WILLIAM GRIER and PRICE COBBS, *Black Rage*

The Founding of the Black Panther Party

All during this time, Bobby and I had no thought of the Black Panther Party, no plan to head up any organization, and the ten-point program was still in the future. We had seen Watts rise up the previous year. We had seen how the police attacked the Watts community after causing the trouble in the first place. We had seen Martin Luther King come to Watts in an effort to calm the people, and we had seen his philosophy of nonviolence rejected. Black people had been taught nonviolence; it was deep in us. What good, however, was nonviolence when the police were determined to rule by force? We had seen the Oakland police and the California Highway Patrol begin to carry their shotguns in full view as another way of striking fear into the community. We had seen all this, and we recognized that the rising consciousness of Black people was almost at the point of explosion. One must relate to the history of one's community and to its future. Everything we had seen convinced us that our time had come.

Out of this need sprang the Black Panther Party. Bobby and

I finally had no choice but to form an organization that would involve the lower-class brothers.

We worked it out in conversations and discussions. Most of the talk was casual. Bobby lived near the campus, and his living room became a kind of headquarters. Although we were still involved with Soul Students, we attended few meetings, and when we did go, our presence was mostly disruptive; we raised questions that upset people. Our conversations with each other became the important thing. Brothers who had a free hour between classes and others who just hung around the campus drifted in and out of Bobby's house. We drank beer and wine and chewed over the political situation, our social problems, and the merits and shortcomings of the other groups. We also discussed the Black achievements of the past, particularly as they helped us to understand current events.

In a sense, these sessions at Bobby's house were our political education classes, and the Party sort of grew out of them. Even after we formally organized we continued the discussions in our office. By then we had moved on to include not only problems but possible solutions.

We also read. The literature of oppressed people and their struggles for liberation in other countries is very large, and we pored over these books to see how their experiences might help us to understand our plight. We read the work of Frantz Fanon, particularly *The Wretched of the Earth,* the four volumes of Chairman Mao Tse-tung, and Che Guevara's *Guerilla Warfare.* Che and Mao were veterans of people's wars, and they had worked out successful strategies for liberating their people. We read these men's works because we saw them as kinsmen; the oppressor who had controlled them was controlling us, both directly and indirectly. We believed it was necessary to know how they gained their freedom in order to go about getting ours. However, we did not want merely to import ideas and strategies; we had to transform what we learned into principles and methods acceptable to the brothers on the block.

Mao and Fanon and Guevara all saw clearly that the people had been stripped of their birthright and their dignity, not by any philosophy or mere words, but at gunpoint. They had suffered a holdup by gangsters, and rape; for them, the only way to win freedom was to meet force with force. At bottom, this is a form of self-defense. Although that defense might at times take on characteristics of aggression, in the final analysis the people do not initiate; they simply respond to what has been inflicted upon them. People respect the expression of strength and dignity displayed by men who refuse to bow to the weapons of oppression. Though it may mean death, these men will fight, because death with dignity is preferable to ignominy. Then, too, there is always the chance that the oppressor will be overwhelmed.

Fanon made a statement during the Algerian war that impressed me; he said it was the "Year of the Boomerang," which is the third phase of violence. At that point, the violence of the aggressor turns on him and strikes a killing blow. Yet the oppressor does not understand the process; he knows no more than he did in the first phase when he launched the violence. The oppressed are always defensive; the oppressor is always aggressive and surprised when the people turn back on him the force he has used against them.

Negroes with Guns by Robert Williams* had a great influence on the kind of party we developed. Williams had been active in Monroe, North Carolina, with a program of armed self-defense that had enlisted many in the community. However, I did not like the way he had called on the federal government for assistance; we viewed the government as an enemy, the agency of a ruling clique that controls the country. We also

---

*Robert Williams was the president of the NAACP in Monroe, North Carolina, when he recruited its male members into an organization that advocated carrying guns for self-defense, a move made necessary for protection against whites who went on regular shooting sprees into the Black community, terrorizing its residents. Williams was one of the first modern Black advocates of self-defense, and he wrote articles supporting his position. In 1961, he fled from the United States when a federal fugitive warrant was issued against him for kidnaping. Members of Williams's organization said that a white couple from the area, whom they had detained for a short period, had been sent into the Black community at night to give police an official excuse for harassment and violence. Williams went to Cuba, China, and Tanzania, where he continued to write. In 1969, he returned to the United States.

had some literature about the Deacons for Defense and Justice in Louisiana, the state where I was born. One of their leaders had come through the Bay Area on a speaking and fund-raising tour, and we liked what he said. The Deacons had done a good job of defending civil rights marchers in their area, but they also had a habit of calling upon the federal government to carry out this defense or at least to assist them in defending the people who were upholding the law. The Deacons even went so far as to enlist local sheriffs and police to defend the marchers, with the threat that if law enforcement agencies would not defend them, the Deacons would. We also viewed the local police, the National Guard, and the regular military as one huge armed group that opposed the will of the people. In a boundary situation people have no real defense except what they provide for themselves.

We read also the works of the freedom fighters who had done so much for Black communities in the United States. Bobby had collected all of Malcolm X's speeches and ideas from papers like *The Militant* and *Muhammad Speaks*. These we studied carefully. Although Malcolm's program for the Organization of Afro-American Unity was never put into operation, he has made it clear that Blacks ought to arm. Malcolm's influence was ever-present. We continue to believe that the Black Panther Party exists in the spirit of Malcolm. Often it is difficult to say exactly how an action or a program has been determined or influenced in a spiritual way. Such intangibles are hard to describe, although they can be more significant than any precise influence. Therefore, the words on this page cannot convey the effect that Malcolm has had on the Black Panther Party, although, as far as I am concerned, the Party is a living testament to his life work. I do not claim that the Party has done what Malcolm would have done. Many others say that their programs are Malcolm's programs. We do not say this, but Malcolm's spirit is in us.

From all of these things—the books, Malcolm's writings and spirit, our analysis of the local situation—the idea of an organization was forming. One day, quite suddenly, almost by chance, we found a name. I had read a pamphlet about voter registration in Mississippi, how the people in Lowndes County had armed themselves against Establishment violence. Their political group, called the Lowndes County Freedom Organization, had a black panther for its symbol. A few days later, while Bobby and I were rapping, I suggested that we use the panther as our symbol and call our political vehicle the Black Panther Party. The panther is a fierce animal, but he will not attack until he is backed into a corner; then he will strike out. The image seemed appropriate, and Bobby agreed without discussion. At this point, we knew it was time to stop talking and begin organizing. Although we had always wanted to get away from the intellectualizing and rhetoric characteristic of other groups, at times we were as inactive as they were. The time had come for action.

17

The only way to police a ghetto is to be oppressive. None of the Police Commissioner's men, even with the best will in the world, have any way of understanding the lives led by the people they swagger about in twos and threes controlling. Their very presence is an insult, and it would be, even if they spent their entire day feeding gumdrops to children. They represent the force of the white world, and that world's real intentions are, simply, for that world's criminal profit and ease, to keep the black man corraled up here, in his place.

JAMES BALDWIN, "Fifth Avenue, Uptown,"
Nobody Knows My Name

Patrolling

It was the spring of 1966. Still without a definite program, we were at the stage of testing ideas that would capture the imagination of the community. We began, as always, by checking around with the street brothers. We asked them if they would be interested in forming the Black Panther Party for Self-Defense, which would be based upon defending the community against the aggression of the power structure, including the military and the armed might of the police. We informed the brothers of their right to possess weapons; most of them were interested. Then we talked about how the people are constantly intimidated by arrogant, belligerent police officers and exactly what we could do about it. We went to pool halls and bars, all the places where brothers congregate and talk.

I was prepared to give them legal advice. From my law courses at Oakland City College and San Francisco Law School

I was familiar with the California penal code and well versed in the laws relating to weapons. I also had something very important at my disposal—the law library of the North Oakland Service Center, a community-center poverty program where Bobby was working. The Center gave legal advice, and there were many lawbooks on the shelves. Unfortunately, most of them dealt with civil law, since the antipoverty program was not supposed to advise poor people about criminal law. However, I made good use of the books they had to run down the full legal situation to brothers on the street. We were doing what the poverty program claimed to be doing but never had—giving help and counsel to poor people about the things that crucially affected their lives.

All that summer we circulated in the Black communities of Richmond, Berkeley, Oakland, and San Francisco. Wherever brothers gathered, we talked with them about their right to arm. In general, they were interested but skeptical about the weapons idea. They could not see anyone walking around with a gun in full view. To recruit any sizable number of street brothers, we would obviously have to do more than *talk*. We needed to give practical applications of our theory, show them that we were not afraid of weapons and not afraid of death. The way we finally won the brothers over was by patrolling the police with arms.

Before we began the patrols, however, Bobby and I set down in writing a practical course of action. We could go no further without a program, and we resolved to drop everything else, even though it might take a while to come up with something viable. One day, we went to the North Oakland Service Center to work it out. The Center was an ideal place because of the books and the fact that we could work undisturbed. First, we pulled together all the books we had been reading and dozens we had only heard about. We discussed Mao's program, Cuba's program, and all the others, but concluded that we could not follow any of them. Our unique situation required a unique program. Although the relationship between the oppressor and the oppressed is universal, forms of oppression vary. The ideas that mobilized the people of Cuba and China sprang from their own history and political structures. The practical parts of those programs could be carried out only under a certain kind of oppression. Our program had to deal with America.

I started rapping off the essential points for the survival of Black and oppressed people in the United States. Bobby wrote them down, and then we separated those ideas into two sections, "What We Want" and "What We Believe." We split them up because the ideas fell naturally into two distinct categories. It was necessary to explain why we wanted certain things. At the same time, our goals were based on beliefs, and we set those out, too. In the section on beliefs, we made it clear that all the objective conditions necessary for attaining our goals were already in existence, but that a number of societal factors stood in our way. This was to help the people understand what was working against them.

All in all, our ten-point program took about twenty minutes to write. Thinking it would take days, we were prepared for a long session, but we never got to the small mountain of books piled up around us. We had come to an important realization: books could only point in a general direction; the rest was up to us. This is the program we wrote down:

OCTOBER 1966

BLACK PANTHER PARTY
PLATFORM AND PROGRAM

WHAT WE WANT
WHAT WE BELIEVE

1. We want freedom. We want power to determine the destiny of our Black Community.
We believe that Black people will not be free until we are able to determine our destiny.

2. We want full employment for our people.
We believe that the federal government is responsible and obligated to give every man employment or a guaranteed income. We believe that if the white American businessmen will not give

full employment, then the means of production should be taken from the businessmen and placed in the community so that the people of the community can organize and employ all of its people and give a high standard of living.

3. We want an end to the robbery by the capitalist of our Black community.

We believe that this racist government has robbed us and now we are demanding the overdue debt of forty acres and two mules. Forty acres and two mules were promised 100 years ago as restitution for slave labor and mass murder of Black people. We will accept the payment in currency which will be distributed to our many communities. The Germans are now aiding the Jews in Israel for the genocide of the Jewish people. The Germans murdered six million Jews. The American racist has taken part in the slaughter of over fifty million Black people; therefore, we feel that this is a modest demand that we make.

4. We want decent housing, fit for shelter of human beings.

We believe that if the white landlords will not give decent housing to our Black community, then the housing and the land should be made into cooperatives so that our community, with government aid, can build and make decent housing for its people.

5. We want education for our people that exposes the true nature of this decadent American society. We want education that teaches us our true history and our role in the present-day society.

We believe in an educational system that will give to our people a knowledge of self. If a man does not have knowledge of himself and his position in society and the world, then he has little chance to relate to anything else.

6. We want all Black men to be exempt from military service.

We believe that Black people should not be forced to fight in the military service to defend a racist government that does not protect us. We will not fight and kill other people of color in the world who, like Black people, are being victimized by the white racist government of America. We will protect ourselves from the force and violence of the racist police and the racist military, by whatever means necessary.

7. *We want an immediate end to POLICE BRUTALITY and MURDER of Black people.*

We believe we can end police brutality in our Black community by organizing Black self-defense groups that are dedicated to defending our Black community from racist police oppression and brutality. The Second Amendment to the Constitution of the United States gives a right to bear arms. We therefore believe that all Black people should arm themselves for self-defense.

8. *We want freedom for all Black men held in federal, state, county and city prisons and jails.*

We believe that all Black people should be released from the many jails and prisons because they have not received a fair and impartial trial.

9. *We want all Black people when brought to trial to be tried in court by a jury of their peer group or people from their Black communities, as defined by the Constitution of the United States.*

We believe that the courts should follow the United States Constitution so that Black people will receive fair trials. The Fourteenth Amendment of the U.S. Constitution gives a man a right to be tried by his peer group. A peer is a person from a similar economic, social, religious, geographical, environmental, historical, and racial background. To do this the court will be forced to select a jury from the Black community from which the Black defendant came. We have been and are being tried by all-white juries that have no understanding of the "average reasoning man" of the Black community.

10. *We want land, bread, housing, education, clothing, justice, and peace. And as our major political objective, a United Nations-supervised plebiscite to be held throughout the Black colony in which only Black colonial subjects will be allowed to participate, for the purpose of determining the will of Black people as to their national destiny.*

When, in the course of human events, it becomes necessary for one people to dissolve the political bands which have connected them with another, and to assume, among the powers of the earth, the separate and equal station to which the laws of nature and nature's God entitle them, a decent respect to the opinions of mankind requires that they should declare the causes which impel them to the separation.

We hold these truths to be self-evident, that all men are created equal; that they are endowed by their Creator with certain unalienable rights; that among these are life, liberty, and the pursuit of happiness. That, to secure these rights, governments are instituted among men, deriving their just powers from the consent of the governed; that, whenever any form of government becomes destructive of these ends, it is the right of the people to alter or to abolish it, and to institute a new government, laying its foundation on such principles, and organizing its powers in such form, as to them shall seem most likely to effect their safety and happiness. Prudence, indeed, will dictate that governments long established should not be changed for light and transient causes; and, accordingly, all experience hath shown, that mankind are more disposed to suffer, while evils are sufferable, than to right themselves by abolishing the forms to which they are accustomed. But, when a long train of abuses and usurpations, pursuing invariably the same object, evinces a design to reduce them under absolute despotism, it is their right, it is their duty, to throw off such government, and to provide new guards for their future security.

With the program on paper, we set up the structure of our organization. Bobby became Chairman, and I chose the position of Minister of Defense.* I was very happy with this arrangement; I do not like to lead formally, and the Chairman has to conduct meetings and be involved in administration. We also discussed having an advisory cabinet as an information arm of the Party. We wanted this cabinet to do research on each of the ten points and their relation to the community and to advise

*All titles in the Black Panther Party were eventually dropped, in July, 1972.

the people on how to implement them. It seemed best to weight the political wing of the Party with street brothers and the advisory cabinet with middle-class Blacks who had the necessary knowledge and skills. We were also seeking a functional unity between middle-class Blacks and the street brothers. I asked my brother Melvin to approach a few friends about serving on the advisory cabinet, but when our plan became clear, they all refused, and the cabinet was deferred.

The first member of the Black Panther Party, after Bobby and myself, was Little Bobby Hutton. Little Bobby had met Bobby Seale at the North Oakland Service Center, where both were working, and he immediately became enthusiastic about the nascent organization. Even though he was only about fifteen years old then, he was a responsible and mature person, determined to help the cause of Black people. He became the Party's first treasurer. Little Bobby was the youngest of seven children; his family had come to Oakland from Arkansas when he was three years old. His parents were good, hard-working people, but Bobby had endured the same hardships and humiliations to which so many young Blacks in poor communities are subjected. Like many of the brothers, he had been kicked out of school. Then he had gotten a part-time job at the Service Center. After work he used to come around to Bobby Seale's house to talk and learn to read. At the time of his murder,* he was reading *Black Reconstruction in America,* by W. E. B. Du Bois.

Bobby was a serious revolutionary, but there was nothing grim about him. He had an infectious smile and a disarming quality that made people love him. He died courageously, the

---

*On the night of April 6, 1968, two days after the murder of Dr. Martin Luther King, Black Panthers riding in three cars transporting food and supplies for a barbecue picnic to be held in the Black community the next day were ambushed by police. In the shoot-out that followed, Little Bobby Hutton and another Black Panther Party member, Eldridge Cleaver, were trapped by the police in the basement of a house on Twenty-eighth Street in Oakland. The police fired upon the house with rifles, pistols, shotguns, tear gas, and fire bombs for ninety minutes, after which Little Bobby came out with his hands in the air. In cold blood, the police shot him dead in the street. He was seventeen years old.

first Black Panther to make the supreme sacrifice for the people. We all attempt to carry on the work he began.

We started now to implement our ten-point program. Interested primarily in educating and revolutionizing the community, we needed to get their attention and give them something to identify with. This is why the seventh point—police action— was the first program we emphasized. Point 7 stated: "We want an immediate end to police brutality and murder of Black people." This is a major issue in every Black community. The police have never been our protectors. Instead, they act as the military arm of our oppressors and continually brutalize us. Many communities have tried and failed to get civilian review boards to supervise the behavior of the police. In some places, organized citizen patrols have followed the police and observed them in their community dealings. They take pictures and make tape recordings of the encounters and report misbehavior to the authorities. However, the authorities responsible for overseeing the police are policemen themselves and usually side against the citizens. We recognized that it was ridiculous to report the police to the police, but we hoped that by raising encounters to a higher level, by patrolling the police with arms, we would see a change in their behavior. Further, the community would notice this and become interested in the Party. Thus our armed patrols were also a means of recruiting.

At first, the patrols were a total success. Frightened and confused, the police did not know how to respond, because they had never encountered patrols like this before. They were familiar with the community-alert patrols in other cities, but never before had guns been an integral part of any patrol program. With weapons in our hands, we were no longer their subjects but their equals.

Out on patrol, we stopped whenever we saw the police questioning a brother or a sister. We would walk over with our weapons and observe them from a "safe" distance so that the police could not say we were interfering with the performance of their duty. We would ask the community members if they were being abused. Most of the time, when a policeman saw us coming, he slipped his book back into his pocket, got into his car, and left in a hurry. The citizens who had been stopped were as amazed as the police at our sudden appearance.

I always carried lawbooks in my car. Sometimes, when a policeman was harassing a citizen, I would stand off a little and read the relevant portions of the penal code in a loud voice to all within hearing distance. In doing this, we were helping to educate those who gathered to observe these incidents. If the policeman arrested the citizen and took him to the station, we would follow and immediately post bail. Many community people could not believe at first that we had only their interest at heart. Nobody had ever given them any support or assistance when the police harassed them, but here we were, proud Black men, armed with guns and a knowledge of the law. Many citizens came right out of jail and into the Party, and the statistics of murder and brutality by policemen in our communities fell sharply.

Each day we went out on our watch. Sometimes we got on a policeman's tail and followed him with our weapons in full view. If he darted around the block or made a U-turn trying to follow us, we let him do it until he got tired of that. Then, we would follow him again. Either way, we took up a good bit of police time that otherwise would have been spent in harassment.

As our forces built up, we doubled the patrols, then tripled them; we began to patrol everywhere—Oakland, Richmond, Berkeley, and San Francisco. Most patrols were a part of our normal movement around the community. We kept them random, however, so that the police could not set a network to anticipate us. They never knew when or where we were going to show up. It might be late at night or early in the morning; some brothers would go on patrol the same time every day, but never in a specific pattern or in the same geographical area. The chief purpose of the patrols was to teach the community security against the police, and we did not need a regular schedule for that. We knew that no particular area could be totally defended; only the community could effectively defend and eventually liberate itself. Our aim was simply to teach them how to go about it. We passed out our literature and ten-point program to the citizens who gathered, discussed community defense, and educated them about their rights concerning weapons. All along, the number of members grew.

The Black Panthers were and are always required to keep their activities within legal bounds. This was emphasized repeatedly in our political education classes and also when we taught weapons care. If we overstepped legal bounds, the police would easily gain the upper hand and be able to continue their intimidation. We also knew the community was somewhat fearful of the gun and of the policeman who had it. So, we studied the law about weapons and kept within our rights. To be arrested for having weapons would be a setback to our program of teaching the people their constitutional right to bear arms. As long as we kept everything legal, the police could do nothing, and the people would see that armed defense was a legitimate, constitutional right. In this way, they would lose their doubts and fears and be able to move against the oppressor.

It was not all observation and penal code reading on those patrols. The police, invariably shocked to meet a cadre of disciplined and armed Black men coming to the support of the community, reacted in strange and unpredictable ways. In their fright, some of them became children, cursing and insulting us. We responded in kind, calling them swine and pigs, but never cursing—this could be cause for arrest—and we took care not to be arrested with our weapons. But we demonstrated their cowardice to the community with our "shock-a-buku."* It was sometimes hilarious to see their reaction; they had always been cocky and sure of themselves as long as they had weapons to intimidate the unarmed community. When we equalized the situation, their real cowardice was exposed.

Soon they began to retaliate. We expected this—they had to get back at us in some way—and were prepared. The fact that we had conquered our fear of death made it possible to face them under any circumstances. The police began to keep a rec-

* "Shock-a-buku" is a term we made up. In the Black community shock-a-buku is a tactic of keeping the enemy off balance through sudden and unexpected maneuvers that push him toward his opponent's position.

ord of Black Panther vehicles; whenever they spotted one, it
would be stopped and investigated for possible violations. This
was a childish ploy, but it was the police way. We always made
sure our vehicles were clean, without violations, and the police
were usually hard-pressed to find any justification for stopping
us. Since we were within the law, they soon resorted to illegal
tactics. I was stopped and questioned forty or fifty times by police without being arrested or even getting a ticket in most instances. The few times I did end up on the blotter it merely
proved how far they were willing to go. A policeman once
stopped me and examined my license and the car for any violation of the Motor Vehicle Code. He spent about half an hour
going over the vehicle, checking lights, horn, tires, everything.
Finally, he shook the rear license plate, and a bolt dropped off,
so he wrote out a ticket for a faulty license plate.

Some encounters with the police were more dramatic. At
times they drew their guns and we drew ours, until we reached
a sort of stand-off. This happened frequently to me. I often felt
that someday one of the police would go crazy and pull the
trigger. Some of them were so nervous that they looked as if
they might shake a bullet out of their pistols. I would rather
have a brave man pull a gun on me, since he is less likely to
panic; but we were prepared for anything. Sometimes they
threatened to shoot, thinking I would lose courage, but I remembered the lessons of solitary confinement and assigned
every silly action its proper significance: they were afraid of us.
It was as simple as that. Each day we went forth fully aware
that we might not come home or see each other ever again.
There is no closeness to equal that.

In front of our first Black Panther office, on Fifty-eighth Street
in Oakland, a policeman once drew his gun and pointed it at
me while I sat in my car. When people gathered to observe, the
police told them to clear the area. I ignored the gun, got out of
the car, and asked the people to go into the Party office. They
had a right to observe the police. Then I called the policeman
an ignorant Georgia cracker who had come West to get away
from sharecropping. After that, I walked around the car and
spoke to the citizens about the police and about every man's

right to be armed. I took a chance there, but I figured the policeman would not shoot me with all those eyes on him. He was willing to shoot me without cause, I am sure, but not before so many witnesses.

Another policeman admitted as much during an incident in Richmond. I had stopped to watch a motorcycle cop question a citizen. He was clearly edgy at my presence, but I stood off quietly at a reasonable distance with my shotgun in hand. After writing up the citizen, he rode his motorcycle over to me and asked if I wanted to press charges for police brutality. About a dozen people were standing around watching us. "Are you paranoid?" I replied. "Do you think you're important? Do you think I would waste my time going down to the police station to make a report on you? No. You're just a coward anyway." With that, I got into my car. When he tried to hold my door open, I slammed it shut and told him to get his hands off. By now people were laughing at the cop, and rather than suffer further humiliation, he drove off, steaming mad. About halfway down the street, he turned around and came back; he wanted to do something and he was about fifty shades of red. Pulling up beside me, he stuck his head close and said, "If it was night, you wouldn't do this." "You're right," I replied, "I sure wouldn't, but you're threatening me now, aren't you?" He got a little redder and kicked his machine into gear, and took off.

The police wanted me badly, but they needed to do their dirty work out of view of the community. When a citizen was unarmed, they brutalized him any time, almost casually, but when he was prepared to defend himself, the police became little more than criminals, working at night.

On another occasion I stopped by the Black Panther office after paying some bills for my father. Since I was taking care of family business, I had not carried my shotgun with me—it was at home—but I did have a dagger, fully sheathed, in my belt. In the office were two comrades. Warren Tucker, a captain in the Party, and another member. As we talked, an eleven-year-old boy burst into the office and said, "The police are at my friend's house, and they're tearing up the place." This house was only about three blocks away, so the two Black Panthers and I hurried to the scene. Warren Tucker had a .45 pistol strapped to his hip in full view, but the other two of us had no weapons. We never kept weapons in the office, since we were there only periodically.

When we arrived, we found three policemen in the house, turning over couches and chairs, searching and pushing a little boy around and shouting, "Where's the shotgun?" The boy kept saying, "I don't have a shotgun," but the police went right on looking. I asked the policeman who seemed to be in charge if he had a search warrant, and he answered that he did not need one because he was in "hot pursuit." Then he told me to leave the house. The little boy asked me to stay, so I continued to question the police, telling them they had no right to be there. The policeman finally turned on me. "You're going to get out of here," he said. "No," I said, "you leave if you don't have a search warrant."

In the middle of this argument the boy's father arrived and also asked the police for a search warrant. When the police admitted they did not have one, he ordered them out. As they started to leave, one of the policemen stopped in the doorway and said to the father, "Why are you telling us to get out? Why don't you get rid of these Panthers? They're the troublemakers." The father replied, "Before this I didn't like the Panthers. I had heard bad things about them, but in the last few minutes I've changed my mind, because they helped my son when you pushed him around."

The police became even more outraged at this. All their hostility now turned toward us. As the whole group went down the steps and out into the yard, more policemen arrived on the scene. The house was directly across the street from Oakland City College, and the dozen or so police cars had attracted a crowd that was milling about. The policeman who had been ordered out of the house took new courage at the sight of reinforcements. Walking over to me in the yard, he came close, saying, "You are always making trouble for us." Coming closer still, he growled at me in a low voice that could not be overheard, "You motherfucker." This was a regular police routine, a transparent strategy. He wanted me to curse him before witnesses; then he could arrest me. But I had learned to be cautious. After he called me a motherfucker, he stood waiting for the explosion, but it did not come in the way he expected. Instead, I called him a swine, a pig, a slimy snake—everything I could think of without using profanity.

By now he was almost apoplectic. "You're talking to me like that and you have a weapon. You're displaying a weapon in a rude and threatening fashion." Then he turned to Warren Tucker—Warren's gun was still in its holster—and said, "And so are you." As if on signal, the fifteen policemen who had been standing around uncertainly stormed the three of us and threw on handcuffs. They did not say they were placing us under arrest. If they had, we would gladly have taken the arrest under the circumstances without any resistance. From the way we went hurtling off in the paddy wagon, with its siren wailing and police cars ahead and behind, you might have thought they had bagged a Mafia capo. After we were booked, they searched us and found a penknife in Warren Tucker's pocket, the kind Boy Scouts use. So, they dropped the charge of "displaying a weapon in a rude and threatening manner" and charged him simply with carrying a concealed weapon. Even that charge was eventually dropped.

This was the kind of harassment we went through over and over again, simply because we chose to exercise our constitutional rights to self-defense and stand up for the community. In spite of the fact that we followed the law to the letter, we were arrested and convicted of all sorts of minor trumped-up charges. They sought to frighten us and turn the community against us, but what they did had the opposite effect. For instance, after this encounter, we gained a number of new members from City College students who had watched the incident and had seen how things really were. They had been skeptical about us earlier because of the bad treatment we had received in the press, but seeing is believing.

The policeman who started this particular incident testified against me in 1968 in my trial for killing a policeman. When my attorney, Charles Garry, questioned him under cross-examination, he admitted his fear of the Black Panthers. He is six feet tall and weighs 250 pounds; I am five feet, ten and a half inches, and weigh 150 pounds; yet he said that I "surrounded" him. Straying further from the facts, he testified that he had not said anything to me, that, on the contrary, he was too frightened to open his mouth. The Black Panthers allegedly frightened him by shaking high-powered rifles in his face, calling him a pig, and threatening to kill him. He was fearful, he said, that I would kill him with the dagger, though it was sheathed. He stated that I had come right up to him, that I was "in his face," and, as he put it, "He was all around me." So much for police testimony.

In addition to our patrols and confrontations with the police, I did a lot of recruiting in pool halls and bars, sometimes working twelve to sixteen hours a day. I passed out leaflets with our ten-point program, explaining each point to all who would listen. Going deep into the community like this, I invariably became involved in whatever was happening; this day-to-day contact became an important part of our organizing effort. There is a bar-restaurant in North Oakland known as the "Bosn's Locker"; I used to call it my office because I would sometimes sit in there for twenty hours straight talking with the people who came in. Most of the time, I had my shotgun with me, if the owners of the establishment did not object. If they did, I left it in my car.

At other times I would go to City College or to the Oakland Skills Center—anywhere people gathered. It was hard work, but not in the sense of working at an ordinary job, with its deadly routine and sense of futility in performing empty labor. It was work that had profound significance for me; the very meaning of my life was in it, and it brought me closer to the people.

This recruiting had an interesting ramification in that I tried to transform many of the so-called criminal activities going on in the street into something political, although this had to be done gradually. Instead of trying to eliminate these activities— numbers, hot goods, drugs—I attempted to channel them into significant community actions. Black consciousness had generally reached a point where a man felt guilty about exploiting the Black community. However, if his daily activities for survival could be integrated with actions that undermined the established order, he felt good about it. It gave him a feeling of justification and strengthened his own sense of personal worth. Many of the brothers who were burglarizing and participating in similar pursuits began to contribute weapons and material to community defense. In order to survive they still had to sell their hot goods, but at the same time they would pass some of the cash on to us. That way, ripping off became more than just an individual thing.

Gradually the Black Panthers came to be accepted in the Bay Area community. We had provided a needed example of strength and dignity by showing people how to defend themselves. More important, we lived among them. They could see every day that with us the people came first.

18

Those who assert this kind of "independence" are usually
wedded to the doctrine of "me first" and are generally wrong
on the question of the relationship between the individual and
the Party. Although in words they profess respect for the Party,
in practice they put themselves first and the Party second. . . .
What are these people after? They are after fame and position
and want to be in the limelight. . . . It is their dishonesty that
causes them to come to grief.

CHAIRMAN MAO, *Little Red Book*

Eldridge Cleaver

One evening in early 1967, Bobby Seale called and asked me to
go with him to a radio station in downtown Oakland. He arrived with Marvin Jackmon, a Black playwright who was in
the process of becoming a Muslim. We had tried to recruit
Jackmon into the Party, but his Muslim beliefs forbade him to
have anything to do with weapons. He and another Muslim
brother arrived with Bobby, driving the car of Beverly Axelrod,
a lawyer active in civil rights cases in California. The purpose
of the trip was to meet Eldridge Cleaver, an ex-convict* of
growing reputation, who would be interviewed that night. I
had heard of Eldridge's speeches in the Bay Area since his release from prison in December, but we had never talked, and I
had not yet read *Soul on Ice*, which was receiving great critical

*Cleaver was released on parole from Soledad Prison to San Francisco on
December 12, 1966, after serving nine years of a one-to-fourteen-year sentence
for rape.

acclaim, or any of his other writings. I knew only that he was an ex-convict with plenty of time behind him.

Because of Eldridge's past experience and his deep involvement in the movement, I was particularly eager to meet him. No ex-convict could be all bad. While we drove to the radio station, we listened to Eldridge's discussion with the interviewer. I liked what he said about his early life and his work in the movement since his release. He was articulate, his insights were good, and he seemed to understand the needs of the community and what Black people had to do to liberate themselves. When we pulled up to the radio station, Eldridge was still on the air.

Immediately after the interview, Eldridge and I fell into a long discussion. It was not much of a dialogue, actually; Eldridge hardly said a word. I tried to persuade him to join the Party then and there by running down our ten-point program and convincing him that we had developed Malcolm's ideas and were carrying them out. I explained that Malcolm's program had been rather vague since he had not had the opportunity to lay it out clearly before he was cut down. A lot of groups were springing up, claiming to bear his standard, but we were the only ones who had armed ourselves and were teaching self-defense to the community. This was Malcolm's program, and we were serious about establishing it.

Eldridge only listened; every once in a while he would nod his head in agreement and say, "I know." But he did not ask any questions or comment one way or the other about the program. When I finished, he told me that he was obligated to Malcolm's widow, Sister Betty Shabazz, and that he had promised to work with her to carry out Malcolm's dream and make it a reality. Then he left.

I was puzzled by this first meeting. Perhaps he had not understood anything I was saying, even though he seemed to by nods and phrases of agreement. I figured that if he really understood, he would have asked some questions or made a criticism or two. When a man is interested, he wants to know more. Eldridge had been as silent as a sphinx. After reading the chapter in *Soul on Ice* that deals with police administration from the local to the international level, I realized that Eldridge did not argue any of the points with me that night because he understood all too well and agreed totally.

A few weeks later, we were together at a meeting in the office of the "Paper Panthers" in San Francisco. This was a group of cultural nationalists in San Francisco who called themselves the "Black Panther Party of Northern California"; they had a similar group in Los Angeles. I do not know when they started or what their goals were, but David Hilliard labeled them the "Paper Panthers" because their activity was confined to a steady production of printed matter. Unlike Bobby and me, they had not grown up on the block. They were more privileged.

Their office was close to the office of an organization called the Black House that Eldridge and Marvin Jackmon had started in San Francisco. This was just a large house in the Fillmore area where people lived upstairs and used the first floor (which had been converted into a meeting room) for political and social activities. LeRoi Jones (now Imamu Amiri Baraka) was teaching for a semester at San Francisco State, and he sometimes gave readings on Friday nights. Other poets also read, and there was plenty of discussion and intellectualizing. It was Oakland and Berkeley all over again. As far as I could see, Black House was exploiting Eldridge, who paid the rent and the huge telephone bills. No one else was doing very much, just lying around "becoming Black."

Early in February, 1967, all these groups banded together to sponsor a program in San Francisco honoring Malcolm on the anniversary of his assassination. The guest of honor was to be Malcolm's widow, Sister Betty Shabazz. They wanted to arrange some security for her, since there was fear that she, too, might be assassinated. Bobby and I attended a meeting to organize an escort, and although we had a good deal of contempt for the Paper Panthers, we agreed to join them in providing security. Eldridge was at the meeting, too, silent as usual. When details for the escort were worked out and the day arrived, we joined the others in San Francisco and headed for the airport to meet Sister Betty.

Before leaving Oakland, I had told the comrades that we were not going to take any arrests on this trip. If anything happened, I said, we would fight right down to the last man, but we definitely would not give ourselves up to the police. We were going out there specifically to provide a bodyguard for Sister Betty, and unless they were willing to give up their lives, they ought not to come.

We made this decision for two reasons. First, she was the widow of Brother Malcolm, our greatest leader and martyr, and the mother of his beautiful children. We would not allow anything to happen to her after the way the Establishment had so treacherously assassinated her husband. Second, her cousin, Hakim Jamal, had told me that when she visited Los Angeles, the police had run off Ron Karenga's group, which was providing an escort for her. They had left her standing alone in the middle of the street. My specific orders were that nobody was to be arrested, because to be arrested was to leave her, and a violation of our main purpose.

We proceeded to the airport. When her plane arrived, we formed a circle around her and led her to the waiting cars. People were standing around staring and wondering what was going on. The airport police were edgy and unhappy about our activity, but we knew what we were doing and we knew the law. We were taking care of Malcolm's widow.

From the airport we took her to the office of *Ramparts* magazine, in downtown San Francisco, for a meeting with Eldridge, Kenny Freeman, Isaac Moore, and some others. While they talked, we remained in an outer office, keeping out the police, who were lurking everywhere. When the group broke up, Sister Betty told us that she did not want any pictures taken by reporters; therefore, as we left the building, we held up copies of *Ramparts* around her. Dozens of reporters were waiting outside, and about thirty policemen. We were ready.

A reporter named Chuck Banks from Channel 7 grabbed for my magazine, but I held on to it and told him to let my property go. I had my shotgun cradled in my right arm and the magazine in my left hand. When he could not wrench the magazine away, he pushed it against my chest. I dropped the magazine and hit him with a left hook; he went down. Just before I hit Banks, I had told four brothers to get Sister Betty out of there because I was sure, from the number of police in the building, that something was cooking outside. We were determined not to pull a Karenga. Finally, she made it to the car and drove off. Then I turned my attention to the situation at hand, telling the police to arrest Banks for hitting me in the chest and also for destroying my property. The police had a predictable reply: "If we arrest anybody, it will be you." That is when I told my men to spread out and hit the street, surrounding the police. At this moment one of the Paper Panthers, Roy Ballard, came running into the street without his weapon and hollered something like "Don't point that gun!" I looked the head policeman in the eye and said, "If you start drawing, this will be bloodbath." My shotgun was in a ready position, safety off, and a shell in the chamber. The police had no shotguns, only revolvers. Had they started something, we would have wiped them out.

This was the extent of the conversation with the police. Otherwise, the air was as quiet as death. I made my statement to the policeman; he saw my weapon and froze. When some of my comrades turned their backs to walk off, I told them not to give the police a chance for "justifiable homicide." Like others of its kind, the scene is chiseled in my memory; I can still see every detail of this tense, brief confrontation. And then we backed away to our cars, guns still held ready, and drove off. We had kept our promise to Sister Betty.

We found out later about the Paper Panthers. Seeing how bad it might be, Roy Ballard had fled inside. He gave his gun to a woman in the office and told her to put it in her briefcase, then he hid, trembling. He did not even leave with us. The Paper Panthers were simply another front for RAM, good for nothing but running a mimeograph machine and fat-mouthing. If Sister Betty had depended on them for security, she would have been stranded.

A short time later, when the Malcolm memorial rally was over and Sister Betty had left town, we learned that the Paper Panthers had not carried loaded weapons that day, either at the airport or in front of *Ramparts*. We had stood down the police alone. Those fellows did not even own any bullets. When I asked Ballard about this later, he admitted it. (A few weeks after this we went to San Francisco, where the Paper Panthers were having a fish fry, and issued an ultimatum: they could merge with us or change their name or be annihilated. When they said they would do none of these things, we waded in. I took on one of them and hooked him in the jaw. It was a short battle, ending a few moments later when somebody fired a shot in the air and people scattered. After that, the Paper Panthers changed their name.)

After the *Ramparts* confrontation we returned to Black House and relaxed until it was time for the memorial rally that night at Hunter's Point Community Center in the middle of San Francisco's low-income Black community. We did not see Sister Betty again until then, although she wanted to meet us. The Paper Panthers had stolen her away. They told her that we were all in the same party, and that night they escorted her to the rally, while we provided security. We were supposed to speak during the program, but Kenny Freeman of RAM—the master of ceremonies—froze us out.

On the way from Black House to the memorial rally, Eldridge rode in the car with me, and while we drove he asked to join the Black Panther Party. This surprised me. I had given up all hope that he would join because he had expressed no interest, and I never try to recruit by keeping after people; once they have heard the program, it is up to them. But Eldridge was a man who kept his peace. He had apparently made up his mind to join much earlier when we went to the Paper Panthers' office to talk about escorting Betty Shabazz.

My surprise quickly turned to pleasure. Eldridge had skills that Bobby and I lacked, skills that were needed for our program. He was an eloquent writer, and his past experiences would make him a strong comrade for the difficult days ahead. I had no reservations about him, although even then something struck me about our conversation that only recently has begun to make sense. He kept calling me "Bobby" and talking about how "that Newton really blew." A short time before, I had been invited to speak on the mall at Provo Park in Berkeley but had sent Alex Papillon in my place. Somehow, the newsmen had mistaken Papillon for me when the announcer used my name in telling the people that I had sent him. To complicate matters further, Eldridge had mistaken Alex Papillon for Bobby Seale. Alex had a gun strapped to his side, and every time he made a strong point he would pat his pistol. He became known as the "Pistol-patting Panther." I do not know how Eldridge was aware of this event—perhaps he was there—but as far as he was concerned the pistol packer was Newton. And so in the car he kept saying, "Newton sure did blow," talking about the fantastic speech. I was so amused by this I let him go on, waiting to see how long it would take Eldridge to get us straight.

I think his desire to belong was a cumulative thing, built slowly—at the meeting about Betty Shabazz, at Provo Park, in front of *Ramparts*. I see now that Eldridge was not dedicated to helping Black people but was in search of a strong manhood symbol. This was a common misconception at the time—that the Party was searching for badges of masculinity. In fact, the reverse is true: the Party acted as it did because we *were* men. Many failed to perceive the difference. As for Eldridge, at that stage of his life he was probing for his own manhood. The Party's uniforms, the guns, the street action all added up to an image of strength. And so he left the Organization for Afro-American Unity and the Paper Panthers to join us in the late spring of 1967.

It must be said in all honesty that Eldridge at the beginning made great contributions to the Party. He is a fine writer, an effective speaker, and an intelligent and talented human being. We felt then that his contribution would be to write for and edit *The Black Panther* paper, which we began publishing in April, 1967. Bobby Seale had thought up the paper, which immediately became an important vehicle for communicating the truth about the Party and the community. But only three of us were working on it, which is a next-to-impossible task for a publication running at least twelve pages an issue and sometimes up to twenty. Publishing first as a monthly, our goal was to have it on the street every two weeks and, if possible, once a week. Eldridge took a good part of the workload.

I soon noticed, however, that Eldridge was not around when the deadlines came; we used to have to "shock-a-buku" him into writing and editing. Because he was a writer, I found his reluctance difficult to understand. He seemed to work with enthusiasm only after something sensational had taken place, a shooting, perhaps, or when he was either out of town or in jail. After Bobby Hutton was killed, in April, 1968, and Eldridge was sentenced to Vacaville, the paper appeared regularly, every week. But once out of prison, he fell back into his old unco-operative ways. He was always somewhat withdrawn, and worked best by himself, doing his own thing in one way or another. And the newspaper suffered.

This kind of independence hurt the Party. It was essential that everyone work together and pitch in, especially when we had a project going. For instance, I wanted Eldridge to talk to Party members, particularly the newer and younger ones, about some of the topics he discussed with the Yippies, the Peace and Freedom Party, radical white youth political organizations, and on campuses. I had great respect for the insight and knowledge he had acquired through study and reading, but when I tried to persuade him to teach a class to the troops, he refused. He never taught one class or attempted to organize any programs. He was always off talking on radio and television and before all sorts of groups that seemed more glamorous and exciting to him.

Eldridge misunderstood the white radical movement. He exploited their alienation and encouraged young whites to think of themselves as "bad" Blacks, thus driving them ever further away from their own community. At the same time, he seduced young Blacks into picturing themselves as bohemian expatriates from middle-class "Babylon" (as he poetically but mistakenly analogized superindustrial America). So we became temporarily alien to the Black community, while the white radicals were plunged deeper into their peculiar identity crisis. Cleaver's genius for political and cultural schizophrenia infected us all, Black and white, and the opportunity was missed for youth of both races to express and make concrete their authentic underlying solidarity and love. This still remains to be done.

Relating as Bobby and I did to the lumpenproletariat of the Black community, we were down on bohemians and white radicals. But when Eldridge joined, he soon took us to meet the Diggers in San Francisco at their store in Haight-Ashbury, and once there, we had no idea why we had come. Eldridge had not explained anything. The store was incredibly disorganized. After fighting our way through piles of garbage, we managed to have a discussion with some of the Diggers. It turned out they wanted us to develop a peace force for them, a kind of protective guard, because they were being harassed by some of the low riders in the area. When this point came up, I tuned out. What right had these people to ask us for protection? I told them to form their own peace force.

Eldridge hung out a lot in Haight-Ashbury and on Telegraph Avenue in Berkeley, and although we avoided further involvement with the Diggers, before long we were attracting hippies and Yippies to the Party. A lot of them were deep into drugs. Because Bobby and I had started out as Black nationalists and were influenced by the Muslims and Malcolm X, we steered clear of the drug scene. Unlike Eldridge, neither of us identified with Haight-Ashbury or Telegraph Avenue, and especially not with drugs.

I had sought out Eldridge because he was an ex-convict, thinking he could not be all bad if he had pulled time. But my trust and belief in him were mistaken. He dealt several serious blows to the Party, not only by welcoming hippies, but also by failing to use his voice to push Black Panther programs or improve our paper or be involved with the poor of the community or create a political vehicle. He talked only empty rhetoric about "dealing blows" and triggering sensational actions. All in all, Eldridge lived in a fantasy world.

As time passed, he drifted away from us and from the ideology and aims of the Black Panther Party. Colossal events were to take place, events that would threaten our very existence, and after each of these setbacks, Eldridge's real position became clearer and clearer, although for a long time I was reluctant to admit or even recognize the truth.

Brothers are bound together by the revolutionary love we have for each other, a love forged through loyalty and trust. It is an element of the Black Panther Party that can never be destroyed. Yet eventually Eldridge betrayed this love and commitment in ways I once never believed possible.

19

It is not often that one encounters in any black ghetto in this country a family that has not experienced some immediate contact with the corrupt judicial system and a repressive prison apparatus. It is not only impossible for a black revolutionary to get justice in the courts, but black people in general have been the victims rather than the recipients of bourgeois justice.

ANGELA DAVIS, *If They Come in the Morning*

Denzil Dowell

North Richmond is an all-Black community of about 9,000 inhabitants on the northwest side of the city of Richmond. It came into being during World War II when this area was used to provide limited and temporary housing for Blacks, like my father, who came from the South to work in the shipyards. Kaiser Industries, the main employers at the time, were responsible for the establishment of the community. They expected the people to go back South after they were no longer needed. But the South had little to offer, and the people had other ideas. When they stayed, the Establishment found ways to punish them. Most of North Richmond is gerrymandered out of the city proper and cut off from any assistance from public agencies except the Contra Costa County agencies. Many of these are run by racists who do not want Blacks there. As a consequence, many people live in poverty and hardship.

On one side of the community is a large garbage dump filled with rats. On another, Standard Oil refineries pour out their wastes and fumes on the community. Some days it is hard to draw a breath without choking and coughing. The industrial needs of the area are obviously more important than the human needs of the people. No more than two or three streets lead into North Richmond and each of these has a number of railroad tracks crossing it. This makes it difficult for the people to get out when emergency situations arise. They have to sit in their cars waiting for the freight trains to pass by. This limited access to the community makes it possible for the police to seal off the area any time they want, and they have used that power often.

About half the population is under nineteen years of age, a fact that presents special problems in terms of education and youth programs, since there is a great need for these functions. Many youths graduate from high school just as illiterate as I was, headed for the social trash heap. Recently, in 1971, one of the new playgrounds built by the people could not be used by children because the rats that came from the dump and the creek terrorized them. Reports in the San Francisco *Chronicle* indicated clearly that city officials believed the people wanted the rats, and that is why they were there. North Richmond is no different from countless Black communities in California and the rest of the United States. Cut off, ignored, and forgotten, the people are kept in a state of subjugation, especially by the police, who treat the communities like colonies.

The family of Denzil Dowell lives in North Richmond, and it was there, on April 1, 1967, that their son and brother was killed by officers of the Sheriff's Department of Contra Costa County. He was twenty-two years old. They said he was running away from a stolen car that had been flagged down by the police. Because he was allegedly in the act of committing a felony, his death was ruled "justifiable homicide."

We were introduced to the Dowell family after Denzil's death by Mark Comfort, a bright, strong man with a long history of organizing Blacks in the Oakland area. The Dowells had asked us to come to their home because of dissatisfaction with the official treatment of Denzil's death. Like most Black families, they recognized the treachery of the police, but they knew how little could be done about Denzil's death through established institutions. The whole Dowell family considered themselves

Black Panthers. Visiting them one Sunday afternoon, we were touched to see the deep sorrow and sense of helplessness so common among Blacks under these circumstances. I had seen it many times in my work, and we were to see it again and again as we became more deeply involved in the life of the people.

Mrs. Dowell, a beautiful and noble Black woman, told us about her son's life. She had spent much of her time and energy trying to survive in North Richmond, supporting her family and raising the children right. She had done her best with what she had, and she had done a good job. Yet nothing could be done about the schools and other institutions that blocked her children from reaching the goals they had been taught to aim for. She was terribly upset about Denzil's death and over the indifferent and contemptuous way the authorities treated it. She knew that her son had been murdered in cold blood.

We began our investigation at the same time the police were carrying out theirs. While they tried to establish a cover for their treachery, we searched for the truth. Policemen were constantly coming to Mrs. Dowell's house and treating her like dirt. They would knock on the door, walk in, and search the premises any time they wanted. I happened to be at the house one day when they came. When Mrs. Dowell answered the knock, a policeman pushed his way in, asking questions. I grabbed my shotgun and stepped in front of her, telling him either to produce a search warrant or leave. He stood for a minute, shocked, then ran out to his car and drove off.

When we read the police report of the incident, we rejected it and continued our own investigation, always carrying our weapons in full view. Together with the Dowells we visited the spot where the murder allegedly took place and checked every possible detail. From my study of police methods in college, I came up with a number of inconsistencies in the official report. For example, the police claimed that Denzil had jumped one fence and was about to jump another when he was shot; but Denzil had a hip injury from an automobile accident and could hardly have run, let alone jump fences. The lot he supposedly ran across was an automobile junkyard full of garbage and oil, yet no oil was found on his shoes. The police said that he bled to death after being shot, but no pool of blood was noted at the site, or anywhere else. We also learned that Denzil's brother and friends had found him lying all alone. After shooting him, the police had made no effort to summon medical aid or to save his life. All this was particularly significant and disturbing in light of the fact that Denzil was known to the police, and they had threatened to get him on a number of occasions. In the dark, far from witnesses, they carried out their murderous treachery.

The same thing happened to Little Bobby Hutton, to Fred Hampton and Mark Clark in Chicago, to the students in the Orangeburg and Jackson State massacres in the South. It has happened to many thousands of unknown Blacks throughout the history of this country, poor and powerless victims, whose families were too terrorized or weak to cry out against their oppressors. The police murder us outright and call it justifiable homicide. They always cook up a story, but simple investigation will expose their lies. That is why we must disarm and control the police in our communities if we want to survive.

When our investigation disproved the official story, we indicted the police for the murder of Denzil Dowell and called a community meeting to discuss our findings. We held a rally on the corner of Third Street and Chesley in North Richmond on a Saturday afternoon. Our troops with weapons at the ready were stationed on all four corners of the intersection. The community was a little timid but proud to see Black men take a stance in their interests, and when we arrived, everybody was very receptive. They asked a number of questions about the guns—if they were loaded and if carrying them was legal. We explained our weapons policy and told them about their right to carry arms. Then a remarkable thing happened. One by one, many of the community members went home and got their guns and came to join us. Even one old sister of seventy years or so was out there with her shotgun.

When they learned of the meeting, the police were again afraid and uncertain. One policeman was sitting in his car on the corner when we arrived. They do that frequently in North Richmond, just drive up to the corner of Third and Chesley and sit there, intimidating the people. But when we arrived and took positions with our guns, followed by a crowd, he took off like a shot.

Bobby spoke first, and I followed. We ran down everything known about the case and exposed the errors in the police version. The people were impressed that some of their own had come forward to confront the police with factual evidence. We called on the community to arm and defend themselves against the racist dogs, stressing that it was their right and we were there to teach them, not only in theory but also through practice.

While we were talking, another policeman drove down to Chesley Street. When he saw the people gathered, he kept coming, but at the first sight of our guns he turned around in the middle of the street and sped away. The people cheered.

Soon after, we had another meeting with the community to discuss the case and what could be done about it. Now that we had presented our findings, we wanted to move their consciousness to a higher level. This meeting was held indoors to permit close discussion. At least two attorneys were there, a white one from the poverty program and a Black lawyer interested in the case. Neither of them took a strong stand. The poverty-program lawyer agreed that Denzil's death was a case of murder but said there was little he could do. Denzil Dowell was dead; he could not stick his neck out too far, since he was hired with public funds to assist the community.

They advised the family to go to Martinez, the county seat, and talk to Sheriff Younger, who was in charge of the police patrolling the community. This seemed a good idea, and after the meeting we took our arms and escorted the family to the sheriff's office. When we arrived, the police had surrounded the building and blocked all the elevators. They told us we could not enter with weapons, but we knew we were not in violation of the law. We asked them to produce the law that forbade us to enter the building with weapons. They could not do it. Although they admitted there was no statute, they still would not give us permission to enter. So we went inside anyway and insisted on seeing Younger. Police and sheriff's office personnel crowded into the elevators and blocked the doors to the stairs.

When we demanded they arrest us or stand aside, they refused, saying they would not arrest us because there was no violation, but they also were not going to permit us to go any farther with our weapons.

This shows again that when the oppressor cannot get his will through legal devices, he will act illegally. We were thoroughly outnumbered and the family, already upset, still wanted to talk to Younger. The Dowells asked us to leave our weapons in the car and come in anyway, mistakenly thinking they would get somewhere by talking. Out of respect for the family we left the weapons behind and escorted the family to the sheriff's office.

Younger refused to suspend the policeman who had killed Denzil. Nor would he discuss the department policy about shooting suspects. If we wanted change in our communities, he said, we ought to go to Sacramento and petition the legislature to change the law. He said that according to the law, even if Denzil Dowell was not armed (and he was not; no weapon was ever found), "reasonable cause" existed to believe that he was in the act of committing a felony. Therefore, the officer had a right to kill him. Despite the evidence we had found, the sheriff said, this was the law, and if we did not like it, only the legislature could help us.

After this interview the family saw even more clearly that no established institution would deal justice in the death of their loved one. Denzil had been executed by a policeman, and the law said that this was legal if any "reasonable policeman" believed that a suspect was in the act of committing a felony. This is a very bitter reality. The policemen assigned to control us are not reasonable men. They are inhuman madmen who see the Black community as a place of aberrant behavior and who therefore feel "justified" in killing us in the dark of night.

No official investigation into the death of Denzil Dowell was ever held, despite a promise from the district attorney's office in Martinez. In the public records Denzil is just another dead suspect, branded as guilty by a corrupt, uncaring police department and an indifferent legal system. The fact that his family mourned his loss or that his name was never cleared does not move them. It was the same old story.

The Black Panther Party had done as much as it could in dealing with the authorities. But another avenue was open to us. We could go beyond Martinez and take our investigation of Denzil's case to the people. Bobby suggested that we put out a leaflet describing the rally and what the Black Panther Party was trying to do for the Dowell family. The boldly headlined leaflet dealt with all aspects of the murder. This was our first newspaper, and when we held it in our hands, it seemed we had taken down another barrier between the Black Panthers and the community.

We had never even thought of putting out a newspaper before. Words on paper had always seemed futile. But the Dowell case prompted us to find a way to inform the community about the facts and mobilize them to action. Lacking access to radio, television, or any of the other mass media, we needed an alternative means of communication. No one would do it for us. The Party had only five or six full-time regulars, but we relied on the community to help us out. Many people knew Denzil Dowell personally and willingly pitched in.

Most of the labor for the first paper was contributed by a hippie underground mimeographing outfit in San Francisco. This was the time when underground newspapers were just beginning: if you took material to them, they would print it for you on an electric stenciling machine. We bought supplies—paper, ink, and staples—and put the leaflet together. Then we took it into the community.

We tried to pay paperboys to insert our paper into the Richmond *Independent,* the Oakland *Tribune,* and the San Francisco *Chronicle* before they delivered them, but when they saw what our sheet was about, they did it for nothing. After delivering their own papers, they went around and passed out ours. We circulated about 3,000 the first time, asking for a donation of ten cents. This went into a fund for the funeral expenses of the Dowell family and also for the costs of printing the paper. If anyone did not have ten cents, we gave him a paper anyway and asked him to read it. But most people gave.

Besides North Richmond we distributed the paper in Parchester Village, a small Black settlement about a mile north, and also in some of the Black sections of South Richmond. We walked everywhere, passing out newspapers, taking them from a borrowed van that went alongside us mile after mile.

We were an unusual sight in Richmond, or any other place, dressed in our black leather jackets, wearing black berets and gloves, and carrying shotguns over our shoulders. Bobby always strapped a .45 pistol to his side. People would stop and call to us, asking what we were distributing. This was a good example of our form of armed propaganda. I say "our form" because it was not exactly the way it happened in Cuba. The Cuban people, impressed by the successes of Castro's guerrillas, left their homes to follow him. Thus, for Castro, guerrilla warfare was a good form of propaganda. Walking armed through Richmond was our propaganda. People showed respect for the Party, not only by wanting to read about Denzil Dowell, but also by wanting to learn more about us. This had always been our aim—to arouse interest in the case and in the Party. Then we could go on to explain the necessity for armed self-defense, an idea that was not hard to put across since the people knew the problems and had been looking for solutions.

The Denzil Dowell case was critical to the development of the Black Panther Party. It led to our first national exposure, and it also helped us launch our paper, which was a way of interpreting events to the community from a Black perspective. Our Intercommunal News Service and weekly paper, *The Black Panther*, have become central in the Black Panther survival programs. So, in one sense, Denzil Dowell's death was not in vain. Every issue continues the struggle we began in his cause. In a way, *The Black Panther* newspaper is a living memorial to him.

20

Sacramento and the
"Panther Bill"

Bobby and I look back on the early days of the Black Panthers
with nostalgia. It was a time of discovery and enthusiasm; we
had hit on something unique. By standing up to the police as
equals, even holding them off, and yet remaining within the
law, we had demonstrated Black pride to the community in a
concrete way. Everywhere we went we caused traffic jams. People constantly stopped us to say how much they respected our
courage. The idea of armed self-defense as a community policy
was still new and a little intimidating to them; but it also made
them think. More important, it created a feeling of solidarity.
When we saw how Black citizens reacted to our movement, we
were greatly encouraged. Despite the ever-present danger of re-
taliation, the risks were more than worth it. At that time, however, our activities were confined to a small area, and we wanted
Black people throughout the country to know the Oakland
story.

In April, 1967, we were invited to appear on a radio talk
show in Oakland, the kind where people phone in questions and
make comments. Early in the program we explained our ten-
point program, why we were focusing on Point 7, and why it
was necessary for Black men to arm themselves. We also made
it clear that we were within our constitutional rights. Hundreds
of calls poured in—the lines were jammed. Some people agreed

with us; others disputed our points. We welcomed the discussion, because criticism helped us to find weaknesses in our program and to sharpen our position.

One of the callers was Donald Mulford, a conservative Republican state assemblyman from Piedmont, one of the wealthy, white sections of Oakland. Mulford was so close to Oakland's power structure that his call could only mean he saw political profit in attacking the Black Panthers. He told us that he planned to introduce a bill into the state legislature to make it illegal for us to patrol with our weapons. It was a bill, he said, that would "get" the Black Panthers. Mulford's call was a logical response of the system. We knew how the system operated. If we used the laws in our own interest and against theirs, then the power structure would simply change the laws. Mulford was more than willing to be the agent of change.

A few days later, the paper carried a story about Mulford's "Panther bill." In its particulars it was what we had expected—a bill intended to suppress the people's constitutional right to bear arms. Until then, white men had owned and carried weapons with impunity. Groups like the Minutemen and the Rangers in Richmond were known to have arsenals, but nobody introduced bills against them. Mulford had been asked by the Oakland police to introduce this bill because some "young Black toughs," as they called us, were walking around with guns. The bill was further evidence of this country's vicious double standard against Blacks. The usual pattern of white racism was gradually being put into effect. They would escalate the killing of Blacks, but this time the police would do the job that the Ku Klux Klan had done in the past.

The Black Panthers have never viewed such paramilitary groups as the Ku Klux Klan or the Minutemen as particularly dangerous. The real danger comes from highly organized Establishment forces—the local police, the National Guard, and the United States military. They were the ones who devastated Watts and killed innocent people. In comparison to them the paramilitary groups are insignificant. In fact, these groups are hardly organized at all. It is the uniformed men who are dangerous and who come into our communities every day to commit violence against us, knowing that the laws will protect them.

Bobby Seale and I discussed the Mulford bill against his background. Sheriff Younger had suggested, facetiously, that the Dowell family attempt to get their case heard at the state capitol. The Dowell family only wanted some good to come out of all the grief inflicted on them. We knew that the Dowells would get no better consideration in Sacramento than they had received from Younger. The legislators would probably tell them to go to the governor, and the governor would point to Washington.

Institutions work this way. A son is murdered by the police, and nothing is done. The institutions send the victim's family on a merry-go-round, going from one agency to another, until they wear out and give up. This is a very effective way to beat down poor and oppressed people, who do not have the time to prosecute their cases. Time is money to poor people. To go to Sacramento means loss of a day's pay—often a loss of job. If this is a democracy, obviously it is a bourgeois democracy limited to the middle and upper classes. Only they can afford to participate in it.

Knowing all this, we nonetheless made plans to go to Sacramento. That we would not change any laws was irrelevant, and all of us—Black Panthers and Dowells—realized that from the start. Since we were resigned to a runaround in Sacramento, we decided to raise the encounter to a higher level in the hope of warning people about the dangers in the Mulford bill and the ideas behind it. A national outcry would help the Dowell family by showing them that some good had come from their tragedy; also, it might mobilize our community even more.

Dozens of reporters and photographers haunt the capitol waiting for a story. This made it the perfect forum for our proclamation. If the legislators got the message, too, well and good. But our primary purpose was to deliver it to the people. Actually, several groups went: four or five members of the Dowell family; a group of brothers from East Oakland, recruited by Mark Comfort, and the Black Panthers. The Black Panthers and Comfort's cadre were armed.

The Party agreed that I ought not to make the trip for two reasons. First, I was on probation from the Odell Lee case, and they did not want to jeopardize my freedom. Second, if any arrests were made in Sacramento, someone should be available to raise bail money and do whatever else was necessary.

Before they left, I prepared Executive Mandate Number One, which was to be our message to the Black communities. It read:

> The Black Panther Party for Self-Defense calls upon the American people in general, and Black people in particular, to take careful note of the racist California Legislature now considering legislation aimed at keeping Black people disarmed and powerless while racist police agencies throughout the country intensify the terror, brutality, murder, and repression of Black people.
>
> At the same time that the American Government is waging a racist war of genocide in Vietnam the concentration camps in which Japanese-Americans were interned during World War II are being renovated and expanded. Since America has historically reserved its most barbaric treatment for nonwhite people, we are forced to conclude that these concentration camps are being prepared for Black people who are determined to gain their freedom by any means necessary. The enslavement of Black people at the very founding of this country, the genocide practiced on the American Indians and the confinement of the survivors on reservations, the savage lynching of thousands of Black men and women, the dropping of atomic bombs on Hiroshima and Nagasaki, and now the cowardly massacre in Vietnam all testify to the fact that toward people of color the racist power structure of America has but one policy: repression, genocide, terror, and the big stick.
>
> Black people have begged, prayed, petitioned and demonstrated, among other things, to get the racist power structure of America to right the wrongs which have historically been perpetrated against Black people. All of these efforts have been answered by more repression, deceit, and hypocrisy. As the aggression of the racist American Government escalates in Vietnam, the police agencies of America escalate the repression of Black people throughout the ghettos of America. Vicious police

dogs, cattle prods, and increased patrols have become familiar sights in Black communities. City Hall turns a deaf ear to the pleas of Black people for relief from this increasing terror.

The Black Panther Party for Self-Defense believes that the time has come for Black people to arm themselves against this terror before it is too late. The pending Mulford Act brings the hour of doom one step nearer. A people who have suffered so much for so long at the hands of a racist society must draw the line somewhere. We believe that the Black communities of America must rise up as one man to halt the progression of a trend that leads inevitably to their total destruction.

When I gave Bobby his instructions, I impressed upon him that our main purpose was to deliver the message to the people. If he was fired upon, he should return the fire. If a gun was drawn on him and it was his interpretation that the gun was drawn in anger, he was to use whatever means necessary to defend himself. His instructions were not to fire or take the offensive unless in imminent danger. If they attempted to arrest him, he was to take the arrest as long as he had delivered the message. The main thing was to deliver the message. In stressing these points, I told him that if he was invited in or allowed inside the legislature, he was to read the message inside, but if it was against the rules to enter the legislature, or if measures were taken to block him, then he was not to enter, but to read the message from the capitol steps.

The Black Panther troops rolled out for Sacramento early on the morning of May 2. As soon as they left, I went to my mother's house. I had promised to mow her lawn that day. But I took a portable radio along and put it on the front step to listen for news; in the house I turned the television set on and asked my mother to keep an eye on it. Then I started mowing.

About noon a bulletin interrupted the radio program. It told of brothers at the capitol with weapons. My mother called out to me that all channels were showing the event. I ran into the house, and there was Bobby reading the mandate. The message was definitely going out. Bobby read it twice, but the press and the people assembled were so amazed at the Black Panthers' presence, and particularly the weapons, that few appeared to hear the important thing. They were concentrating on the weapons. We had hoped that after the weapons gained their attention they would listen to the message.

Later, another bulletin came on saying the brothers had been arrested, Bobby for carrying a concealed weapon—although he was wearing his gun openly on his hip. Some of the other brothers were charged with failing to remove the rounds from the chambers of their guns when they put the weapons back in the car. I got on the phone and finally made contact with one of the Black Panther women who had gone along. She told me what had happened, and I began to initiate the next phase of our plan—raising bail money. That night I went to a local radio station, where a talk show was on. People calling in to discuss the incident had been told that I was in jail, and I decided the best way to deal with that was by confrontation. So I went in there, as Malcolm would have done, and asked for equal air time. One of the startled program directors looked at me and said, "Well, you're sort of in jail." I said, "Yes, I am in jail, but let me have equal time anyway."

On the air I explained the Sacramento ploy. My explanation was not very effective, I felt, because people who call these shows are always more interested in themselves than in issues, and you have to fight through that first. But I was able to make an appeal for money. We were faced with $50,000 bail in Sacramento, and within twenty-four hours I had raised the $5,000 needed to get the troops back on the streets. Our plans had worked exactly as we hoped.

Looking back, I think our tactic at Sacramento was correct at that time, but it was also a mistake in a way. It was the first time in our brief existence that an armed group of Black Panthers had been arrested, and it was a turning point in police perceptions. We took the arrests because we had a higher purpose. But it was not until then that the police started attempting to disarm the Party. They leveled shotguns on the brothers, handcuffed them, and generally pushed them around. I had given orders not to fire unless fired upon. Maybe the order should have been to fire on everybody in there; then they would have realized we were serious. But our purpose was not to kill; it was to inform, to let the nation know where the Party stood. The police, however, took it to mean that the Party was only a front with weapons, that we would not defend ourselves. This attitude caused a number of problems for us, and it took some time to restore caution to the police after Sacramento. Now, everything is as it used to be, because they know they will have a fight on their hands if they try to attack us.

Sacramento was certainly a success, however, in attracting national attention; even those who did not hear the complete message saw the arms, and this conveyed enough to Black people. The Bay Area became more aware of the Party, and soon we had more members than we could handle. From all across the country calls came to us about establishing chapters and branches; we could hardly keep track of the requests. In a matter of months we went from a small Bay Area group to a national organization, and we began moving to implement our ten-point program.

21

I have made up my mind, wherever I go I shall go as a man and not as a slave. . . . I shall always be courteous and mild in deportment towards all with whom I come in contact, at the same time firmly and constantly endeavouring to assert my equal right as a man and a brother.

FREDERICK DOUGLASS, *My Bondage and My Freedom*

Growing Pains

The Mulford bill passed the California legislature in July, 1967, by a huge majority. As soon as the law was changed, making it illegal to carry loaded weapons, we stopped the armed patrols. The police understood this to mean that we were ready to submit, and they stepped up their campaign of harassment. Only a month after the Sacramento trip, we were subjected to another stupid and childish incident.

One night in June a bail-fund party was held in Richmond. As soon as we arrived, the police miraculously appeared, but remained outside in their parked cars. This was an ominous sign. We decided to ignore them, however, and remained inside all evening having a fine party. When the party began breaking up about 2:00 A.M., we decided to stay a while longer to avoid trouble, since we thought the police might leave when the place emptied out a little. But it turned out they wanted us, the Black Panthers. It became a waiting game: the police cut their motors and lights and sat in the darkness; we stayed inside and went right on enjoying ourselves.

Finally, all of us had to leave, about 5:00 A.M.; we came out and got into our cars. One of the Black Panther members, John

Sloane, made a U-turn in the middle of the block and drove off, away from the police. To my knowledge, such a turn in a residential area is perfectly legal, but the police pursued him, stopped him about a block away from the house, and began writing out a ticket. We stopped our cars a reasonable distance from this exchange and got out to watch.

Sloane refused to sign for the ticket. He had been drinking at the party, and this may have affected his behavior, but at any rate he would not sign where he was supposed to. When an argument broke out, I walked over to his car and said, "Sign the ticket. If there's any problem, we'll take it up in court, but sign the ticket." Sloane went right on arguing, and soon seven or eight more policemen arrived. Among them was a young recruit—no more than twenty-two or twenty-three—who went up to all of us standing on the sidewalk and began stepping heavily on one foot after another. When he got to me, I pulled my foot back. It was no time for a fight. After he passed, I ignored him and tried to get John Sloane to calm down and sign the ticket. Sloane finally came around and was about to sign when the recruit stepped on the feet of a brother, who promptly helped him off in a vigorous fashion. That was all the police needed. They charged the brother and began to beat him with their clubs. I ran up to them, saying, "This isn't necessary! It's not necessary!" None of us were armed, or the situation would have been different. But, cowardly as ever, they were unrestrainedly attacking an unarmed man, overpowering him.

When I saw how brutally they were beating the brother, I went over to one of the policemen and put my hand on his arm to restrain him. This man was big and powerfully built. He spun around and charged me, backing me against the car in a choke hold so tight I could not move. The other brothers ran to my assistance. The policeman had reached for his gun because he was afraid the people would storm him, but I told them not to do anything, and I took the arrest, along with John Sloane and the brother who had shoved the policeman off his foot.

All the way to the station Sloane and the other brother angrily cursed the policeman. I tried to calm them down; we were handcuffed and there was no point in further struggle. But they kept right on protesting and cursing, and when we got to the station, the police began working them over. Their arms were still restrained. Since I said nothing, I got off lightly. The police provoked me, but I refused to respond. I just kept telling the other guys to shut up, but they would not, and so they got a real beating. The big guy who had charged me was right in the middle of it, giving as many blows as he could, really enjoying his work. After the brothers were subdued, he mopped his brow, straightened out his clothes, and told the others, "I have to go now because I promised to take my wife and the kids to church at nine."

When we began to receive requests for assistance in starting new branches of the Party, we realized our need for more than courageous troops. We lacked an administrative body that could handle these requests and supervise a large-scale organization. The brothers on the block had none of the bourgeois skills needed for this. Yet these skills were necessary, even though we did not want bourgeois values, so we looked for ways to solve our administrative problems while continuing our work with the street brothers.

I had to respect the Student Nonviolent Co-ordinating Committee (SNCC) for having some of the most disciplined organizers in the country. When we had first talked of forming a party, Bobby and I read about their work in the South—registering people to vote and organizing co-operatives and the like. We felt they could do a good job of administering the Party because they were all committed people and highly skilled. Their leadership came from college campuses.

Our original plan was to draft Stokely Carmichael of SNCC into the Party and make him Prime Minister, then to add all the SNCC leadership to the Party's administrative positions, including H. Rap Brown and James Forman. By doing this, we hoped to create a merger, not a coalition, since it seemed to us that only by merging could we produce the strong leadership we needed.

The movement was cresting around the country. Brothers on the block in many northern cities were moving angrily in response to the problems that overwhelmed them. New York and other eastern cities had exploded in 1964, Watts went up in 1965, Cleveland in 1966, and in 1967 another long hot summer was approaching. But the brothers needed direction for their energies. The Party wanted no more spontaneous riots, because the outcome was always the same: the people might liberate their territories for a few short days or hours, but eventually the military force of the oppressor would wipe out their gains. Having neither the strength nor the organization, the people were powerless. In the final analysis, riots caused only more repression and the loss of brave men. Blacks bled and died in the riots and went to jail on petty or false charges. If the brothers could be organized into disciplined cadres, working in broadly based community programs, then the energy expended in riots could be directed toward permanent and positive changes.

The matter was urgent. Police were being strengthened nationwide and given more power. In order to deal with this, we had to organize our resources and develop an administrative body. On the other hand, although SNCC had skills, we felt they were headed for a decline, because the thrust of the movement was diminishing in the South and moving into the cities of the North and West. At this point in time, it seemed clear to us that SNCC and the Black Panther Party needed each other, and Black people needed us both.

By making Stokely Prime Minister—head of the Party—we were in effect voting to give leadership of the Party to SNCC. We even considered moving our headquarters to Atlanta, where we would be under SNCC, in their buildings, with access to their duplicating equipment and other sorely needed materials. Our long-range plan was to organize the communities of the North, especially the brothers on the block, using SNCC's administrative talent to co-ordinate the activities. Combining their work in the South and ours in the North would give the forces of Black liberation a powerful striking force.

We drew up our plans, drafting Stokely Carmichael as Prime Minister, H. Rap Brown as Minister of Justice, and James Forman as Minister of Foreign Affairs. Our own position was clear; we would accept whatever places in the administration they had for us; we were not hung up on status. Eldridge, Bobby, and I were in full agreement about this. A party as such did not interest me. I was more concerned about the revolution and the freedom of the Black people, and getting the best personnel in positions of authority to bring these goals about. From the beginning, Black Panther leadership had been a casual thing, designed only to give our ideas a form and a structure.

Eldridge got in touch with Stokely about the merger. They had met early in 1967 when Eldridge traveled with Stokely on an assignment for *Ramparts*. We had met other SNCC people then, too, so Eldridge handled communications. We also got in touch with Rap Brown and James Forman, who both seemed to go along with the plan. They in turn were supposed to inform the rest of the governing body of SNCC, and we thought this had been done when Brown and Forman indicated that SNCC approved of the merger. But the scheme never worked out as we had hoped.

We later found out that it had all been empty talk on their part. According to others on the governing body of SNCC, the matter was never brought up formally, despite assurances to us by Brown and Forman. Nor was the entire membership notified of any plans for a merger. So when we announced the merger—that we were delivering the Black Panthers to them— some of the SNCC people reacted in a paranoid way; they thought we were trying to co-opt them. As a result, some SNCC members—Julius Lester and others—wrote articles criticizing us, saying that we had not approached the right people in attempting to accomplish the merger. We took offense at this. We had gone through the people we knew and those who spoke publicly for SNCC since we thought the organization was behind them. But apparently it was not.

I think the main problem was a basic lack of trust. If we supported each other and were honest, I felt sure that a certain level of trust would be reached. This is very crucial in any good relationship, more crucial perhaps in this case, since the merger was susceptible to misrepresentation and misunderstanding. But there was no real trust, because SNCC's people believed we wanted to take over their organization, whereas the reverse was true: we intended to give them complete control. They just did not see it that way. Later, when I was in jail, I was told that they had totally rejected any plans for a merger because I never answered a letter they wrote me. I was in solitary confinement all this time and did not receive the letter from SNCC. But they held me responsible nonetheless.

It worked out for the best in the end, however, because when SNCC took their turn in the wrong direction we were not dragged along. They had talked socialism for a while, but then they backtracked and started to advocate a separate nation and to ignore the world class problem. Any relationship with Stokely would have been problematical. We realized this when we first got in touch with African guerrilla groups and other freedom fighters. They said they had had confidence in Stokely at first, believing him to be a revolutionary. But when he aligned himself with reactionary African governments, he lost his credibility. He had come into their countries, barely acknowledging them, talking about the new alliance he was forming with Nkrumah, and making himself the spokesman for African freedom fighters. Then the revolutionaries found out that Nkrumah did not really support Stokely's position on race.

I first met Stokely in May, 1967, when he came to speak in the Bay Area. We met once at Eldridge's house, and another time at Beverly Axelrod's. Several times we drove to San Mateo together to meet with small community groups. Stokely wrote in a recent book that when he visited the Bay Area, Bobby and I had asked his permission to start an organization and call it the Black Panther Party. This is untrue. Bobby and I together had chosen the Party's name, taking it from the symbol of the black panther used by the Lowndes County Freedom Organization, which Stokely had helped found in Mississippi. We never asked Stokely's advice about starting the Party; we were organized before we met him.

Anyway, we broke with SNCC, not really wanting to, but realizing we could accomplish little without their trust. Later I was glad of the break, because Stokely's views are so inconsistent you never know where he is coming from. When a man is consistent, you at least know what is happening and what to expect. Stokely says one thing one day and another the next. He accuses us of misleading people by our coalitions with whites, but I say he confuses people when he goes to Washington and tries to prevent a Black policeman from being kicked off the force—a policeman who takes orders to kill his own people and who protects the Establishment. Stokely told me he would support anyone—he did not care who—if the person were Black. We consider this viewpoint both racist and suicidal. If you support a Black man with a gun who belongs to the military arm of your oppressor, then you are assisting in your own destruction.

Our plans for a merger with SNCC probably would not have come in time to prevent the summer riots of 1967. In July and August, when the Black communities of Newark and Detroit erupted in rage and frustration, our worst expectations came true. In each instance trouble had begun when the police had brutalized a brother or sister. In a larger sense, the younger Blacks particularly were expressing their frustration. The consequences of these bitter uprisings would surely be more right-wing political reaction and a move to conservative politics throughout the nation. The eruption in Watts had come in 1965, and Ronald Reagan was elected governor in 1966. Now, with the cities rocked by riots again in 1967, the ruling circles would undoubtedly respond with more repressive controls. The California story would be repeated in other states and then on a national level.

All that summer we sought to prevent this chain of events. We organized, recruited, and worked hard at putting out our paper. We tried especially to be aware always of what was happening on the streets of the inner cities so that we could ride the crest of the movement by directing the people's energies in constructive ways. We particularly wanted people to understand their constitutional rights, rights that were constantly violated by police and authorities. With only an elementary knowledge of these rights, many of their problems could be avoided in tense situations.

To impart that knowledge we began a series of pieces in the

earliest issues of our newspapers called "Pocket Lawyer of Legal First Aid." Using lawbooks and various legal pamphlets, I put together in simple form a number of rules for people to follow.

POCKET LAWYER OF LEGAL FIRST AID

This pocket lawyer is provided as a means of keeping Black people up to date on their rights. We are always the first to be arrested and the racist police forces are constantly trying to pretend that rights are extended equally to all people. Cut this out, brothers and sisters, and carry it with you. Until we arm ourselves to righteously take care of our own, the pocket lawyer is what's happening.

1. If you are stopped and/or arrested by the police, you may remain silent; you do not have to answer any questions about alleged crimes; you should provide your name and address only if requested (although it is not absolutely clear that you must do so). But then do so, and at all times remember the Fifth Amendment.

2. If a police officer is not in uniform, ask him to show his identification. He has no authority over you unless he properly identifies himself. Beware of persons posing as police officers. Always get his badge number and his name.

3. Police have no right to search your car or your home unless they have a search warrant, probable cause or your consent. They may conduct no exploratory search, that is, one for evidence of crime generally or for evidence of a crime unconnected with the one you are being questioned about. (Thus, a stop for an auto violation does not give the right to search the auto.) You are not required to consent to a search; therefore, you should not consent and should state clearly and unequivocally that you do not consent, in front of witnesses if possible. If you do not consent, the police will have the burden in court of showing probable cause. Arrest may be corrected later.

4. You may not resist forcibly or by going limp, even if you are innocent. To do so is a separate crime of which you can be convicted even if you are acquitted of the original charge. Do not resist arrest under any circumstances.

5. If you are stopped and/or arrested, the police may search you by patting you on the outside of your clothing. You can be

stripped of your personal possessions. Do not carry anything that includes the name of your employer or friends.

6. Do not engage in "friendly" conversation with officers on the way to or at the station. Once you are arrested, there is little likelihood that anything you say will get you released.

7. As soon as you have been booked, you have the right to complete at least two phone calls—one to a relative, friend or attorney, the other to a bail bondsman. If you can, call the Black Panther Party, 845-0103 (845-0104), and the Party will post bail if possible.

8. You must be allowed to hire and see an attorney immediately.

9. You do not have to give any statement to the police, nor do you have to sign any statement you might give them, and therefore you should not sign anything. Take the Fifth and Fourteenth Amendments, because you cannot be forced to testify against yourself.

10. You must be allowed to post bail in most cases, but you must be able to pay the bail bondsmen's fee. If you cannot pay the fee, you may ask the judge to release you from custody without bail or to lower your bail, but he does not have to do so.

11. The police must bring you into court or release you within 48 hours after your arrest (unless the time ends on a week-end or a holiday, and they must bring you before a judge the first day court is in session).

12. If you do not have the money to hire an attorney, immediately ask the police to get you an attorney without charge.

13. If you have the money to hire a private attorney, but do not know of one, call the National Lawyers' Guild or the Alameda County Bar Association (or the Bar Association of your county) and ask them to furnish you with the name of an attorney who practices criminal law.

Carrying our message as it did right into the homes of the people, the paper was a source of great satisfaction and pleasure to us. It explained events from a community point of view. For instance, in *The Black Panther* the people read the true explanation of why we went to Sacramento and what happened there. We reported on events and meetings in Black communities all over the Bay Area. Until that time the Black Panther Party had been maligned by the Establishment press, which was interested only in the kind of sensationalism that sells papers. But once we began to give our own interpretation of events, Black people realized how facts had been twisted by the mass media. They were glad to get our point of view, and the paper sold well. It became a steady source of funds to help us continue developing our programs.

I was satisfied with our movement in 1967. Our newspaper was reaching the people; the Sacramento stance had received tremendous support; new chapters were springing up in many cities; we were exploring new ways to raise the consciousness of Black people. Everything was working well.

My only sadness was that Bobby Seale was going away to jail for six months in August as a result of the Sacramento confrontation. We had made a deal with the courts in Sacramento: Bobby would do six months for a misdemeanor in exchange for the charges being dropped against the others. Six months was not long in the life of our struggle, but Bobby was a good organizer, a man who got things moving. He would be missed. Still, we expressed no sorrow when Bobby was taken away from us. This was a small price to pay for the liberation of the people. Also, it was only a question of time before they would be after me, and then Eldridge. When Bobby left in August, 1967, we were not to be together on the streets again until June, 1971.

PART FOUR

Black men and women who refuse to live under oppression are dangerous to white society because they become symbols of hope to their brothers and sisters, inspiring them to follow their example.

22

The mobilization of the masses, when it arises out of the war of liberation, introduces into each man's consciousness the ideas of a common cause, of a national destiny, and of a collective history. In the same way the second phase, that of the building-up of the nation, is helped on by the existence of this cement which has been mixed with blood and anger.

FRANTZ FANON, *The Wretched of the Earth*

Nommo: Swahili for "the power of the word"

Raising Consciousness

The Black Panthers have always emphasized action over rhetoric. But language, the power of the word, in the philosophical sense, is not underestimated in our ideology. We recognize the significance of words in the struggle for liberation, not only in the media and in conversations with people on the block, but in the important area of raising consciousness. Words are another way of defining phenomena, and the definition of any phenomenon is the first step to controlling it or being controlled by it.

When I read Nietzsche's *The Will to Power,* I learned much from a number of his philosophical insights. This is not to say that I endorse all of Nietzsche, only that many of his ideas have influenced my thinking. Because Nietzsche was writing about concepts fundamental to all men, and particularly about the meaning of power, some of his ideas are pertinent to the way Black people live in the United States; they have had a great impact on the development of the Black Panther philosophy.

Nietzsche believed that beyond good and evil is the will to power. In other words, good and evil are labels for phenomena, or value judgments. Behind these value judgments is the will to power, which causes man to view phenomena as good or evil. It is really the will to power that controls our understanding of something and not an inherent quality of good or evil.

Man attempts to define phenomena in such a way that they reflect the interests of his own class or group. He gives titles or values to phenomena according to what he sees as beneficial; if it is to his advantage, something is called good, and if it is not beneficial, then it is defined as evil. Nietzsche shows how this reasoning was used by the German ruling circle, which always defined phenomena in terms complimentary to the noble class. For example, they used the German word *gut,* which means "godlike" or "good," to refer to themselves; nobles were *gut.* On the other hand, the word *villein,* used to describe the poor people and serfs who lived outside the great gates of the noble-man's home, suggested the opposite. The poor were said to live in the "village," a word that comes from the same root word (Latin: *villa*) as the term "villain." So the ruling class, by the power they possessed, defined themselves as "godlike" and called the people "villains" or enemies of the ruling circle. Needless to say, when the poor and common people internalized these ideas, they felt inferior, guilty, and ashamed, while the nobles took their superiority for granted. Thought had been shaped by language.

We have seen the same thing in the United States, where, over a period of time, the adjective "black" became a potent word in the American language, pejorative in every sense. We were made to feel ashamed and guilty because of our biological characteristics, while our oppressors, through their whiteness, felt noble and uplifted. In the past few years, however—and it has been *only* a few years—the rising level of consciousness within our Black communities has led us to redefine ourselves. People once ashamed to be called Black now gladly accept the label, and our biological characteristics are sources of pride. Today we call ourselves Black people and wear natural hair styles because we have changed the definition of the word "black."

This is an example of Nietzsche's theory that beyond good and evil is the will to power.

In the early days of the Black Panthers we tried to find ways to make this theory work in the best interests of Black people. Words could be used not only to make Blacks more proud but to make whites question and even reject concepts they had always unthinkingly accepted. One of our prime needs was a new definition for "policeman." A good descriptive word, one the community would accept and use, would not only advance Black consciousness, but in effect control the police by making them see themselves in a new light.

We thought up new terms for them. At first I figured that the reverse of god—dog—would be a good epithet, but it did not catch on. We tried beast, brute, and animal, but none of them captured the essential quality we were trying to convey. One day, while working on the paper, Eldridge showed us a postcard from Beverly Axelrod. On the front was the slogan "Support Your Local Police"; there was a sheriff's star above the phrase, and in the center of the star a grinning, slobbering pig. It was just what we were looking for. We began to show policemen as pigs in our cartoons, and from time to time used the word. "Pig" caught on; it entered the language.

This was a form of psychological warfare: it raised the consciousness of the people and also inflicted a new consciousness on the ruling circle. If whites and police became caught up in this new awareness, they would soon defect from their own ranks and join us to avoid feelings of guilt and shame.

Nietzsche pointed out that this tactic had been used to good effect by the Christians against the Romans. In the beginning the Christians were weak, but they understood how to make the philosophy of a weak group work for them. By using phrases like "the meek shall inherit the earth," they imposed a new idea on the Romans, one that gave rise to doubt and led to defections to the new sect. Once Christians stated that the meek shall inherit the earth and won over members, they weakened the strength of those in power. They were to be the victors. People like to be on the winning side. We have seen the same principle work on college campuses in this country. Many white youths now identify with Blacks; the identification is manifested in clothes, rhetoric, and life styles.

Thus, even though we came to the term "pig" accidentally, the choice itself was calculated. "Pig" was perfect for several reasons. First of all, words like "swine," "hog," "sow," and "pig" have always had unpleasant connotations. The reason for this probably has theological roots, since the pig is considered an unclean animal in Semitic religions. In the English language well-established "pig" epithets are numerous. We say that someone eats like a hog, is a filthy swine, and so on. In *Portrait of the Artist as a Young Man,* James Joyce uses swine as a destructive, devouring image when he describes Ireland as "an old sow that eats her farrow." So the word "pig" is traditionally associated with grotesque qualities.

The pig in reality is an ugly and offensive animal. It likes to root around in the mud; it makes hideous noises; it does not seem to relate to humans as other animals do. Further, anyone in the Black community can relate to the true characteristics of the pig because most of us come from rural backgrounds and have observed the nature of pigs. Many of the police, too, are hired right out of the South and are familiar with the behavior of pigs. They know exactly what the word implies. To call a policeman a pig conveys the idea of someone who is brutal, gross, and uncaring.

"Pig" has another point in its favor: in racial terms "pig" is a neutral word. Many white youths on college campuses began to understand what the police were really like when their heads were broken open during demonstrations against the draft and the Vietnam war. This broadened the use of the term and served to unify the victims against their oppressors. Even though white youths were not victimized in the same way or to the same extent that we were, they nonetheless became our allies against the police. In this case the ruling circle was not able to set the victims against each other, as the racists in the South had done by setting poor whites against Blacks.

Our greatest victory, however, lay in the effect on the police themselves. They did not like to be called pigs, and they still do not. Ever since the term came into use, they have conducted a countercampaign by using slogans like "Pigs Are Beautiful" and wearing pig pins; but their effort has failed. Our message, of course, is that if they do not want to be pigs, then they ought to stop their brutalization of the victims of the world. No slogan will change the people's opinion; a change in behavior is the only thing that will do it.

Another expression that helped to raise Black people's consciousness is "All Power to the People." An expression that has meaning on several levels—political, economic, and metaphysical—it was coined by the Black Panther Party around the same time as "pig," and has also gained wide acceptance. When we created it, I had in mind some distinct philosophical goals for the community that many people did not understand. The police and the press wanted everyone to believe that we were nothing more than a bunch of "young toughs" strutting around with guns in order to shock people. But Bobby and I always had a clear understanding of what we wanted to do. We wanted to give the community a wide variety of needed programs, and so we began in a way that would gain the community's support. At the same time we saw the necessity of going beyond these first steps. In developing our newspaper, we were working toward our long-range goals of organizing the community around programs that the people would come to believe in strongly. We hoped these programs would come to mean so much that the people would take up guns for defense against any maneuvers by the oppressor.

All these programs were aimed at one goal: complete control of the institutions in the community. Every ethnic group has particular needs that they know and understand better than anybody else; each group is the best judge of how its institutions ought to affect the lives of its members. Throughout American history ethnic groups like the Irish and Italians have established organizations and institutions within their own communities. When they achieved this political control, they had the power to deal with their problems. Yet there is still another necessary step. In the Black community, mere control of our own institutions will not automatically solve problems. For one thing, it is difficult to get enough places of work in the community to produce full employment for Blacks. The most important element in controlling our own institutions would be to organize them into co-operatives, which would end all forms of exploitation. Then the profits, or surplus, from the co-operatives would be returned to the community, expanding opportunities on all levels, and enriching life. Beyond this, our ultimate aim is to have various ethnic communities co-operating in a spirit of mutual aid, rather than competing. In this way, all communities would be allied in a common purpose through the major social, economic, and political institutions in the country.

This is our long-range objective. Although we are far from realizing it, it is important that the people understand what we want for them and what are, indeed, their natural rights. Therefore, the slogan "All Power to the People" sums up our goals for Black people, as well as our deep love and commitment to them. All power comes from the people, and all power must ultimately be vested in them. Anything else is theft.

Our complete faith in the people is based on our assumptions about what they require and deserve. The first of these is honesty. When it became apparent in the early days that the Black Panthers were a growing force, some people urged us to take either accommodating positions for small gains or a "Black line" based solely on race rather than economic or social strategy. These people were talking a Black game they did not really believe in. But they saw that the people believed and that the Black line could be used to mobilize them. We resisted. To us, it was both wrong and futile to deceive the people; eventually we would have to answer to them.

In the metaphysical sense we based the expression "All Power to the People" on the idea of man as God. I have no other God but man, and I firmly believe that man is the highest or chief good. If you are obligated to be true and honest to anyone, it is to your God, and if each man is God, then you must be true to him. If you believe that man is the ultimate being, then you will act according to your belief. Your attitude and behavior toward man is a kind of religion in itself, with high standards of responsibility.

It was especially important to me that I explore the Judaeo-Christian concept of God, because historically that concept has had an enormous impact on the lives of Black people in America. Their acceptance of the Judaeo-Christian God and religion has always meant submission and an emphasis on the rewards of the life hereafter as relief for the sufferings of the present. Christianity began as a religion for the outcast and oppressed. While the early Christians succeeded in undermining the authority and confidence of their rulers and rising up out of slavery, the Afro-American experience has been just the opposite. Already a people in slavery, when Christianity was imposed upon them, the Blacks only assumed another burden, the tyranny of the future—the hope of heaven and the fear of hell. Christianity increased their sense of hopelessness. It also projected the idea of salvation and happiness into the afterlife, where God would reward them for all their sufferings on this earth. Justice would come later, in the Promised Land.

The phrase "All Power to the People" was meant to turn this around, to convince Black people that their rewards were due in the present, that it was in their power to create a Promised Land *here and now.* The Black Panthers have never intended to turn Black people away from religion. We want to encourage them to change their consciousness of themselves and to be less accepting of the white man's version of God—the God of the downtrodden, the weak, and the undeserving. We want them to see themselves as the called, the chosen, and the salt of the earth.

Even before we coined the phrase, I had long thought about the idea of God. I could not accept the Biblical version; the Bible is too full of contradictions and irrationality. Either you accept it, and believe, or you do not. I could not believe. I have arrived at my understanding of what is meant by God through other means—through philosophy, logic, and semantics. My opinion is that the term "God" belongs to the realm of concepts, that it is dependent upon man for its existence. If God does not exist unless man exists, then man must be here to produce God. It logically follows, then, that man created God, and if the creator is greater than that which is created, then we must hold that man is the highest good.

I can understand why man feels the need to create God, particularly in earlier periods of history when scientific understanding was limited. The phenomena that man observed around him in the universe sometimes overwhelmed him; he could not explain or account for them. Therefore, he created something in his mind that was "greater" than these phenomena, something that was responsible for the mysteries in nature. But I think that when man clings to the idea of a God, whom he has created and placed in the heavens, he actually reduces himself and his own potential. The more he attributes to God, the more inferior he becomes, the less responsible for his own destiny. He says to God, "I am weak but thou art mighty," and therefore accepts things as they are, content to leave the running of the world to a supernatural force greater than himself. This attitude embodies a kind of fatalism, which is inimical to growth and change. On the other hand, the greater man becomes, the less his God will be.

None of this means that I am completely hostile to the many beautiful and admirable things about religion. When I speak of certain aspects of society to Black people, the use of religious phraseology flows naturally, and the audience response is genuine. I also read the Bible frequently, not only for its poetry, but also for its wisdom and insight. Still, much of the Bible is madness. I cannot accept, for example, the notion of divine law and responsibility to "God." As far as I am concerned, if men are responsible beings, they ought to be responsible to each other. And so, when we say "All Power to the People," we mean to convey a sense of deep respect and love for the people, and the idea that the people deserve complete truth and honesty. The judgment of history is the judgment of the people. That is the motivating and controlling idea of our very existence.

23

Crisis: October 28, 1967

When I was convicted of assaulting Odell Lee in 1964, the court sentenced me to three years' probation under condition that I first serve six months in the county jail. After release I reported regularly to my probation officer, all through the months that we founded the Black Panther Party and began our work in the community. The probation officer was better than average, really a pretty nice guy, intelligent and fair, and we got along well. Nonetheless, I was relieved when he told me early in October, 1967, that my probation would end on October 27 and parole begin. One of the requirements of parole was that I avoid some parts of Berkeley; in any case, no more reporting; October 27 was going to be a very special day, and my girl friend, LaVerne Williams, and I agreed that we would celebrate the occasion.

On the afternoon of October 27, I was scheduled to speak at a forum on "The Future of the Black Liberation Movement," sponsored by the Black Students Union of San Francisco State College. Requests for speaking engagements had been coming in frequently since the end of the summer. The Sacramento publicity prompted a number of college groups to ask for an explanation of our approach to the problems of Blacks. They were also interested in hearing why we opposed spontaneous rebellions in Black communities and how we viewed the recent riots in Newark and Detroit. Bobby was in jail, and I was filling as many of these requests as possible, even though I am not very good at talking to large groups; nor do I enjoy it. Abstract and theoretical ideas interest me most, but they lack the rhetorical fire to hold audiences. I went to San Francisco State, anyway, because I was eager to increase our contacts with Black college students. Sharing the platform with me that afternoon was Dr. Harry Edwards, the sociology professor from San Jose State College, who was organizing the Olympic boycott by Black athletes.

That session was particularly challenging because it offered the opportunity for a lively discussion with people who disagreed with my ideas. (This was in 1967, just after one of the longest, hottest summers in American history. Student consciousness had never been higher.) I talked about the necessity for Black people to gain control of the institutions in their own communities, eventually transforming them into co-operatives, and of one day working with other ethnic groups to change the system. When I had finished speaking, an informal dialogue began; almost all the students' questions and criticisms were directed at the Black Panthers' willingness to work in coalition with white groups. We maintained this was possible as long as we controlled the programs, but the students were opposed to working with white groups, or, for that matter, almost anyone but Blacks. While this viewpoint was understandable to me, it failed to take into consideration the limitations of our power. We needed allies, and we believed that alliances with young whites—students and workers—were worth the risk.

I pointed out that many young whites had suddenly discovered hypocrisy; their fathers and forefathers had written and talked brotherhood and democracy while practicing greed, imperialism, and racism. While speaking of the rights of mankind and equality for all, of "free enterprise," the "profit system," "individualism," and "healthy competition," they had plundered the wealth of the world and enslaved Blacks in the United States. White youths now saw through this hypocrisy and were trying to bring about changes through traditional electoral politics. But reality is impervious to idealism. These youngsters were discovering what Blacks knew in their bones—that the military-industrial complex was practically invincible and had in fact created a police state, which rendered idealism power-less to change anything. This led to disillusionment with their parents and the American power structure. At that point of disillusionment they began to identify with the oppressed people of the world.

When the Black Panthers saw this trend developing, we understood that their dissatisfaction could help our cause. In a few years' time, almost half of the American population would be composed of young people; if we developed strong and meaningful alliances with white youth, they would support our goals and work against the Establishment.

Everywhere I went in 1967 I was vehemently attacked by Black students for this position; few could present opposing objective evidence to support their criticisms. The reaction was emotional: all white people were devils; they wanted nothing to do with them. I agreed that some white people could act like devils, but we could not blind ourselves to a common humanity. More important was how to control the situation to our advantage. These questions would not be answered overnight, or in a decade, and time and again the students and I went for hours, getting nowhere. We talked right past each other. The racism that dominated their lives had come between us, and rational analysis was the victim. When I left San Francisco that afternoon, I reflected that many of the students who were supposedly learning how to analyze and understand phenomena were in fact caught up in the same predicament as the prisoners in Plato's cave allegory. Even though they were in college, they were still prisoners in the cave of exploitation and racism that Black people have been subjected to for centuries. Far from preparing them to deal with reality, college kept their intellects in chains. That afternoon I felt even more strongly that the Party would have to develop a program to implement Point 5 of our program, a true education for our people.

When I returned home around 6:30, I had a happy, righteous dinner of mustard greens and corn bread with my family. We

discussed the college students and their attitudes and how difficult it had been to get through to them. That was our last meal
together as a family for thirty-three months. But I had no pre-
monition of this when I left the house and set out on foot for
LaVerne's. The friends with me at San Francisco State had
taken the car after driving me home. On the way, I planned our
evening together, and thought about some of the things I might
do now that I no longer had to report to my probation officer.
At LaVerne's house, I found to my disappointment that she was
ill and did not feel like going out. Although I wanted to stay
with her, she insisted that I take her car and celebrate. She knew
how much it meant to me that probation was over. By this time
it was getting late, close to ten, so I decided to visit a few of my
favorite places.

Nothing about my movements that evening was out of the
ordinary. I went first to the Bosn's Locker, the bar where I had
started recruiting. Most of the people there were close or casual
friends, and I talked, discussing my new freedom and celebrating with a liberation drink, Cuba libre, a rum and Coke. From
there I went to a nearby church where a social was in full swing.
Every Wednesday night this church held an Afro-history class,
and on Friday nights a well-attended social with dancing and
punch. I had one more place to go—a party being given by
friends on San Pablo Street in Oakland. About 2:00 A.M., when
the social was ending, I set out for the party with Gene McKinney, a friend I had known since grammar school. By now it was
October 28; I was officially a free man, and feeling great. Even
though the food was gone by the time we got to San Pablo
Street, I did not mind. It was good to mingle with the people
and talk about the Black Panthers and answer their questions.
We stayed until the very end, 4:00 A.M.

Then Gene McKinney and I headed for Seventh Street, the
center of the action for West Oakland. There are a number of
bars and soul-food restaurants on the street, a few nightclubs,
and at almost any hour you can find something going on. Some
of the restaurants serve up barbecue that is really saying something. Gene and I were hungry, and Seventh Street is the place
to get righteous soul food.

As I turned into Seventh Street, looking for a parking place, I saw the red light of a police car in my rear-view mirror. I had not realized that I was being trailed by a policeman, and my initial reaction was here we go again, more harassment. But, having been stopped so many times before, I was ready. The police had a list of the licenses on cars Black Panthers frequently used, so we always expected this. I kept my lawbook between the bucket seats, and I knew that once I began to read the law to the "law enforcer" he would have to let me go. I wondered what his excuse would be this time; I had obeyed all the traffic regulations.

I pulled the car over to the curb, and the police officer stopped behind me, remaining in his car for a minute or so. Then he got out and came up to my window. When he got a good look at me, he stuck his head in the window within six inches of my face and said very sarcastically, "Well, well, well, what do we have here? The great, *great* Huey P. Newton." I made no reply but merely looked him in the eye. He acted like a fisherman who had just landed a prize catch he had never dreamed of landing. Then he asked for my driver's license, which I gave to him. "Who does the car belong to?" he asked. I told him, "It belongs to Miss LaVerne Williams," and showed him the registration. After comparing it with the license, he gave me the license back and went to his car with the registration. While I sat in the car waiting for him to finish, another police officer pulled up behind the first one. This was not unusual, and I attached little significance to it. The second officer walked up to the first officer's car, and they talked for a moment. Then the second officer came to my window and said, "Mr. Williams, do you have any further identification?" I said, "What do you mean 'Mr. Williams'? My name is Huey P. Newton, and I have already shown my driver's license to the first officer." He just looked at me, nodding his head, and said, "Yes, I know who you are." I knew they both recognized me, because my picture and name were known to every officer in Oakland, as were Bobby's and most of the other Black Panthers'.

The first officer then came back to my car, opened the door, and ordered me out, while the second officer walked around to the passenger side and told Gene McKinney to get out. He then walked Gene to the street side of the car. Meanwhile, I picked up my lawbook from between the seats and started to get out. I thought it was my criminal evidence book, which covers laws dealing with reasonable cause for arrest and the search and seizure laws. If necessary, I intended to read the law to this policeman, as I had done so many times in the past. However, I had mistakenly picked up my criminal lawbook, which looks exactly like the other one.

I got out of the car with the book in my right hand and asked the officer if I was under arrest. He said, "No, you're not under arrest; just lean on the car." I leaned on the top of the car—a Volkswagen—with both hands on the lawbook while the officer searched me. He did it in a manner intended to be degrading, pulling out my shirttail, running his hand over my body, and then he pat-searched my legs, bringing his hands up into my genital area. He was both disgusting and thorough. All this time the four of us were in the street, the second officer with Gene McKinney; I could not see what they were doing.

The officer then told me to go back to his car because he wanted to talk to me. Taking my left arm in his right hand, he began walking, or rather pushing me toward his car. But when we reached it, he kept going until we had reached the back door of the second police car, where he brought me to an abrupt halt. At this, I opened my lawbook and said, "You have no reasonable cause to arrest me." The officer was to my left, just slightly behind me. As I was opening the book, he snarled, "You can take that book and shove it up your ass, nigger." With that, he stepped slightly in front of me and brought his left hand up into my face, hooking me with a smear that was not a direct blow, but more like a solid straight-arm. This momentarily dazed me, and I stumbled back four or five feet and went down on one knee, still holding on to my book. As I started to rise, I saw the officer draw his service revolver, point it at me, and fire. My stomach seemed to explode, as if someone had poured a pot of boiling soup all over me, and the world went hazy.

There were some shots, a rapid volley, but I have no idea where they came from. They seemed to be all around me. I vaguely remember being on my hands and knees on the ground, disoriented, with everything spinning. I also had the sensation of being moved or propelled. After that, I remember nothing.

24

Black brother, think you life so sweet
That you would live at any price?
Does mere existence balance with
The weight of your great sacrifice?
Or can it be you fear the grave
Enough to live and die a slave?
O Brother! be it better said,
When you are gone and tears are shed,
That your death was the stepping stone
Your children's children cross'd upon.
Men have died that men might live:
Look every foeman in the eye!
If necessary, your life give
For something, ere in vain you die.

RAY GARFIELD DANDRIDGE,
"Time to Die"

Aftermath

Long after I was shot I hovered between consciousness and un-
consciousness. I remember some things and have no memory of
others. It was a terrifying time: the blood was pounding in my
head, waves of pain engulfed me, and everything around me
receded into a vast blur. I lost all sense of minutes and hours.
The next thing I recall is arriving at the entrance to Kaiser Hospital, which is about five miles from the scene of the shooting.
I have no idea how I got there. I remember a platform at the
entrance about the height of my waist; it seemed to have no
steps leading up to it, and I wondered how I would get up on

it. Although I was in excruciating pain, I managed to roll onto the platform. Then I rose and somehow staggered into the hospital, where I asked for a doctor. I do not remember the person I spoke to, but whoever it was would not call a doctor and kept mentioning the police. The time seemed endless, and I grew weaker and weaker. Someone finally helped me into a room and put me on a gurney, and a doctor came at last.

As he began to examine the wound in my stomach, the police burst in. Although I was in terrific pain and completely helpless, they grabbed my hands and stretched them above my head, handcuffing them to the gurney on both sides. This pulled and stretched my stomach, causing real agony; then they began to beat on my handcuffs, already too tight and cutting into my flesh (for more than a year after I had a pinched nerve, where they pounded the steel into my wrists). Before long the pain in my arms was more intense than the pain in my stomach. It was more than I could stand, and I screamed, begging the doctor, who was watching this, to make the police loosen the handcuffs. He told me to shut up.* There was also a Black nurse in the room, and she became very upset, but there was nothing she could do. The police were all around me, hitting me in my face and head, and calling me names. They said I had killed one policeman, John Frey, had wounded another, Herbert Heanes, and that my life was no longer worth anything. "You're going to die for this," they promised. "If you don't die in the gas chamber, then when you're sent to prison we'll have you killed there, and if you're acquitted we'll kill you in the streets." Some of the police spat on me, and I spat back, getting rid of some of the mucus and blood in my throat. Each time they came at me I spat blood in their faces and over their uniforms. Finally, the doctor put a towel over my mouth, and the police continued

*This doctor, Thomas Finch, a young man of thirty-five, committed reactionary suicide shortly after my first trial, in 1968. He had been a witness for the prosecution at the trial, testifying about the nature of my wound and the sequence of events at Kaiser Hospital the morning of October 28, 1967. It is generally believed that he took his own life out of a sense of remorse and despair over his conduct in the emergency room that morning; because he had violated all medical ethics in his treatment of a suffering human being, his conscience would give him no peace.

their attacks. I was still screaming in pain when I passed out completely.

I regained consciousness in Highland-Alameda County Hospital in East Oakland, having been moved there because I was not a member of the Kaiser health plan. My wound had been treated, and I was in bed with a penile catheter and tubes running into my nose and abdominal area. Machines arranged around the bed removed the excess fluids and mucus from the tubes. The police had awakened me. Whenever I fell asleep, they would wake me up again.

I was so heavily drugged for the first few days it is difficult to remember everything that went on. When I first regained consciousness, I seem to remember thinking about my situation and wondering if it was hopeless. My fear was not of death itself, but a death without meaning. I wanted my death to be something the people could relate to, a basis for further mobilization of the community. I remember a radio playing in the room and the announcer saying something about a song dedicated to the Minister of Defense. However, I was not sure I had really heard it. Perhaps it was my imagination. At that point a nurse came into the room, and seeing I was awake, asked if I had heard the song dedicated to me. Then I knew that my situation was not hopeless and that the people were relating to the incident, whatever it was. This gave me much comfort at the time, even though I was in the hands of my oppressors. I knew that the Establishment would do everything in its power to destroy me, but this small sign of community response helped me to begin to deal with the police in my room.

During the time this was happening I kept waking up and drifting back to sleep. I soon discovered that my feet were shackled, the chains connecting one ankle to the other, with both fastened to the bed. It was a strange feeling to wake up and find your feet in chains. At first I wondered if I was having a nightmare, but then I remembered the officer drawing his service revolver and the scene at the Kaiser Hospital, and I decided it was no dream. I really was shackled, and police were there guarding me; they meant to kill me, as they had long wanted to and as the officer who shot me had attempted to do. Under the circumstances, my survival was a miracle.

Shortly after the incident, I received a letter from a physician, Dr. Aguilar, which was printed in *The Black Panther* newspaper. It read:

> I can remember nothing in my medical training which suggested that, in the care of an acute abdominal injury, severe pain and hemorrhage are best treated by manacling the patient to the examining table in such a way that the back is arched and belly tensed. Yet this is precisely the picture of current emergency-room procedure which appeared on the front page of a local newspaper last weekend. Looming large in the foreground of the same picture, so large as to suggest a caricature, was a police officer. Could it have been he who distracted the doctor in charge of the case to position the patient in this curious way?
>
> Unusual as it was, this picture probably did not disrupt very much the pleasant weekend enjoyed by my neighbors nor disturb more than momentarily the consciences of my medical colleagues. To me, upon whose mind's eye it is permanently engraved, this photograph is a portentous document of modern history: it represents an end and a beginning. Further, for me, there has been enough of listening, of reading, of pondering. The time has now come to speak, to act, to fight back.
>
> I have read essays written by the patient, Huey P. Newton; I have heard him patiently and painstakingly articulating his ideas and his hopes to a parade of questioners: hour after hour he continues to address the convinced and the unconvinced alike without malice. I have listened to him paraphrasing the concepts set forth in Dr. Fanon's books in a dozen brilliantly succinct sentences. I have listened to him and marvelled that a young man of twenty-five years can interpret in such scholarly fashion the historic, socioeconomic, and political implications of the trend of modern society, while I, on the other hand, after forty-five years—seventeen of them spent in study at college and in postdoctoral education—discover I learned little of human value and must begin again.

The beginning again for me dates from the last time I saw the patient, several weeks ago, in a discussion with a group of people, many of whom came by, listened awhile, and left. One such young man called later in the evening to say that he was in jail. He had been detained by the police for what they suspected might be a minor infraction of the Motor Vehicle Code, mistakenly, as it turned out, for they quickly determined that no law had been broken. Not content, the police undertook lengthy investigation which ultimately revealed that the young man had not satisfactorily replied to a charge of driving with an invalid license one year ago. For this reason he was now jailed with bail set at $550. It took three hours to fill out the requisition form, pay the requisite fees, and see the requisite people in order to extricate this Black boy from his cell.

Two days later I was driving with a friend on the highway when she was apprehended because of four concurrent infractions of the Motor Vehicle Code, including driving without a valid permit for the trailer we were pulling. Nothing happened in spite of the fact that we were detained momentarily some miles farther on for still another infraction—this time a moving violation; we still arrived home in time for dinner, two white ladies in their comfortable white neighborhood. My friend told me later her total bail for all of this lawlessness came to $15! So please do not waste my time, my white brothers and sisters, in telling me that justice is dispensed equally under the law to all Americans. I will not believe you.

I apologize, Mr. Newton, for any aggravation of suffering inflicted upon you during the course of treatment of your injuries. I apologize for the subhuman conditions and horrors of the ghetto in which an immoral political and social system . . . makes it inevitable that men like you are gunned down in the streets of your own town.

Mary Jane Aguilar, M.D.

All the time I was in the hospital, the police did their best to exhaust me. Every time I dropped off they kicked the bed or shook me. One of them held a sawed-off shotgun up to my face, warning me that it was going to go off accidentally. Another showed me a razor blade and threatened to cut the tubes and let me suffocate. One of them predicted I would commit suicide by pulling the tubes out of my nose. Sometimes they even moved the tubes. They told me I was going to "burn." They repeated their threat that I would be gassed in the little green chamber at San Quentin; if I escaped, they said they would have me killed. They even took bets among themselves on whether I would get the gas chamber or life in prison. They made remarks like "the nigger's going to die. He's done for now; he's going to die in the gas chamber."

I never replied, but I did complain to the nurses about the abuse. The supervisor of nurses paid a visit, smiled at the police apologetically, and asked them if they were bothering me. Oh, *no,* of course not, they said, smiling back. When she left, the harassment started again. They even prevented a Black nurse from treating me. White nurses came and went at will, but when a Black nurse tried to take my blood pressure, the police grabbed her, and she ran terrified from the room. Then the supervisor came back. "Now, you know she works here," she said. "You shouldn't bother her like that." This cruel game went on until my family—who could scarcely afford it—hired private nurses to be with me all the time. Things improved then, because the nurses watched the police and made them leave me alone.

From the moment my family heard about the incident, they did everything to help me. They had rushed to Kaiser Hospital and stayed close by me while I underwent surgery. Then, at Highland Hospital, they hired private nurses to protect me from police abuse. My brother Melvin and my sister Leola, with Eldridge Cleaver and other Black Panthers, began the arrangements for my legal defense. They knew it was going to be difficult since the police were determined to have me convicted and ruin the Party. To the police it was a golden opportunity; Bobby was in jail, and they had what looked to be an open-and-shut case against me.

The efforts of my family to get me the best legal help soon brought encouraging results. One afternoon, after I had been in Highland Hospital a few days, I heard a commotion outside my door. The police were trying to keep out someone—a woman—

who was determined to come in, and she was raising all kinds of hell. It was Beverly Axelrod, the lawyer who had done so much to get Eldridge Cleaver out of prison, and with her was a Black attorney. Because I was still so weak Beverly did not stay long that day, just long enough to assure me that every effort was being made to find the best lawyer to fight my case. Beverly felt it was too big and difficult a case for her, but I sensed in her someone who would stand by me, no matter what the cost.

Beverly has never betrayed that confidence. Most of the time I have never thought of her as a white person. Politically, she is left-wing, but more important, she is a generous and open human being, capable of growth and change. I have known her now for many years, and often in the past I had discovered while talking to her that she had certain unconscious racist ways of looking at things. Whenever this was pointed out to her, she would examine her attitudes and deal with them in ways that changed her life. It was this ability to change that convinced me she was genuine and could be trusted. So when she spoke of the lawyer Charles Garry during that first visit, I knew I could have confidence in her opinion of him. Beverly had met Garry in the early 1950's when she was a parole officer. She had become a protégé of his; he had given her cases and helped her to establish a law practice.

She told me that Charles Garry had a long history of defending the politically, racially, and socially depressed. His concern for social justice came from his father, who had fled Armenia after the 1896 massacre and settled in Bridgeport, Massachusetts. There, he had been involved in the early labor movement and led a strike against a factory paying low wages to workers. The family moved to San Francisco in 1915, and Charles put himself through law school, specializing in labor law after graduation. In the early days of his practice, when labor unions did not have the respectability they later enjoyed, he represented sixteen unions. Over the years, he became more and more involved in political cases, defending dissenters and activists in unpopular but important causes. He developed a strong sense of commitment to the underprivileged and those whose rights were not fully protected. Because the political dissenter, the accused criminal, and the early trade union organizer were looked upon as social outcasts, Garry maintained that they were most in need of justice and should have the best legal talent. Garry had a reputation as a brilliant trial lawyer, with a remarkable gift for cross-examining witnesses, and an acute understanding of the jury's importance in political cases. He believed that in political trials a defense lawyer must try to select a jury that is not so much concerned with law and order as with basic principle— the moral principle of law.

During World War II Garry had insisted on serving as a combat infantryman, although he was an obvious candidate for a commission in the Judge Advocate's Corps. He made this choice because of his strong opposition to fascism; he wanted to be totally involved in helping defeat it. Charles Garry was obviously an extraordinary man.

The same day that Beverly came to see me, John George, a Black attorney who had previously handled a number of cases for me, arrived at the hospital. The police barred him from my room. It was typical of their racism: a white lawyer could demand to see me and get in, but a Black lawyer was chased away. Regardless of position or education, color was all that mattered. Soon after, however, John did manage to get in and brought Beverly with him. He felt, as she did, that an explosive case like mine required someone with more experience than he had, someone with a large office staff and the necessary investigative and research facilities.

In between these visits, the police talked loudly about Beverly and John. They hated Beverly Axelrod passionately because she had gotten Eldridge out of the penitentiary; the fact that she was white only made her more culpable, I think. They viciously ridiculed her and mocked John George, making fun of his physical characteristics. All through this, I lay shackled to the bed, half-drugged and in pain, while they swaggered about with their guns, waiting for visitors to leave the room, then threatening to kill me.

Other people visited. I remember nothing distinctly about the first week or so, but I know that my family came regularly, and I remember seeing my brothers and sisters in the room from

time to time. My mother was terribly upset by the whole experience and could not bring herself to come to the hospital. It was
almost impossible for people who were not relatives or lawyers
to get in to see me. Yet, waking up one day, I became aware of a
complete stranger in my room, a Black man—neither a lawyer
nor a relative. He was probably a police agent trying to lure me
into a damaging statement, but he went about his task in such
a clumsy, transparent way that he got nowhere. I knew he could
not have entered the room without an assignment to investigate the case for the police, so I let him do the talking.

Finally Charles Garry came to visit me. Before Beverly mentioned his name, I had never heard of him, but my respect and
trust for her transferred to him. The Party and my family had decided to put the whole matter into his hands, from a legal point
of view. I was only half-conscious, and Garry showed deep concern for my pain. That first day we did not discuss strategy. Garry
said simply that he admired my stand and would be proud to represent me. I returned the compliment.

As I lay recovering from my wounds, I tried to assess my position, to think of the immediate emergency and also its larger
meaning and significance. No doubt about it, I was in serious
trouble. I was fully under the control of my oppressors, and I
was charged with a major crime that could carry the death
penalty. As a matter of fact, I expected to die. At no time before
the trial did I expect to escape with my life. Yet being executed
in the gas chamber did not necessarily mean defeat. It could be
one more step to bring the community to a higher level of consciousness. I was not trying to be heroic, but I had been preparing myself for death over a long period of time.

When the Party was first organized, I did not think I would
live for more than one year after we began; I thought we would
be blasted off the streets. But I had hoped for that one year to
launch the Party, and any additional time was just a bonus.
When I landed in Highland Hospital, I was already living on
borrowed time. More had been accomplished in one year than
Bobby and I had dreamed of when we drew up our ten-point
program in the North Oakland Service Center. Despite my le-

gal predicament and the prospect of death, I was not discouraged or unhappy. There would be time to make a few more political statements and to make my ordeal a part of Black consciousness.

This was important. For more than 350 years Black men in this country have been dying with courage and dignity for causes they believe in. This aspect of our history has always been known to Black people, but for many the knowledge has been vague. We knew the names of a few of our martyrs and heroes, but often we were not acquainted with the circumstances or the precise context of their lives. White America has seen to it that Black history has been suppressed in schools and in American history books. The bravery of hundreds of our ancestors who took part in slave rebellions has been lost in the mists of time, since plantation owners did their best to prevent any written accounts of uprisings. Millions of Black schoolchildren never learned about two great Black heroes in the nineteenth century, Denmark Vesey and Nat "The Prophet" Turner, who died for freedom.

White people had good reason to destroy our history. Black men and women who refuse to live under oppression are dangerous to white society because they become symbols of hope to their brothers and sisters, inspiring them to follow their example. In our time, Malcolm X is the supreme example. His life and accomplishments galvanized a generation of young Black people; he helped us take a great stride forward with a new sense of ourselves and our destiny. But meaningful as his life was, his death had great significance, too. A new militant spirit was born when Malcolm died. It was born of outrage and a unified Black consciousness, out of the sense of a task left undone.

In light of this, I was able to stand back a little and consider my own death. The Black Panther Party had been formed in the spirit of Malcolm; we strove for the goals he had set for himself. When Black people saw Black Panthers being killed not only by the police but also by the judicial system, they would feel the circle closing around them and take another step forward. In this sense, my death would not be meaningless.

After fifteen days in Highland-Alameda Hospital my condition improved, and I was transferred to the medical unit on Death Row in San Quentin. Officially I was there for my own protection. When the ambulance neared Quentin, the police told me to take a good look at its walls because I was going to be inside them a long, long time. As my gurney rolled through the halls of San Quentin toward Death Row, one by one the guards called ahead, "Dead man, dead man, dead man." No prisoner is allowed to talk to a man bound for Death Row.

The hospital tank at Quentin is right next door to the psychotic ward. While my cell was well secured—it had three locks—most of the psychotic cells were left open because those inmates became restless in a small space. Out in the hall there were things to keep them occupied—weight-lifting equipment, a card table and chairs, some games.

One of the mental cases was a Chicano named, I think, Robilar. Robilar and I hit it off because he identified with the Muslims, and so did I. All day he would stand outside my cell playing his guitar and singing to me and saying, "Don't you worry now; everything's going to be all right."

Robilar had been in and out of prison all his life. This time the beef was murdering a former cellmate. Like me, he had defended himself and lost the case, but the death sentence had been overturned when Robilar was declared incompetent to defend himself. After that, he was brought to the Quentin psychotic ward and locked up. There, he tried to cut his wrists, so they left his cell open and made him a trusty. Robilar liked to see the doctors dress my wound, and when they came and removed the bandages, he would move from one end of the bed to the other and hover over the doctors, chattering with excitement.

On my third day at Quentin a new man, a white, was placed in the cell next to mine. We never learned his name, but we knew he was scheduled for release in six months. All that day Robilar sang to me, and when night came, he slipped into the new man's cell and slit his throat and smashed his skull with a weight-lifting dumbbell. Then he went back to his own cell and sang over and over:

> Hang down your head Tom Dooley,
> Hang down your head and cry;
> Hang down your head Tom Dooley,
> Poor boy you're bound to die.

He was still singing when I fell asleep about ten. Although it happened right next door, I never knew, and neither did anybody else, until the guards found the new man dead in his bunk the next morning. Robilar was finally declared incurably insane. It was his seventh murder, his fourth in prison; all the other prison murders had been cellmates.

After two weeks in San Quentin I was well enough to leave. They had carried me in, but I walked out, and from Quentin they took me to the Alameda County Jail in downtown Oakland, where I had been before. This time I was to stay there eleven months, before and during my trial.

25

The hypocrisy of Amerikan fascism forces it to conceal its attack on political offenders by the legal fiction of conspiracy laws and highly sophisticated frame-ups. The masses must be taught to understand the true function of prisons. Why do they exist in such numbers? What is the real underlying economic motive of crime and the official definition of types of offenders or victims? The people must learn that when one "offends" the totalitarian state, it is patently not an offense against the people of that state, but an assault upon the privilege of the privileged few.

GEORGE JACKSON, *Blood in My Eye*

Strategy

On November 12, 1967, the Alameda County grand jury returned an indictment against me. I was accused of three felonies: the murder of Patrolman John Frey; the assault of Patrolman Herbert Heanes with a deadly weapon; the kidnapping of a Black man named Dell Ross near the scene of the crime, which included my forcing him to drive me in his car to another part of the city. This is supposedly how I got to Kaiser Hospital. Dell Ross testified before the grand jury that I and another man had climbed into his car, pointed a gun at him, and told him to drive us to the hospital. But before we arrived at the hospital, he testified, we had jumped out of the car and disappeared into the night.

Evidence presented to the grand jury included the bullet taken from Patrolman Frey's back, the bullet taken from Patrolman Heanes's knee, Heanes's revolver, two nine-millimeter cartridge cases that had been found in the street, two match-boxes containing marijuana found under the seat of the car I had been driving, various photographs of the cars at the scene, and a Xerox of the Kaiser Hospital records of my emergency treatment. Patrolman Heanes's gun was the only weapon found at the scene; the nine-millimeter casings were not fired from it. In addition to this meager evidence, the grand jury heard the testimony of Heanes, Dell Ross, the police officers who arrived at the scene after the shooting, the nurse who had admitted me to Kaiser Hospital, and ballistics experts. It was estimated that seven shots had been fired on the morning of October 28. Patrolman Heanes had received three wounds, and Frey had been shot twice, in the thigh and back. A completely flattened slug, which had probably ricocheted off some other surface, was found in a door of LaVerne's Volkswagen.

The grand jury took evidence after I was removed from San Quentin to the County Jail in Oakland. Although severely wounded only a few weeks earlier, I was recuperating rapidly and was strong enough to begin planning the political strategy for my trial. I did not want to deal with the legalities—just political strategy. The number-one political decision made by the Party was that the attorneys stay out of all political decisions concerning the trial. I needed to know the legal ramifications of any move, of course, and I would not question them, but legal niceties were definitely secondary. The ideological and political significance of the trial was of primary importance.

By political strategy I mean this: I wanted to use the trial as a political forum to prove that having to fight for my life was the logical and inevitable outcome of our efforts to lift the oppressor's burden. The Black Panthers' activities and programs, the patrolling of the police, and the resistance to their brutality had disturbed the power structure; now it was gathering its forces to crush our revolution forever. Public attention was assured. Why not use the courtroom and the media to educate our people? To us, the key point in the trial was police brutality, but we hoped to do more than articulate that. We also wanted to show that the other kinds of violence poor people suffer—unemployment, poor housing, inferior education, lack of public facilities, the inequity of the draft—were part of the same fabric. If we could organize people against police brutality, as we had begun to do, we might move them toward eliminating related forms of oppression. The system, in fact, destroys us through neglect much more often than by the police revolver. The gun is only the *coup de grâce,* the enforcer. To wipe out the conditions leading up to the *coup de grâce*—that was our goal. The gun and the murder it represented would then fade away. Thus, for the Black Panther Party, the goal of the trial was not primarily to save my life, but to organize the people and advance their struggle.

Our goal was not to save my life, because I had accepted what I thought was a certain fate: they would kill me. Everything we did in the next eleven months was predicated on my death. My life had to come to an end sometime, but the people go on; in them lies the possibility for immortality. The dialectic teaches that all men long for immortality, and this longing is one of the contradictions between man and nature. Man tries to resolve the certainty of death through reversal, by bringing it under control, which is a form of the will to power. But since each man eventually gives up his life, death can be controlled only through the ongoing life of the people.

Because I saw my death growing closer, I often wondered how I would prepare for it. A person never knows how he will act prior to the experience itself. Knowing that the most valuable thing anyone has is his life, I could not be sure in what way I would give it up, particularly under the threat of the gas chamber. I had faced death before, but under different circumstances. There had been a spontaneity and a suddenness in each confrontation, and the possibility of outwitting death. But when the state kills you, there are no odds; the inevitability of death is absolute. To face execution by the state demands a special kind of courage—the ability to act with grace and dignity in a totally degrading situation. It is the ultimate form of truth.

The first defense strategy that Charles Garry decided upon was a series of pretrial motions in state and federal courts questioning the validity of grand juries—to prove that my indictment was both illegal and unjust. Garry not only presented arguments against the composition of grand juries, which rarely represent a cross-section of the community, but also maintained that the system itself is unconstitutional. An indictment by a grand jury, he argued, imperils the right to a fair trial. In a grand jury hearing, which is always held in secret, the defendant and his lawyer are not present. Evidence against the accused is presented to the jury by the district attorney, but no cross-examination is allowed, and no evidence can be introduced by the defendant. While it is true that grand jury testimony is inadmissable at trials, the fact that the transcript of a grand jury hearing can be published by the press offers little chance of public impartiality toward the accused. Public opinion can be greatly influenced by these transcripts, especially since all evidence and testimony are presented at the discretion of the district attorney, who is out to prove the defendant's guilt. So it hardly seems fair that a trial jury can then be selected from citizens who have heard of or read the evidence that was responsible for an indictment. After all, an indictment means only that the grand jury felt there was enough evidence of guilt to bring the accused to trial.

Garry also argued that in asking for a grand jury hearing in my case the prosecutor was doing something unusual and prejudiced. Alameda County statistics show that only 3 per cent of all cases go before grand juries. The rest are heard in what are known as "informations," where both sides argue before a judge, who then has the sole decision of calling a trial. In an "information" witnesses can be cross-examined, a procedure not allowed in grand jury hearings. In my case the prosecutor clearly wanted testimony presented to a grand jury in order to influence public opinion against me.

Garry also criticized the whole process of grand jury selection. In California, each of the twenty Superior Court judges recommends three persons as grand jurors; these nominees are supposed to be known to the judge personally. Obviously, few judges in Alameda County would be acquainted with many of the 200,000 Black people who live there. As a matter of fact, the only Black person who sat on my grand jury was absent on the day evidence was presented. Judges tend to choose white upper-middle-class citizens—businessmen, conservative house-wives, brokers, bankers, retired army officers, and so forth, who are for the most part middle-aged and without the faintest understanding of the lives of poor Black people. Most of them, in fact, are hostile to Blacks. How, then, are they qualified to have any insight into the events or attitudes that bring such defendants before them?

One of Garry's presentations concerned the physical movements of the grand jury. After examining the official court transcripts of my hearing, Garry proved that the grand jury could not possibly have considered or discussed any of the evidence presented to them. He did a very thorough job of analyzing the minute-by-minute movements of the jurors on the final day of deliberations. The result was astonishing. The time sequence of the jury's movements that day, as recorded in the official transcript, proves that there could not have been any discussion or deliberation about my case. After all the evidence had been presented, the members of the grand jury went into the room where they were supposed to consider the evidence and shut the door. Almost immediately they came out. Since the evidence concerning my guilt was nonexistent—not one person had testified that I carried or fired a gun—their failure to spend any time weighing the issue is incredible. In exposing their indifference and fraudulence, Garry strongly reinforced his contention that grand juries are insensitive to the problems of the poor and oppressed.

After filing briefs that questioned the constitutionality of the grand jury system, Garry turned to the inequities in the trial system itself. He and his staff did research on how jurors are chosen to serve. Alameda County, like most of the country, selects its juries from the county voter-registration list, and there, as elsewhere, the number of registered voters from Black communities is far smaller than those from the white population. Furthermore, if selected for jury duty, many Black people have legitimate reasons for declining: economic hardship and inconvenience are involved. Because of this, few members of minority groups are available to decide the fate of their peers. Again,

Garry raised the question of whether, under these circumstances, a Black man can receive a fair trial in America.

From November until the following July, when my trial began, Garry was busy and overworked, filing these motions in the California courts. Nine months is an exceptionally long time between indictment and trial. The delay in my case was not only inevitable, because of the time-consuming pretrial hearings, but desirable. The media had made me a celebrity through television and hysterical newspaper accounts. The death of a policeman always incites a large percentage of the population to cry vengeance. Many people believed I was guilty. Then, too, the Oakland police were in a state of frenzy. On October 17, less than two weeks before the Frey shooting, they had once again demonstrated their brutality at a protest rally of 4,000 demonstrators in Oakland. That day they attacked the demonstrators so viciously and with so little provocation that the entire media, even William Knowland's *Tribune,* criticized their behavior. The day became known as "Bloody Tuesday." As a result, the police were very much on the defensive and anxious to vindicate themselves. To do this, they had to keep demonstrating how threatened they were, particularly by the Black Panthers. Their attacks on the brothers increased. At one point David Hilliard was arrested on the street for handing out leaflets about my case; as far as I know, leafletting has never been against the law. At any rate, Garry wanted emotions to subside to improve my chances for a more objective trial.

While the police were stepping up their harassment of the Black Panthers, other people in the Oakland area were rallying to help me. The Party decided that a broad base of support would be necessary in order to win allies and raise funds for my defense. So in December the Black Panther Party announced a coalition with the Peace and Freedom Party. This organization was made up mostly of young whites who opposed the war in Vietnam and who also felt that the two-party system was no longer working. They saw a need for a third party that could run strong antiwar leaders in the 1968 national election as well as combat the evils in our society. Ultimately, when the Peace and Freedom Party became a legal party in most states, Eldridge was its candidate for President, along with Jerry Rubin for Vice-President. But mainly the alliance between the Black Panthers and the Peace and Freedom Party was meant to demonstrate that racism and police oppression were responsible for my being in jail and that I was falsely accused of the murder of Patrolman Frey. The phrase "Free Huey" was created out of this coalition; it became a rallying cry for people who believed in my innocence.

Meanwhile, all across the country, Black people were relating to my imprisonment. The Black Panthers were recruiting members in every major city and also in some of the rural areas. In some cases, people just formed a group and called themselves Black Panthers without even getting in touch with central headquarters. Sometimes, groups would form around our ten-point program and use another name. It was all the same: the community was becoming educated; their consciousness was being raised.

We were also gaining international attention. Soon, groups in other countries began to ask us to send speakers. At that time we still considered ourselves revolutionary nationalists, that is, Black nationalists who took a revolutionary position in the United States. We had not as yet developed an international policy. But some Black Panthers made trips out of the United States to explain our position and describe the nature of American oppression. One of these trips was to Japan, where a group of revolutionary Japanese students, *Zengakuren,* invited the Black Panthers to speak at a number of conferences organized by left-wing students. We chose Kathleen Cleaver, whom Eldridge had recently married, and Earl Anthony, a Black Panther, to make the trip. Earl was a Party member from Los Angeles with a college degree. Even though the Los Angeles chapter had had some problems with him, he was considered competent and articulate enough to speak for the Party. However, in Hawaii, both Kathleen and Earl experienced some delay in getting their visas cleared by the Japanese consulate. Kathleen decided to return to California, and Earl went on by himself.

When Anthony got to Japan, everything went wrong. Instead

of stating the Party's position, he presented a personal platform, a strictly white and Black line—about how the Black
world would fight the white world, and that would be the end
of it. His whole talk was just that simple, the same line Stokely
Carmichael was following. He showed no awareness of class
issues and did not even try to describe them in terms of this
country. To him the whole problem was a matter of racism,
which cried out for separatism.

I heard a tape recording of some of the Japanese sessions—
a friend brought it to me—and I was angered. The Japanese
students put Anthony down left and right. They asked good
questions—questions that dealt with contradictions in a dialectical way—whereas Anthony was dealing in absolutes. For him,
all meaning lay in the white world's oppression of Blacks. Certainly, this is much of the problem, but it fits into a larger context. Ironically, it was the Japanese students who stated the
Party's actual position by pointing out other reasons and circumstances that complicate the Black-white situation. Anthony
betrayed the purpose of his visit by going on a solo trip and nar-
rowing the possibilities of international solidarity. No wonder
the Japanese students were disillusioned with the Party. To this
day, I do not know whether Kathleen Cleaver had anything to
do with Anthony's confusion. She has always been a kind of
cultist in her Black nationalism, so she may have influenced
him. Kathleen really loved the Party, but I doubt that either she
or Eldridge ever completely accepted our ideology.

Anyway, when we heard the tapes, we were disgusted. The
Central Committee censured Anthony and relieved him of all
duties dealing with sensitive issues. He went back to Los Angeles and worked with the Party for a while, but eventually
dropped out and wrote a shallow and opportunistic book about
the Party. For this, he was expelled. At the time, we needed
writers to help our cause, not people on ego trips.

Incidents like this are depressing when you are unable to deal
with them directly. At the time, since I was the victim of a police frame-up, it was probably best that I remain in prison. In
this way, my incarceration was a continual reminder to the outside world of the outrageous tactics of the police. Every day

they kept me there I grew as a symbol of the brutalization of the poor and Black as well as a living reproach to society's indifference to the inequities of the legal system. "Free Huey" became a powerful slogan, and the words went far beyond me to become a cry for liberation of all Blacks.

But the eleven months I spent at the Alameda County Court House waiting for trial were not easy. The prison routine was deadly, the food bad, and the guards corrupt. Most of my stay was spent in solitary—because I had protested the way prisoners were treated. My cell was four and a half feet by six feet with no window in it, not even in the door (eventually they did cut out a small hole in the door and covered it with thick wire). It was so swelteringly hot that I often took off all my clothes to get relief; even breathing was hard work, since there was no ventilation in the cell. A bunk, a wash basin, and a toilet were there—nothing more. I got out only three afternoons a week— Monday, Wednesday, and Friday—when my family came or when I saw my lawyers. Even visiting was unpleasant. The visiting rooms were tiny cubicles with a steel wall between prisoners and visitors. You had to talk through a round, screened hole and put your ear to another hole to hear the reply. Usually the babble from other visitors and prisoners made conversation strained. Fortunately, I was able to send letters and tapes out with my lawyers to friends and the Party. (The tapes were made in the attorney's room.) I was never actually out of touch, and never tempted to give up, largely because of the strong support I had, not only from the people but also from Charles Garry and the attorneys who were working with him on my case. These were Alexander Hoffmann, a lawyer active in civil rights cases in the Bay Area; Fay Stender, who was later to be involved in George Jackson's case at Soledad and thereafter; John Escobedo, a Chicano lawyer; and Carlton Innis, a Black lawyer. Later, attorney Edward Keating, the founder of *Ramparts* magazine, joined the others.

The brothers on the outside worked unceasingly for my defense. They went into Black communities in the Bay Area collecting money; they moved onto college campuses and talked to students; they spoke and held forums and organized rallies. When Bobby Seale got out of jail in December (he had been released before his six months were up), he worked full time organizing for my defense. The police never let up on him, either, and one night in February they busted into his apartment and arrested him for having a weapon, which they had planted there. It was such an obvious frame-up that the judge let him off. On February 17, my birthday, and the next day, two huge rallies were held, one in Oakland and one in Los Angeles. Many leaders of the Black revolutionary movement in the United States spoke at them, including H. Rap Brown, then chairman of SNCC, and James Forman, then head of SNCC's New York office.

Among them, also, was Stokely Carmichael, who came to the jail to see me. He had just returned from a trip around the world—to Africa, Cuba, and Vietnam—and a lot of his ideas had changed in a short time.

Our visit lasted just long enough for us to disagree. Stokely began by telling me what it would take to get me out of jail. The only thing that would do it, he said, was armed rebellion, culminating in a race war. I disagreed with him. While I acknowledged the pervasiveness of racism, the larger problem should be seen in terms of class exploitation and the capitalist system. In analyzing what was happening in the country, I said that we would have to accept many alliances and form solidarity with any people fighting the common oppressor. He objected to the Black Panther alliance with the Peace and Freedom Party and said we should not associate with white radicals or let them come to our meetings or be involved in our rallies. Stokely warned that whites would destroy the movement, alienate Black people, and lessen our effectiveness in the community. Later, he proved right in terms of what happened to the Party, although he was wrong in principle. As a result of coalitions, the Black Panthers were brought into the free speech movements, the psychedelic fad, and the advocacy of drugs, which we were and are dead set against. All these causes were irrelevant to our work, which was concerned with deeper and more fundamental issues, in fact, survival. When these things happened, Stokely warned, whites would try to take the leadership from us.

I did not believe him while he was running these things down to me. We were not into a racist bag, I told him, and these developments were not inevitable. At the time I felt sure that Stokely was afraid of himself and his own weaknesses. I responded to his racist analysis with a class analysis. We could have solidarity and friendship in a common struggle against a common oppressor without the whites taking over. But in the thirty-three months I spent in jail our leadership did falter, and serious frictions developed between the Black Panthers and white radicals. Not until I got out of jail nearly three years later were we able to start putting everything together again.

One of my most unhappy moments during the period I was awaiting trial was when I learned of Little Bobby Hutton's murder on April 6, 1968. News of the shoot-out came over the prison radio. I was shocked but not surprised. The police claimed Little Bobby was shot trying to escape, but we knew that for the same lie told by southern sheriffs for years. Black people were not fooled either. A terrible frustration and rage arose in the community. Little Bobby was murdered only two days after Martin Luther King's assassination, and the people were still staggering under that blow. After King's death Police Chief Gain had canceled all police leaves and doubled the number of occupying troops in our community, which only intensified the sense of anger and despair. With Bobby's murder, tension mounted in Oakland, along with the fear that the Black community would riot.

On the morning of April 7, Charles Garry and Bobby Seale came to see me. Eldridge had been arrested after the shooting, and Garry was going to defend him. He and Bobby were on their way that morning to a press conference at the police station, and they wanted a message for the people. I gave them a tape I had made, urging the people not to riot spontaneously. This would only give the police an opportunity to continue the massacre. The people should arm themselves for protection when the police moved in to brutalize them, but not make themselves targets for defenseless slaughter. Charles Garry delivered my message at the press conference and also made a statement to the media about the deliberate murder of Little Bobby by the police. Of course, Police Chief Gain exploded at that and accused Garry on radio and television of intemperate and false statements. However, a former member of the Oakland Police Department, a Black man, recently confirmed to us in private that Little Bobby was murdered outright. He had witnessed the murder that night. Bobby's death really tore me up. I became even more determined to use my trial as an organizing point against these murders.

Meanwhile, Charles Garry was persevering in his motions to challenge the jury selection system. As a matter of fact, his efforts continued right up until the day my trial began. His investigations have had a profound effect on the whole judicial system, and their repercussions can be seen all over the country today. It is largely because of Garry's work that courts all over the country have become aware of a defendant's right to be tried by a jury of his peers. But in the summer of 1968, he was still fighting for this right as the date of my trial came nearer and nearer.

PART FIVE

Let us go on outdoing ourselves; a revolutionary man always transcends himself or otherwise he is not a revolutionary man, so we always do what we ask of ourselves or more than what we know we can do.

26

We knew before Huey's trial began in mid-July that the whole power structure wanted to hang Huey. We understood that William Knowland (the publisher of the Oakland Tribune), the mayor, the other politicians, the D.A., and the cops were all so treacherous that they would do anything to get a conviction and send Huey to the gas chamber.

We asked Charles Garry a number of times what he thought would happen. He would run it down, how Huey was really innocent, and how the two cops had shot each other in an attempt to kill Huey.

BOBBY SEALE, *Seize the Time*

Trial

The morning my trial began on July 15, 1968, in the Alameda County Court House, 5,000 demonstrators and about 450 Black Panthers gathered outside to show their support. Busloads of demonstrators came from out of town and joined the throng that crowded the streets and sidewalks outside the courthouse. Across the street from the building a formation of Black Panthers stood, lined up two deep, and stretching for a solid block. At the entrance to the building a unit of sisters from the Party chanted "Free Huey" and "Set Our Warrior Free." In front of them, on both sides of the courthouse door two Party members held aloft the blue Black Panther banner with FREE HUEY emblazoned on it. Black Panther security patrols with walkie-talkie radio sets ringed the courthouse.

The building was under heavy guard. At every entrance and patrolling every floor, armed deputies from the sheriff's office prowled up and down, and plain-clothes men were assigned positions throughout the building. On that first day nearly fifty helmeted Oakland police stood inside the main entrance, and on the rooftop more cops with high-powered rifles stared down into the street. The trial was conducted in the seventh-floor courtroom, a small depressing room kept ice cold throughout the trial. Security was so tight that the courtroom was carefully inspected before every session; everyone, even my parents, was searched before entering. The spectators' section had only about sixty seats: two rooms were reserved for my family; the press had twenty-five or so seats; and the rest was for the general public. Every morning around dawn people began lining up outside for the few remaining places.

Presiding was Superior Court Judge Monroe Friedman, seventy-two years old, dour and humorless. Of course, no one admits prejudice, but Judge Friedman betrayed his in countless ways throughout the trial. Clearly, from the beginning he thought I was guilty, and his sympathies lay with the prosecution. For one thing, he condescended to Black witnesses, speaking to them as if they were not capable of understanding the issues. It was obvious that he was totally unaware of the development of Black consciousness in the past decade. Even his tone of voice was revealing. As the trial progressed, he constantly overruled my lawyer and sustained almost every objection of the prosecutor. Sometimes, when he did not like the way things were going, he looked over to the prosecutor's table as if inviting an objection, which he would then sustain. On interpretation, he was extremely rigid. Whenever a legal point could not be solved by legal mechanics, he would pass it off as unimportant, thereby leaving it for some higher court to deal with or for some political statement to be made through the legislature. Nothing was considered that was not in the book. He acknowledged that some laws were good and reluctantly followed those he disliked. Never for one moment did I consider him a fair arbitrator.

The most crucial aspect of the trial was the jury selection, and on that first trial day several hundred prospective jurors

came to the courthouse. Charles Garry wanted a certain kind
of juror, and he faced terrific odds in finding him. For one thing,
everyone in the Oakland area had read or seen prejudicial accounts of the shooting. It was difficult to find anyone without
an opinion about the case. Then, too, we wanted some Black
people. This was a vital issue and, as we learned through our
investigations, a formidable hurdle to overcome. Our inquiries
revealed that the assistant district attorney and prosecutor in
my trial, Lowell Jensen, had developed a system whereby Blacks
would ostensibly be on jury panels called for duty but would
always be eliminated before they were seated in an actual trial.
Under Jensen's direction whenever a Black was removed from
a prospective jury for cause, or through peremptory challenges,
he was then returned to the jury panel and called in another
trial. That way, it always appeared the Blacks were an active
part of the system, even though it was unlikely a Black would
ever serve on an actual jury. When my trial began, the routine
changed; other district attorneys in the area did not remove
Blacks from their jury panels. Therefore, while my trial was in
session there were juries in other courts with as many as six
Blacks on them.

The Party instructed Garry to use all his peremptory challenges on prospective jurors. In a capital case in the state of
California each side is allowed twenty, that is, both defense and
prosecution can reject twenty jurors without giving a reason.
We gave Garry these instructions to demonstrate to the people
that something is wrong with a trial system that defies the right
of a defendant to be tried by a true cross-section of his community. We used all our peremptory challenges to emphasize
this point. The prosecution did not exhaust all theirs, since it
was not hard for them to find their kind of people. (Charles
Garry found racism in almost every prospective juror he questioned.)

Selecting the jury took a long time—about two weeks. All in
all, three panels of prospective jurors—about 180 people—
were questioned before a jury and four alternates were chosen.
Out of the nearly two hundred people available for my jury,

there were sixteen Blacks, a few Orientals, and one or two Chi-canos. The population of Oakland was then 38 per cent Black.

The final jury consisted of eleven whites and one Black. The Black man, David Harper, actually looked enough like me to pass as a relative, although we were strangers before the trial. At the time, he was an executive in a branch of the Bank of America, but he has since become president of a Black bank in Detroit. I wondered why the district attorney did not excuse him from serving. Perhaps he figured it would help his case in the Appeals Court to have at least one Black on the jury. Also, he had tried to get a safe one. I figured that the district attorney saw Harper as a "house nigger," a Black bank official who "had it made," so to speak. They probably thought Harper could be counted on because of his status and his ambition to go further in the white world.

Throughout the trial I studied Harper, trying to get the mea-sure of the man. Would he go along with the madness of the system? With a jury it is always a guessing game. You know the judge and the prosecutor are your enemies and will do any-thing to keep you down. Every other paid employee in the courtroom, regardless of his color, is a slave to the system. But the jurors are something else. I watched every move Harper made, yet I could not detect where he was, or where he was go-ing. I began to wonder if the fact that he had a good job in a bank gave him satisfaction. I asked myself whether he was so blinded by the crumbs the system offered him that he would go along with the racists on the jury and a corrupt state apparatus to secure his future—or what he hoped might be his future.

These questions went through my mind almost daily as the proceedings crept along. Sometimes, pondering Harper, I found myself paying no attention at all to the boring testimony of the prosecution witnesses, such as the ballistics experts. Not until I took the stand myself and began talking to the jury did I feel Harper knew his friends better than the district attorney had estimated. When I finally testified, I directed my words to Harper. He was my audience. An unspoken bond grew up be-tween us that convinced me he not only understood but he also agreed with me. Only then did I see a glimmer of hope with the jury—he was it. However, I never placed much confidence in his ability to sway the others.

The prosecutor in my case was Lowell Jensen, who later became district attorney of Alameda County. Jensen is a witty and intelligent man and a worthy opponent as far as the law is concerned. He appears to have a photographic memory, and on the basis of legal knowledge alone he is a good lawyer. In my case, he meant to get a conviction of first-degree murder, no matter how far he had to stretch the law, and to that end, he ignored the possibility that there were a number of grounds for reversal and that in time a higher court would decide against the verdict of this trial. A conviction was all he cared about. He knew that if he won his case against me—a person hated by the Establishment—he would be regarded with fame and rising fortune. What would a reversal matter? A ruling by a higher court would take from two to five years, and by that time he would have achieved what he wanted. My trial was nothing more than an ego trip for him.

Throughout the trial an unspoken "game" or challenge went on in the courtroom between Jensen, the judge, and myself, although a lot of people—especially the jury—knew nothing about it. The jury probably believed that the prosecutor and the judge were honorable men, with only their jobs and justice on their minds. But my lawyers and I understood the undercurrents and intangibles that were always present, difficult as they were to expose. And we knew that if the jury were aware of them also they would see the political nature of much that went on in the courtroom. For example, we surmised from the very start of the trial that Jensen had engineered the racist system by which Blacks would be on jury panels called for duty but eliminated before they could be seated for trial. And we knew that Jensen did not have justice on his mind but wanted victory at any cost to further his own personal ambitions. These were some of the things that made the whole trial scene like a game— a grim game with my life at stake—but a game nonetheless.

In his opening statement to the jury Jensen charged that I had murdered Officer John Frey with full intent, that I had shot Officer Herbert Heanes, and that I had kidnaped Dell Ross. He said that when the first policeman stopped me I had given him false identification, but when the second officer came up, I had correctly identified myself. Then the first officer, Frey, placed me under arrest. He claimed that when the police officer walked me back to his car, I produced a gun and began firing. According to Jensen, I shot Officer Frey with my own gun, which I pulled from inside my shirt, then took his gun and continued shooting. I was charged with shooting Officer Frey five times and Officer Heanes three times. Officer Heanes was supposed to have shot me once. After this, the prosecutor said, I escaped and forced Dell Ross to take me to another part of Oakland.

The most crucial challenge facing the prosecution was to establish motivation for my alleged actions. Jensen claimed that I had three motives for my alleged crimes. First, he said, I had had a prior conviction for a felony and was on probation. Because of this, I knew that having a concealed weapon on my person could lead to another felony conviction if the police officers found the gun on me. Second, they claimed that I had marijuana in the car and that bits of marijuana had been found in the pocket of my pants; this, too, could lead to another felony beef. And, third, they claimed that I had given false identification to the police officer, which was a violation of the law. For these reasons, the prosecutor claimed I was so desperate to escape another felony charge that I killed an officer, wounded another, and kidnaped a citizen. As I said before, the prosecutor was willing to go to any lengths to win his case.

The truth of the matter is that when Frey stopped me, he knew full well who I was, as did every other policeman on the Oakland force, and he tried to execute me in an urban variation of the old-style southern lynching. My attorneys had investigated Frey's background, and they found a long history of harassing and mistreating Black people and making racist statements about Blacks and to Blacks. Unfortunately for Frey, his habits boomeranged that time. I do not know what happened because I was unconscious, but things did not work out as he wanted or expected them to. I guess he thought that if he could bring me in dead, he would be given a promotion.

The marijuana charge was sheer fabrication. First of all, no member of the Black Panther Party uses drugs. It is absolutely forbidden. Anyone discovered violating this rule is expelled from the Party. Narcotics prohibition is part of the Black Panther principle of obeying the law to the letter. Both Charles Garry and I believed that the marijuana found in the car and in my trousers was planted there by the police. Having been stopped by members of the Oakland police force more than fifty times in the past year, why would I take the risk? Knowing that at any moment of the day or night I was liable to be thoroughly searched and my car inspected, I would never have been reckless enough to carry marijuana, even if I had wanted to use it—which I didn't. If the matchboxes really were in LaVerne's car that night, there is no way of knowing how they got there. Dozens of people used her car, many of whom she knew only slightly, since they were friends of friends. But it is far more likely that the police were behaving as usual, leaving out no possibility in their determination to railroad me to jail.

As for being a felon with a gun, I, of course, was not carrying a weapon but had been out celebrating the end of my probation that night. There was no reason for me to have a gun and no reason to avoid arrest on this count. Nor did I consider myself a felon. The original conviction of felony was a complicated one, anyway, going back to the Odell Lee case in 1964. Under California law, the sentence a defendant receives determines whether he is a "felon" or a "misdemeanant." If he is sentenced to a state prison, he is a felon; a misdemeanant usually goes to a county jail. When I was convicted of assaulting Odell Lee with a deadly weapon, I was sentenced to three years' probation, a condition being that I serve six months in the county jail. This meant I was a misdemeanant. However, in my murder trial the judge testified that I had been sentenced to the state prison and that then the sentence had been suspended. As a condition of my probation I spent six months in the county jail. Technically the state considered me a felon. In the end, this proved to be reversible error. Although I could have changed my legal status in the courts, I never petitioned because I did not consider myself a felon.

But the prosecution did, and planned its whole case around

the point. Not only did they want to show I would commit murder to avoid arrest, but they also wanted to take advantage of
the fact that a felon's testimony can be discredited and he can
receive a severer sentence. Despite Charles Garry's objections
and arguments, Judge Friedman ruled that I had been convicted
of a felony in 1964, and this charge against me was added to
the other three. This question of the Odell Lee conviction came
up repeatedly during the trial, since the prosecution needed to
establish a motive. Eventually, when I testified, I told the jury
again that I had not considered myself a felon. It was actually a
ridiculous basis for motivation, since I had dozens of witnesses
who saw me out celebrating on the night of October 27—a fact
which proved beyond doubt that I had no reason to resist arrest as a felon.

When my trial was just beginning, Eldridge Cleaver put out a
leaflet that was widely distributed in the Black community. In it
he charged that the police, with murder on their minds, had violated the territorial integrity of the Black community and that I
had dealt with their transgression in a necessary way. The leaflet went on to say that Black people are justified in killing all
policemen who do this. Behind Eldridge's message lay the infer-
ence that I had killed the police officer, even though I had not.

The leaflet could not have been used against me in the courts.
Even so, my family was very upset over it, and they protested
strongly to Eldridge. They felt he cared little about me and that
he was, in effect, trying to gas me. I told them as gently as I
could not to interfere with anything Eldridge or other Party
members did during the trial because such actions could not be
brought into the legal proceedings. As far as I was concerned,
Eldridge was free to write and mobilize the community by any
means necessary; I supported him in that. Issuing the leaflet
was a political act using the trial to heighten the consciousness
of the community. I was willing to go along with Party actions
in the interest of educating the people, mobilizing the community, and taking the contradictions to a higher level. After that
my family did not interfere with political activities.

The trial caused much grief and worry to my family. They
wanted to save me, but I felt death was ahead, and my main

concern was the community. Because my family continued to hope, I could not tell them this, however, and I was very moved by their faith and support. In fact, the only strain I felt during the trial was the pull between trying to comfort my family and carrying out the political activities I knew were necessary. It has all worked out for the best now, but at the time it was a tremendous weight on my family, and on me.

Another matter of concern was whether to reveal to my attorneys the name of Gene McKinney, my passenger on the night the incident went down. Gene had never been apprehended by the police, despite a diligent search. What is more, they did not even know his name. From the start, the police had cleared Gene, and Heanes had testified before the grand jury that my companion had not taken part in any violence. Right after I was captured, the police sent broadcasts all through California saying that they had apprehended the "guilty" party and they wanted the passenger to come in for questioning. They repeatedly said in these broadcasts that the passenger had nothing to do with the incident. I suspected that they wanted to use him against me, and at first I refused to give his name to my attorneys. I saw no point in involving Gene, even though I knew his testimony might help free me. Only when my lawyers had convinced me that legally the prosecution could not do anything to him did I agree to reveal Gene's identity. From my own knowledge of the law, I became aware that the courts were powerless to hurt him. However, Gene was skeptical. When my lawyers finally met him, they explained very carefully that he could not be hurt by testifying for the defense, and he did eventually testify despite his doubts. This showed supreme courage on his part, because the prosecutors were not above pulling some trick to involve him.

The prosecution took about three weeks to present its case and called about twenty witnesses to the stand. They included people like the nurse who had admitted me at Kaiser Hospital, the doctor who did the autopsy on Officer Frey, ballistics experts from the police department, various policemen who arrived at the scene of the shooting, and so on. But their three most important witnesses were Patrolman Heanes, Henry Grier, the bus driver who allegedly witnessed the shooting, and Dell Ross, who claimed that McKinney and I had kidnaped him. The first of these to testify was Herbert Heanes.

When Officer Heanes took the witness stand, it soon became apparent that he was a very disturbed man. He told of recurring dreams in which the Black Panthers were attacking him. Heanes is not very bright, and as time and again he had trouble keeping his story straight, the impression grew that he was completely confused. The prosecutor had obviously rehearsed him, but Heanes was so tense that he made mistakes; with each mistake he dropped his head as if to say, I'll try the script over again. He was no good at all at improvisation and reconciling contradictions in his testimony.

Heanes testified that after Frey ordered me out of my car, the two of us walked to Heanes's patrol car (parked behind La-Verne's Volkswagen) while he, Heanes, remained near the front door of Frey's patrol car, about thirty-five feet away from us. As Frey and I reached the rear of Heanes's car, Heanes testified that I "turned around and started shooting," and that Frey and I then started to "tussle" on the trunk of his car. At this point, Heanes said, he was shot in the right arm, whereupon he switched his gun to his left hand. Immediately after this, he noticed out of the corner of his eye that the passenger in my car (McKinney) had gotten out of the Volkswagen and was standing on the curb with his arms up in the air. Heanes turned his gun on him, but after the passenger assured him he was not armed, Heanes turned back to Frey and me. By this time, Heanes said, Frey and I had separated, although Frey was still hanging on to me, and he, Heanes, shot at my stomach as I faced him. He did not say that he saw his bullet hit me, only that he fired at my "midsection." After that, Heanes said he remembered only two things: first, sending out a 940B—the police emergency number— over the police radio; and second, seeing two men run into the darkness.

When Garry cross-examined Heanes after his testimony, many contradictions and unanswered questions emerged. Heanes repeatedly stated that he never saw a gun in my hand, yet he testified that I had turned around and started to shoot. He was never able to say who had shot him in the arm, although when he shot me in the stomach, he said I was facing him. He would not state that I had shot him, even though, as a police officer, he is supposedly trained to observe such facts as whether or not a suspect has a gun. He was confused in his descriptions of what McKinney was wearing; some of his testimony contradicted the description given later by Henry Grier, the bus driver.

Perhaps the greatest weakness of his testimony, which Garry skillfully brought to the jury's attention, was that Heanes had turned his back on McKinney, having only McKinney's word that he was unarmed. Since the Oakland police distrusted and hated all Black Panthers, and since McKinney, who was unknown to Heanes, and who was riding with the Black Panther Minister of Defense, could very well have been a Black Panther, why had he left himself so unprotected, particularly since he said he did not know where all the shots were coming from? As Garry suggested in his cross-examination of Heanes, it was probably because Heanes was more worried about what Frey would do. Among the police Frey was known to need watching in the Black community; he was even worse than the normal cop, which made him extremely dangerous.

It was clear from Heanes's testimony and the way he had been coached by the prosecutor that great pains had been taken to avoid any implication that Frey and Heanes had shot each other. Charles Garry's first question on cross-examination dealt with this: "Did you shoot and kill Officer Frey?" Heanes said no. Yet several facts pointed that way, and Heanes's evasions were not helpful to the prosecution. For instance, Heanes made a point of saying that he fired at me only when Frey and I had broken apart after our struggle on the car. A more damaging piece of evidence came from the ballistics section of the police department itself. The expert who testified concluded that the bullets that had hit both Frey and Heanes came from police revolvers. They were lead bullets—not copper-jacketed, as were the two nine-millimeter casings found on the ground at the scene of the shooting. This damaged the prosecution's case, because Jensen had maintained from the beginning that I had shot Heanes and Frey with my own .38 pistol whose bullets would have matched the nine-millimeter casings found on the ground. Of course, this mythical gun was never found.

All in all, Heanes's testimony did little for the prosecution. He became even more muddled during my second trial, and by the time he appeared at the third trial, he found it impossible to deal with his own inconsistencies. It was then that he broke down on the stand and admitted seeing a third party at the scene of the shooting. But even at my first trial his testimony was too vague and inconsistent to be taken seriously.

The testimony of Henry Grier, a Black man, and the next major witness for the prosecution, was therefore all-important. He was the only person besides Heanes who claimed I had had a gun at the scene of the shooting. Grier was a bus driver for the Alameda-Contra Costa Transit system in Oakland. According to his testimony, he had been driving his bus along Seventh Street shortly after 5:00 A.M. on the morning of October 28, 1967, when he stopped his vehicle and under its bright lights witnessed the shooting of Frey and Heanes from a distance of about ten feet or less. Asked by Jensen to identify the gunman, Grier left the stand, walked over to where I sat with my attorneys, and put his hand on my shoulder.

When he testified for the first time, on the afternoon of August 7, 1968, a feeling of disgust for him overwhelmed me; he was obviously a bought man who had sold out from terror of the white power structure and perhaps because the district attorney had promised him a few handouts. My attorneys also had reason to suspect, after investigation, that he was in some kind of trouble with his job or the law, and only by co-operating with the district attorney's office could he get out of his predicament. Yet, as the first trial wore on, my feelings of disgust turned to pity. He was, after all, a brother. As a Black, I understood that he was coerced into selling his integrity for survival, and I knew he must have been disgusting to himself. After the first trial, I felt Grier would not be able to live with himself, but when he came back and did it twice again, in the second and third trials, I realized he had been totally destroyed as a person, too corrupt even to feel shame. He was a complete mystery to me.

It is an indication of Grier's importance to the prosecution that Charles Garry learned of his existence only on August 1, six days before he appeared on the witness stand. On August 1, jury selection had been completed, and under the rules of the court, the prosecution was required to give the defense the names and addresses of all the witnesses it intended to call during the trial. It was on this day that Garry first saw Grier's name and learned who he was. During the entire nine months of preparation for the trial, Jensen had seen to it that Grier was kept completely out of sight and never mentioned. He did not appear before the grand jury. In all the police reports, in all the official statements that were issued covering every detail of the incident, the name of the most important "witness" to the shooting was withheld. Jensen had carried out his Machiavellian tactics with supreme cunning. Only when it was no longer possible to hide Grier did Garry learn of his identity and that he claimed to have witnessed the incident.

At the time my lawyers received the prosecution list with Grier's name on it, they were also given another staggering piece of evidence: a transcript of a recorded conversation between Grier and Police Inspector Frank McConnell, which took place at the Oakland police station only ninety minutes after the shooting on October 28. The police had brought Grier to the station house for a statement almost immediately after the incident, and in it he described everything he had allegedly seen. He also identified me as the gunman from a photograph in the police files that Inspector McConnell showed him.

When my attorneys read Grier's statement, given to the police while everything was still fresh in his mind, we learned why the police and prosecution had hidden him away. If Charles Garry had had a chance to talk to him earlier, he would have convinced Grier in a very short time that his eyewitness account of the shooting would never stand up in court. First of all, Grier did not make a "statement" to the police. His interview at the police station was a classic case of verbal entrapment. The inspector led Grier, who was not only weak but also in many instances unsure of everything he had seen, and fed him the questions that would produce answers the police wanted. Whenever Grier hesitated or stopped while trying to remember what he had seen, Inspector McConnell put words in his mouth or suggested the way things had happened; then Grier would agree. But, serious as this was, some of Grier's most crucial statements were so damaging to the prosecution's case it seems incredible that Jensen was willing to gamble everything on him as a principal witness. The fact that Grier swore I had a gun in my hand must have affected Jensen's judgment concerning the rest of Grier's testimony.

First, in describing the gunman whom he later identified as me, Grier said he was no taller than five feet; "sort of a pee-wee type you might call him" were his exact words to Inspector McConnell. Since I am five feet ten and a half inches, Grier's impression of my height was wildly inaccurate. He also said I was wearing a black shirt, a light tan jacket, and that I was clean-shaven. The police had kept all the clothing I was wearing that night, and it was a matter of record that I wore a black jacket, a white shirt, and had two weeks' growth of beard (this was confirmed by a close-up photograph taken by the police when I was lying on the gurney at Kaiser Hospital). Then, too, many of the things Grier said in the transcript were at variance with Officer Heanes's depiction of what took place.

Grier told Inspector McConnell that he had first come upon the scene while driving his bus westbound on Seventh Street. As he approached Willow Avenue on Seventh, directly across from the construction site of a new post office, he said, he observed two parked police cars and near them two policemen and two civilians standing in the street. It was Grier's impression that the police were probably giving the two civilians a ticket or making a routine check, and so he thought little of it as he continued west to the end of his run. (This contradicted the testimony of Heanes, who said that the second passenger [McKinney] had remained in the Volkswagen until after he, Heanes, was shot.) Grier related how he went to the end of his route, turned around, and began his eastbound run back along Seventh Street, picking up three passengers on his way. When he got back to where the police cars were, he said he arrived at the moment Frey and I were walking toward one of the police cars, with Officer Heanes walking behind us. (Heanes had testified that he stayed beside Frey's car as we walked toward the other police car and had not accompanied us.) At this point, Grier said, while Frey was walking beside me, I reached into my jacket, pulled out a gun, and fired at Heanes, who was walking behind me. Heanes fell to the ground. By this time, Grier told McConnell, he had stopped the bus about thirty or forty yards away from us. Then, he continued, Frey and I began wrestling, and he heard a second shot. He reached for the phone in his bus to call the central dispatcher of the transit system, and when he looked again, Frey had fallen on his back, and I was standing over him and firing three or four more shots at him while he lay on his back on the ground. The next thing he knew, said Grier, I had turned and fled west, and within minutes people and police were arriving at the scene from every direction. He told Inspector McConnell that he had not seen the second civilian after he first passed the four of us on his eastbound trip. During the shooting, the man was nowhere to be seen, according to Grier's testimony (Heanes had testified that McKinney was standing near the curb with his hands in the air).

As soon as Garry and my other attorneys read this transcript and received Grier's name and address on August 1, they tried to get in touch with him. He did not appear at work for the next six days. They called his home over and over again, but could never reach him; a recorded message said that the number was out of order. For six days a constant vigil was maintained outside his home. No one was there, and neither he nor any member of his family could be found. Grier had simply disappeared. None of my lawyers laid eyes on Henry Grier until he walked into the courtroom on August 7 to testify for the prosecution. On the afternoon his name had been given to the defense, Grier had been taken into protective custody by the district attorney's office and secretly installed in the Lake Merritt Hotel in downtown Oakland, completely unavailable for questioning by the defense. When Grier finally appeared, Garry had only a matter of hours to prepare his cross-examination on the basis of prosecution testimony. However, he had had six days to go over Grier's sworn statement to Inspector McConnell, enough time to discredit totally Grier's statements on the witness stand, because—unbelievably—Grier changed a lot of his earlier testimony under questioning by Jensen.

At this point the jury had not read the transcript of Grier's sworn statement to Inspector McConnell. And so, when Jensen put Grier on the stand on August 7, the jurors were hearing for the first time Grier's account of the shooting. Jensen handled his testimony very slickly, emphasizing particularly that part in which Grier said I pulled a gun from inside my shirt, shot at Heanes, and then shot and killed Frey, standing over him and firing three or four more shots into his body. When Grier walked over and identified me, the jury must have been convinced of my guilt, for Grier was a calm, assured witness.

But Jensen made a crucial mistake. He thought he could get away with the inconsistencies between Grier's statements made an hour and a half after the shooting and what Jensen coached him to say on the stand. He had Grier tell the jury that he was less than ten *feet* away from the participants in the shooting, whereas in his sworn statement to McConnell, Grier had said he was thirty or forty *yards* away. He told the jury in the courtroom that I had reached into my *shirt* for my gun, but in his original statement, he had said I reached into the pocket of my *jacket* or *coat* to get it. Grier testified during the trial that Frey fell forward, face down, while he had told McConnell that Frey fell on his back. On the stand Grier claimed that the bus lights were shining directly on the scene and he could see plainly, but he had told McConnell that he could not tell how old the gunman was because he had his head down and he "couldn't get a good look." He told Jensen on the stand that I had fled toward the post office construction site, but when McConnell had asked him if that was where I was headed when he had last seen me, Grier said no, that I was running northwest, toward a gas station.

It took only about three and a half hours of cross-examination for Charles Garry to demolish Grier's credibility. In his examination of him and in his final summation, Garry showed that there were at least fifteen crucial statements in which Grier's two sworn testimonies were in conflict. "For a while," Garry said to the jury near the end of the trial, "I thought Mr. Grier was making an honest mistake. I really thought that for a long time. But I've now come to the conclusion that this man was either deliberately lying or that he is a psychopath and that he can't be depended upon in relating any kind of facts. As far as Huey Newton is concerned, either choice is deadly."

In his cross-examination of Grier, Garry first demonstrated that there had been absolutely no reason for his having been taken into protective custody. Over the strenuous objections of Jensen, who constantly leaped up and called Garry's questions "incompetent, irrelevant, and immaterial," Garry got Grier to admit that not only had the district attorney's office never told him why he was being taken into custody, but also that Grier himself had always felt perfectly safe, had never been threatened, and had never felt a need for any protection. This was an effective beginning, because it showed the jury that the trial was being conducted by a ruthless prosecutor who had denied the defense lawyers their legal right to question a prospective witness.

Then Garry proceeded to develop his masterly strategy to expose Grier's fraudulence. He had him describe all over again in the same words the story he had told the jury for the prosecution. Garry wanted the jury to understand very clearly what was happening (the jury was still unaware of Grier's first statement to McConnell). When Grier had finished, Garry took off. He demonstrated in one instance after another all the discrepancies in Grier's two stories. This is how his cross-examination went at one point:

Garry: How was the civilian dressed?

Grier: Well, sir, he had on a dark jacket and a light shirt.

Garry: As a matter of fact, sir, didn't he—didn't that civilian have on a *dark* shirt and a *light* tan jacket?

Grier: No, sir.

Garry: I want you to think about this before you answer it. I am going to ask you again. Isn't it a fact that the person you have described as the civilian was a person who had a dark shirt on, a black shirt on, and a light tan jacket?

(Silence) . . .

Garry: A light tan jacket?

Grier: No, sir. It was dark.

Judge Friedman: What was the answer?

Grier: Dark.

Judge Friedman: Dark what?

Grier: The outer garment was dark.

Garry: How tall was that civilian?

Grier: From up in the coach, sir, to look down at an angle like that, I wouldn't dare say, sir.

Garry: Isn't it a fact that that civilian was under five feet?

Grier: I do not know, sir.

Garry: Would you say that that civilian was heavy-set, thin, or otherwise?

Grier: I didn't pay that close attention, Counselor.

Garry: Mr. Grier, you know that you are under oath, do you not?

Grier: I do, sir. I do.

Jensen: Object to that as being argumentative, Your Honor.

Garry: Mr. Grier, you made a statement to Inspector McConnell on the twenty-eighth day of October, 1967, at the hour of 6:30 A.M.?

Grier: That's right, sir.

Garry: And in that statement didn't you tell Inspector McConnell that the person that was involved was under five feet?

Grier: I could have, sir.

Garry: Did you or did you not say so?

Grier: I don't recall making any specific statement, sir, as to that fact, sir.

At this point the court adjourned for the day. Next morning, Thursday, August 8, in the absence of the jury, Garry made two motions for a mistrial. The first was based on the evidence that the prosecution had hidden a witness from the defense. "We found out for the first time yesterday," said Garry to Judge Friedman, "that immediately after these documents were given to us and the list of the witnesses, that the prosecution immediately took this man out of circulation to a point where we did not know where he was, under the guise of so-called protective custody. He was put into the Hotel Merritt, and we didn't find this out until he was on the stand yesterday afternoon. Our motion is based upon the grounds that the prosecution has gone out of its way to circumvent the right and the obligation and the duty of the defense to prepare its case and to present it in a serious case as this one is. I feel hamstrung, I feel tied up. And I am asking the court for relief."

Jensen immediately responded that if Garry had wanted to talk to any witness he should have come to the district attorney's office the following day and talked to him there.

"I have a right to see the witnesses under my own circumstances and my own conditions. . . . I spent hours and hours of investigation time trying to locate this man, and all the time he had him under wraps," Garry replied. Then he went on to present his second motion for a mistrial:

"My second motion is based upon the atmosphere of the courthouse. I feel impelled to call to the court's attention that the entire courthouse, as you walk in through the front door, is permeated and surrounded by deputies of the Alameda County Sheriff's Department and other police agencies, making it embarrassing and insulting, and has, in my opinion, a direct bearing and effect on the jury itself.

"In this particular case, under these circumstances, I feel impelled to call to the court's attention that we don't feel we can get a fair trial with a jury walking through these same doors with bailiffs finding out who they are and what they are doing in the building, and this kind of atmosphere; and for that same reason I am going to renew a motion for mistrial."

Judge Friedman: Motion is denied. Bring the jury down.

With that, the jury returned, and Garry resumed his cross-examination of Henry Grier.

Garry: Mr. Grier, isn't it a fact that you first saw this officer and this civilian walking alongside of each other, as you have described it, when your bus was at least thirty to thirty-five yards from the scene?

Grier: I did not, sir.

Garry (reading from transcript): ". . . And then I noticed as I approached—I saw the officer walking—one guy towards the second patrol car and this guy was short, sort of a small-built fellow. He—just as I approached within thirty, thirty or forty yards of it I noticed the man begins going into his jacket—" You gave that answer to Inspector McConnell on that hour of the morning, did you not, sir?

Grier: I did, sir.

Garry: Mr. Grier, this man was under five feet, isn't that right? Would you answer that question either yes or no. . . .

Grier: I don't know, Counselor.

Garry (reading from transcript):   "Q. And how tall would
                                         you say he was?
                                     A. No more five feet.
                                     Q. Very short?
                                     A. Very short."

You gave that answer, did you not, at the time?

Grier: I did.

Garry: Mr. Grier, how much did this man weigh?

Grier: I don't know.

Garry: In your estimation?

Grier: I don't know, Counselor.

Garry (reading from transcript):   "Q. About how much
                                         would you say he
                                         weighed?
                                     A. Oh, 125."

Did you give that answer to that question?

Grier: I could have, Counselor.

Garry: Was this fellow, this man that you saw on that morning, was this fellow a husky fellow or a thin person, or a medium person, or what?

Grier: Medium, I would say.

Garry: As a matter of fact, the person you have described was a little pee-wee fellow, isn't that right?

Grier: He was not, sir.

Garry (reading from transcript):   "Q. Was he heavy, husky?
                                                        A. No.
                                                        Q. Slender?
                                                        A. Sort of pee-wee type
                                                             fellow, you might call
                                                             him."
Isn't that right, that is what you said?

Grier: I could have, Counselor.

Garry: That is what you did say, isn't it, sir?

Grier: Possibility, yes. I could have said that, yes, sir.

Garry: Not possibility; that is exactly what you did say, isn't it, sir?

Grier: As I said before, Counselor, without any mistake, I could have.

Garry: It was the truth, wasn't it, sir?

Grier: It was, sir.

After this, and while Jensen registered his disapproval, Garry read to the jury the entire transcript of Grier's statement to Inspector McConnell. There could be no question in the jurors' minds then that something was suspicious, if not rotten, about the prosecution's star witness.

Garry's most dramatic refutation of Grier's testimony—and the one that went to the heart of the matter—came during his final summary for the defense. He walked over to the table in the courtroom where all the evidence for the trial was on display and picked up the black leather jacket I had been wearing on October 28. Then he picked up Heanes's .38 revolver and walked over to the jury box. Standing before the jurors, he quoted Grier's original statement that I had gone into my jacket or coat pocket and pulled out a gun. The gun that the prosecution claimed I had hidden, a .38 pistol, could not have been much smaller than Heanes's revolver, Garry said, as he put the gun into the jacket pocket. It immediately fell out. He put it into the other pocket, and it fell out again. He tried putting the gun in the pockets several times, and each time it fell out; the pocket was too small to hold it. He reminded the jury again of Grier's statement. "And if this isn't a diabolical lie," he said, "then I don't know what a lie is. That's the reason that he changed it from his coat to his shirt. Could it be doctored in any more fashionable way? Try it. This is a shallow pocket. It's about three and one half inches deep. That's why his testimony was changed. And it was changed with the condonation and the knowledge of the prosecution in this case. To get a conviction."

On Monday morning, August 12, Dell Ross, accompanied by his own lawyer, arrived at court to testify for the prosecution. At this point Jensen needed him desperately. The first two major witnesses—Heanes and Grier—had not been as strong as he had hoped. Ross was his last chance. Dell Ross had testified before the grand jury in November, 1967, that right after the shooting I had jumped into his car with another man and forced him at gunpoint to flee the scene. He was the second person to claim I had had a gun in my hand. The kidnaping charge was important, too, since it demonstrated that I knew I had committed a crime and was using desperado tactics to escape. Ross had told the grand jury that I had jumped into the back seat of his car, and my companion had gotten into the front. At first, he said, he had refused to drive us to the corner of Thirty-second and Chestnut as we requested, but when I pulled a gun on him, he complied. He testified that I had said to him, "I just shot two dudes," and "I'd have kept shooting if my gun hadn't jammed." When a picture of me was shown to him, Ross identified me as the man with the gun.

When Jensen put him on the stand on August 12, he had no reason to suspect that Ross would not repeat all his grand jury testimony. Ross answered his first few questions about where he lived, whether he had owned a car in October, 1967, what make it was, et cetera, et cetera. But when Jensen asked him where he had been at five o'clock on the morning of October 28, Ross would not tell him. "I refuse to answer on the grounds it would tend to incriminate me," he said. Jensen could not believe his ears. He asked the court reporter to read the answer back to him, as if to reassure himself of what he had just heard. Ross was a *prosecution* witness. Moreover, he was a *victim*, not a defendant, and victims do not take the Fifth Amendment. When Ross persisted in refusing to answer, Jensen became furious.

From his point of view, Ross's insistence on not answering could damage his case seriously and result in bad publicity. It would look as if something fishy was going on (which, of course, it was) and put the district attorney's office in an unfavorable light. He appealed to Judge Friedman, asking that the witness be obligated to respond to his questions, pointing out that he had already testified fully on the case before the grand jury nine months before. At this point, the judge ordered the jury to retire from the courtroom. Ross's lawyer argued that Ross was making a personal claim for his own protection under the Fifth Amendment. He pointed out that questions put to Ross during the trial might well go beyond the factual answers he had given to the grand jury and lead to further questions that could incriminate him. Ross's lawyer suggested that Ross perhaps knew more about what had happened on the morning of October 28 than he had told the grand jury.

Here was a dilemma for both prosecutor and judge. Judge Friedman responded by cutting short the proceedings for that day. The next day he granted Ross immunity and told him he could not be prosecuted for anything that arose out of his testimony, except perjury or contempt for failing to answer questions directed at him. Now, Ross had to answer Jensen's questions and could no longer invoke the Fifth Amendment. But when the prosecutor began all over again and asked the same question Ross had refused to answer the previous day—where he had been at 5:00 A.M. on October 28, 1967—Ross again refused to answer on the grounds that it would incriminate him. The judge became totally exasperated and told him that he must now answer the questions since he had immunity. Otherwise, he would go to jail for contempt. Ross just sat there stolidly, refusing to go on. Just as Judge Friedman was preparing to sentence him for contempt, Jensen suddenly realized what he could do with this intransigent witness in order to save the day for the prosecution.

"Mr. Ross," he asked him, "do you *remember* what happened on the morning of October 28, 1967?" Ross stalled. Judge Friedman was quick to interject, "If you don't remember what happened that morning," he said, "why, you should say you don't remember. The court does not desire to force you into anything. Is it perhaps that you don't remember what happened that morning?" Ross agreed that he couldn't remember.

It was incredible to see the way the judge aided Jensen. What they planned to do was clear. The judge chose to point out that a witness cannot be punished for having a faulty memory, and so the prosecution was going to help Ross remember by reading back to him all his grand jury testimony, which ordinarily is never allowed as evidence in a trial. Charles Garry protested strongly, but Judge Friedman was adamant. Jensen read all Ross's testimony back to him in front of the jury, and it went into the official record of the trial.

Never was Judge Friedman's bias in favor of Jensen more blatantly obvious than in his dealings with Dell Ross as a witness. It was typical of the arbitrary way the trial was conducted. When their man would not testify because of self-incrimination, they gave him immunity so that anything he said could not be used against him. Then the judge actually coaxed Ross into saying he could not remember what he had said before the grand jury so that the prosecution had an excuse to read his testimony into the transcript. On the other hand, when our man, Gene McKinney, refused to testify twelve days later, because of self-incrimination, they did not offer him immunity or coax him in any way; they just threw him into jail. The police had already exonerated McKinney of any involvement in the incident, but they still would not offer him immunity to protect himself. This was the only time that the contradiction between justice and what the judge and prosecution were doing came out in open court. Their people got immunity when they knew their testimony would incriminate them. Our people, who had been exonerated but who did not trust the system anyway, got tossed into jail. The whole trial was nothing but a big charade to get me railroaded into the gas chamber.

But all their chicanery to get Dell Ross's testimony came to nothing in the end, because Charles Garry had called the last trump. Two weeks before the trial, he had interviewed Ross in his office and taped the conversation, during the course of which Ross admitted that he had lied to the grand jury. He had gone along with the authorities, he said, because they had warrants out on him for parking violations, and he was afraid of them. Ross told Garry in this interview that I did not have a gun that night, that I was barely conscious and had said nothing at all to him. Of course, when Garry got up to cross-examine him during the trial, Ross could not remember this interview, either, so Garry played the whole tape in court, over Jensen's vehement objections.

As a result, the kidnaping charge against me was dropped for lack of evidence—and I was now being tried on three counts instead of four. Ross's appearance as a witness for the prosecution had been a complete failure. Yet he was brought back for my second and third trials, and both times he repudiated his position during the first trial. Despite this, I felt no anger toward him. Like Grier, he was a crushed and broken man, pathetically terrified of the power of the state. I felt more angry at the prosecution for using him as a dupe of the state than against Ross, who could not defend himself.

Ross was the last important witness that Jensen produced, and after he appeared the prosecution rested its case. In any trial the burden of proof lies with the prosecution to establish beyond reasonable doubt the evidence of guilt. Jensen had not achieved this. Many of his accusations were made through implication and innuendo, not facts. Despite his single-minded determination to place me at the scene with a gun in my hand, a lot of his evidence had backfired in ways he had not anticipated. In addition to weaknesses in the testimony of both Grier and Heanes—and the fact that their two stories did not jibe at crucial points—there were a number of serious flaws and omissions in the prosecutor's case.

Jensen never dealt satisfactorily with the shooting—for instance, the location of the two nine-millimeter casings that were found at the scene by police officers. Jensen had suggested throughout the trial that these casings, which did not match police guns, belonged to the .38 revolver I allegedly carried that night. The casings were found lying twenty to twenty-five feet apart, one between the two police vehicles and one near the rear left fender of Heanes's car, right where Frey was shot. Since both Heanes's and Grier's testimony coincided in stating that Frey and I had walked to the back of Heanes's car and that no shooting had occurred until we reached this point, how could the second casing have gotten twenty-five feet away? I could not have been in two places at once. This was an insurmountable puzzle in the prosecution argument. The only possible solution seems to be that a third person was firing at the scene, and the prosecution had totally excluded this possibility since it wanted only one assailant—me.

Then, too, my lawyers found the police tapes from that morning very mystifying. They carefully went over the transcript of all the police conversations that were recorded between the police cars at the scene and Radio Dispatch in the police administration building. The tapes began with a request from Officer Frey just after he had stopped me shortly before 5:00 A.M. The request was for information about me and the car I was driving. They continued through all the communications that took place after other police cars arrived at the scene following the shooting. In analyzing the messages that passed between Radio Dispatch and the patrol car radios, my lawyers found indications that the police dispatcher in the administration building was sending out information to other police in the Oakland area that was not being radioed in by the police at the scene. This suggested that either the tapes were tampered with or that witnesses were phoning in accounts of the shooting and giving descriptions that the police at the scene did not have.

For instance, the dispatcher assumed that I was connected with the crime since Frey had asked information about me before he was shot, and so he sent out a bulletin about 5:15 A.M. describing me as the "suspect" and stating that I was wearing a tan jacket. Half an hour later, he inexplicably sent out another bulletin that said I was wearing "dark clothing." There had been no incoming police radio message on the tape to tell him this, and no indication of how he got this information. How did he learn that I was wearing dark clothing? Henry Grier, too, had mentioned in his interview with Inspector McConnell a "pee-wee" type wearing a tan jacket. Was there a

third person answering this description at the scene? Throughout the trial Jensen never allowed this possibility to be suggested to the jury, even though the police had interviewed
witnesses who had heard the shots and arrived at the scene seconds after the shooting. My lawyers even suspect that a number of people in the area were close and had witnessed the
incident. One woman, a Black prostitute, told the police that
she had seen three men running away in the direction of the gas
station at the corner of Seventh Street and Willow Avenue. Another witness, a young man, told the police that he had seen
two cars speeding away north on Seventh Street. Jensen never
called these people to testify because he wanted to create the
impression that I was the only person who could possibly have
killed Frey. Yet the accounts of others who were there (and
later Heanes's own admission at my third trial that there had
been a third person present) contradicted his theory.

Another piece of evidence that Jensen found hard to dismiss
was the lawbook I was carrying when Frey ordered me to the
back of Heanes's car. Charles Garry pointed out that I could
not very well have carried a gun and a lawbook in my right
hand at the same time. But even more crucial was my reason
for carrying it. Reading to the police from lawbooks was the
only defense I had in case of unlawful arrest. I had done it
countless times in the past, and there are hundreds of people in
the Black community who have seen me do it and can testify
that it was my common practice. I carried it again on the morning of October 28 to read the law to Officer Frey. It was an action that Jensen could not distort for his own ends.

Perhaps Jensen's most grievous and callous omission during
the entire trial was his failure to point out that a vital word in
the transcript of Grier's conversation with Inspector McConnell had been changed. It was only by accident that Charles
Garry discovered that this word had been incorrectly tran-
scribed by a typist in the district attorney's office from the tape
that Inspector McConnell had made with Grier. And yet this
one word was so important that it called into doubt Grier's
identification of me from the picture McConnell showed him at
police headquarters. To make matters worse, Garry discovered

this error only after the trial proper was over and the jury had been out deliberating the verdict for a day.

On September 5, the jury requested to see the transcript, and Judge Friedman called Garry and Jensen into his chambers to ask them for a copy. There was no court copy (the trial clerk had forgotten to acquire one as evidence), and Charles Garry had lent his only copy to someone else. So Jensen went to get his and came back with the original working copy of the transcription. As Garry quickly looked through it, he paused in disbelief over a section of Grier's testimony. There, over the crucial word, was a handwritten correction, completely reversing the meaning of the sentence. This section read:

Q. About how old?

A. I couldn't say because I had only my lights on. I couldn't—
I DID get a clear picture, clear view of his face, but—
because he had his head kind of down facing the
headlights of the coach and I couldn't get a good look—.

Over the word "did" someone had written in the correct word: "didn't." But throughout the trial, Jensen, knowing that this issue was crucial, had neglected to inform Garry, the jury, and the court that there was a question in the transcript of how clearly Grier had been able to see. Indeed, Jensen's contention was that Grier *had* gotten a good look and was therefore in a position to identify that person as me. As long as there was the slightest doubt in his mind about whether the word was "did" or "didn't" he had a moral obligation to inform the court and the defense counsel, and it was an absolute matter of conscience that he listen again to the tape to see what the word actually was. He never bothered.

In this important matter and in all the other dubious issues—the position of the bullet casings, the police tapes, the hiding of Grier, the keeping of important witnesses off the stand, the changing of Grier's original testimony—Lowell Jensen proved less than honorable. It is the prosecutor's job to convict a *guilty* man—not an *innocent* one. And in my case Jensen had many reasons to believe I was innocent. He chose to ignore them all.

When the prosecution rested its case, Charles Garry, on the morning of August 19, moved for another mistrial. He based his motion on the fact that it was impossible for me to receive a fair trial in Oakland because of the atmosphere of hatred, violence, and controversy. As proof of this, he read to the court samples of hate mail that he and I had been receiving. One of the letters was from four retired marines who said they had known Frey. The letter stated that neither Garry nor I would be alive ten days after the trial was over, no matter what the verdict. Another letter was signed "KKK" and read:

Nigger Lover:

I guess you feel that the murdering coon's gonna get off because the jury and witnesses have all been intimidated to the extent that no one dares convict. I hope he will be gunned down in the streets by some friends of the poor policeman he killed. The Black Panthers parade all over the place and I don't see why the KKK and American Nazi Parties couldn't do the same. It is supposed to be a free country for everybody. It is too bad we ever stopped lynching. At least the dam niggers knew their place in those days and didn't cause any trouble. I remember reading about one time they strung up some coons and pulled out pieces of their flesh with corkscrews. That must have been a lot of fun. I wish I had been there to take part in the good work. I hope this race war that we are having starts right away. We outnumber the blacks ten to one, so we know who will win. And a lot of damn nigger lovers will be laying right there beside them. I wish Hitler had won and then we could have kicked off the shinnies and started in on the coons.

KKK

Garry's request for a mistrial was denied by Judge Friedman, who refused to acknowledge that I was receiving anything but a fair trial. He felt the letters were negligible and unimportant.

After this, Garry opened the defense and began on the morning of August 19 to show the jury where the truth lay. He introduced a group of witnesses who were essential to those political aspects of the case that we had been so determined to explore from the beginning. These were people from the Black community—ordinary, honest working people—who could testify with sincerity and conviction about how their lives were frequently made difficult by the occupying army of racist police. These people described being stopped, questioned, bullied, pushed around, and insulted for no reason other than the sadistic whim of some southern cracker who hated Blacks. These were the people brutalized by intruders in their own community. All had one thing in common: encounters with Officer John Frey.

Daniel King, sixteen, related on the stand how he had met Frey around four o'clock one morning in West Oakland, where he was visiting his sister. They had gone out to get something to eat on Seventh Street, and there, incredibly enough, had encountered a white man with no pants on. He was with Frey. Frey told King he was violating curfew, and the white man accused him of knowing the girl who had taken his pants. When King denied this, both Frey and the white man called him "nigger," "pimp," and other "dirty words." Frey had held King while the white man hit him. Then he put him in a paddy wagon and took him to Juvenile Hall where he spent the rest of the night. Frey did not even bother to call King's parents.

Luther Smith, Sr., who worked with a youth organization in Oakland, told of a number of run-ins with Frey. He testified that Frey was "awful mean" and had used racial epithets when talking to him. Frey had called Smith's brother a "little Black nigger" and his son's wife a "Black bitch."

Belford Dunning, an employee of the Prudential Life Insurance Company, described an encounter with Frey the day before he died. When Frey pushed Dunning around while he was being given a ticket by another policeman for a minor violation on his car, Dunning had said to him, "What's the matter with you? You act like you're the Gestapo or something." Frey's hand went to his revolver. "I *am* the Gestapo," he said.

A young white schoolteacher, Bruce Byson, who had taught Frey in high school, invited him to come back and speak to the class about his work as a policeman. While he was talking to the high school students, Byson testified, Frey referred to people in the Black community as "niggers" and spoke disparagingly of them as criminals and lawbreakers.

Garry wanted the jury to understand what Black people are subjected to by cops like Frey, hung up on power. He also wanted them to realize that Frey's bloodthirstiness was responsible for his own death. Belford Dunning, the insurance man, had said to him the day before he died, "Man, if you don't lick this, you are not going to last very long around here." As a matter of fact, Frey's superiors had already decided to move him out of the Black community into another area, where he would be less of a lethal threat to innocent human beings. But they were too late, and Frey himself fulfilled Dunning's prophecy. Garry stressed this aspect of Frey's behavior (and by implication, most other policemen) over and over again during his defense. Frey was not only a bully to helpless people; he was also determined to exterminate anyone whom he considered a threat to his own dubious masculinity. "You know," Garry said to the jury during his summation, "since the day I got into this case, one thing has bothered me. Why in tarnation was Officer Frey so headstrong in stopping Huey Newton's automobile? I wake up at night trying to find an answer to that, and I can't find an answer. This bothers me. It is just not part of legal due process. It is not part of any understanding of justice. It is not part of any understanding of the proper administration of the law. Frankly, it is not the type of police action that I have personally witnessed, but then again, I am not a Black man. I am not a Black Panther. I am part of accepted society. I don't think any officer would stop me unless I was actually, openly, overtly violating the law.

"What was Huey Newton doing when he was driving down Seventh Street, between 4:50 and 5:00 o'clock in the morning, that warranted this officer to call in and ask for PIN [Police Intelligence Network] information, saying 'I got a Black Panther car. See if there is something on it.'

"In my opening statement I told you that there was a plan, a concerted plan by the Oakland Police Department, together with other police departments in Alameda County, to get Huey Newton, to get the Black Panther Party. Huey Newton above all. . . .

"Another thing that bothers me, and bothers me very, very much about the evidence, and it should bother you when you start analyzing it. If it is true that Officer Frey intended to arrest Huey Newton and, in fact, said, 'I now place you under arrest,' which we contend is not so, but let's assume for the sake of argument that he did, I don't understand why he didn't put handcuffs on him, since the Panthers are supposed to be such desperadoes.

"I further don't understand, if he was placing him under arrest, why he passed his own automobile. I don't understand why Officer Frey took Mr. Newton to the third automobile, to the back end of it. Why? Was he going to beat him up? You know, he could very well do it. He was a heavier man, weighing 200 pounds. He went to the gym regularly, according to Officer Heanes. Huey is a 165-pounder and Huey had a lawbook in his hand."

Perhaps the most significant comment that can be made about the testimony of these defense witnesses from the Black community is that Jensen offered no rebuttal. His silence was eloquent. I guess no one could be found to speak well of Frey. What can you say about a policeman who owned three guns, carried extra ammunition on his cartridge belt, and was the only member of the Oakland force who did not use the regular bullets issued by the department but spent his own money to buy a special high-velocity type?

On August 24, Charles Garry called Gene McKinney to the witness stand. When McKinney entered the courtroom that afternoon with his lawyer, Harold Perry, a feeling of excitement and expectation could be felt among the spectators. Here was one of the most important witnesses to the shooting of Heanes and Frey. Up until then, there had been considerable speculation about whether even the defense lawyers knew the name of my companion that morning. Throughout the trial reporters and newsmen had been asking Charles Garry whether the mysterious witness would testify.

When McKinney took the stand, Garry rose and asked him first his name and then whether he had been a passenger in the Volkswagen with me at the corner of Seventh and Willow on the morning of October 28, 1967. "Yes, I was," McKinney answered. His response electrified the courtroom. But those two questions were the only ones he ever answered. When Garry asked, "Now, Mr. McKinney, at the time and place on that morning, at approximately five o'clock in the morning, did you by chance or otherwise shoot at Officer John Frey?" McKinney said, "I refuse to answer on the grounds it may tend to incriminate me." Jensen was outraged. He jumped to his feet and demanded that Judge Friedman direct the witness to answer. "Inasmuch as he has already started to testify," said Jensen, "saying he was there at the scene, he has obviously waived [his right to silence]. Let's hear him tell what he knows. He said he was there, and I ask that that question now be read to him and the court direct him to answer."

Then followed a discussion between the prosecutor, Perry, and the judge about McKinney's constitutional rights, with Perry claiming McKinney need only be cross-examined on the two questions he had chosen to respond to—his name and where he was on October 28. Beyond that, Perry claimed, he was entirely within his rights to claim the Fifth Amendment. When Jensen insisted on cross-examining him, McKinney refused to answer. Here Garry was trying to raise the question of "reasonable doubt"—doubt about whether there could have been only one possible person who did the shooting—me, as the prosecution claimed.

But Garry and Harold Perry were also using another brilliant strategy, and Jensen understood immediately what was involved. The prosecution believed that McKinney was inviting Judge Friedman to grant him immunity in his testimony—the same immunity he had given to Dell Ross—whereby nothing he said could be used against him. Then, with this protection, he could say that *he* had killed Frey and shot at Heanes, and that he had escaped with me. Because no evidence had been submitted during the trial to prove otherwise, he could not have been convicted of perjury. Thus, having absolved me of the crime and having freed himself of any danger of prosecution, since his testimony could not be used against him, both of us could have walked out of the courtroom—at liberty.

But Jensen and Friedman, believing this to be the strategy, were having none of it. After questioning McKinney carefully to make sure he realized he was liable for contempt, Judge Friedman ordered him immediately sent to jail for refusing to testify. He later sentenced him to six months, but the California Superior Court reversed the decision, stating that McKinney had acted within his constitutional rights. After spending a few weeks in the county jail, McKinney was released on bail. As I said, he is a courageous man.

Finally, on the morning of August 22, I took the witness stand. A number of people had doubted I would testify because they thought I would not be able to handle a merciless cross-examination by Jensen. But actually I looked forward to it. For six weeks I had sat beside Charles Garry in the courtroom and listened to Jensen claim that I had murdered Frey in cold blood. I had watched him try to sell the jury on the fact that I loved violence, that I had a history of provoking policemen, and that there was reason to believe I did not tell the truth. I wanted to set the record straight and prove to the jury that I was innocent. I also was determined to let him know what it meant to be a Black man in America and why it had been necessary to form an organization like the Black Panther Party. After that, I hoped they would understand why Frey had illegally stopped my car on the morning of October 28.

Garry opened up by asking me the two all-important questions: whether I had killed Officer John Frey and whether I had shot and wounded Officer Herbert Heanes. I gave the only possible answers—the truth. No, I had not. After that, we went through the necessary background leading up to the incident, which in this case began the day I was born. I told the court about my family, about growing up in Oakland, where there was no place to play except in the rubble and garbage-strewn streets and vacant lots, because Black kids have no swimming pools, no parks, no playgrounds. I told them about degrading experiences in the public school system, experiences that countless thousands of other Black children have endured and continued to endure in an oppressive and indifferent world. I told them how the Black community is occupied by police who need no excuse to harass and bully its inhabitants. I told them that when I graduated from Oakland Technical High School I was unable to read or write and that most of my classmates were in the same boat, because no one in the school system cared whether we learned to read or write. Then I told how, under the influence of my brother Melvin, I had taught myself to read by going again and again through Plato's *Republic*. I tried to explain what a deep impression Plato's allegory of the cave had made on me and how the prisoners in that cave were a symbol of the Black man's predicament in this country. It was a seminal experience in my life, I explained, for it had started me thinking and reading and trying to find a way to liberate Black people. Then I told of meeting Bobby Seale at Oakland City College and how the Black Panther Party grew out of our talks.

Garry led me through an exposition of what the Black Panther Party stood for and an explication of its ten-point program. I recited the ten points in the courtroom and explained them. Blacks, I said, are a colonized people used only for the benefit and profit of the power structure whenever it suits their purposes. After the Civil War, Blacks were kicked off plantations and had nowhere to go. For nearly one hundred years they were either unemployed or used for the most menial tasks, because industry preferred to use the labor of more acceptable immigrants—the Irish, the Italians, and the Jews. However, when World War II started, Blacks were again employed—in factories and by industry—because, with the white male population off fighting, there was a labor shortage. But when that war ended, Blacks were once again kicked off "the plantation" and left stranded with no place to go in an industrial society. Growing up in the late forties, I was aware of it in Oakland, because major defense plants had been built there during the war, and a large Black population was condemned to unemployment after the war. I quoted the second point in our program as a way of changing all this: "We want full employment for our people. We believe that the Federal Government is responsible and obligated to give every man employment or a guaranteed income. We believe that if the white American businessman will not give full employment, then the means of production should be taken from the businessmen and placed in the community so that the people of the community can organize and employ all of its people and give a high standard of living."

Sometimes, while I was explaining Black history and the aims of the Black Panther Party to the court, I forgot that I was on trial for my life. The subjects were so real and important to me that I would get lost in what I was saying. There were moments when I even enjoyed myself, especially when I had a chance to score points against Judge Friedman and Jensen.

On one occasion I saw an opportunity to show my contempt for the judge, and I took it. I was describing how some immigrant groups had been subjected to oppression and discrimination when they first arrived in this country, but that after they began to make economic gains some of them had joined their oppressors, even when the oppressors continued to discriminate against the immigrants' own people. I used as an example Jews who join the Elks Club, even though they know that this organization is racist and anti-Semitic. Judge Friedman had been the first Jew admitted to the Elks Club in Oakland, a fact that had been given a great deal of publicity. The Elks wanted it believed that they were no longer anti-Semitic, but everybody knew better.

Another time, talking about contemporary racism in American society, I deliberately used the Mormon church as one of the most blatant proponents of ethnic discrimination. Knowing that Jensen was a Mormon, I looked at him when I said this, instead of at the jury. He gave me a smirk, and I kept right on looking at him. He could say nothing in front of the jury lest they learn the truth about him.

Jensen often became impatient with the way Garry was conducting his examination of me and frequently interrupted, but even he sometimes seemed interested in what I was saying. Throughout, however, those meaningful glances passed between Jensen and Judge Friedman, the judge asking for an objection and Jensen giving it to him. Friedman could hardly hide his disapproval of everything I was saying and kept telling me to stick to the present and the incident itself. Then Garry would remind him that everything I said was relevant to the defense. Somehow, we managed to get in all the most important political aspects of the case, and that was what mattered most. Only when that was accomplished did I turn to my version of what had happened that morning. I described it exactly as it took place up until Frey shot me. After that, of course, I had passed out, so I could describe only those things I remembered and my hazy impressions of them.

I had spent nearly the entire day on the stand when Garry turned me over to the enemy. For the first time in eight weeks Jensen and I were face to face.

My sister Leola had told me of an incident that occurred at the beginning of the trial when she was standing on the courthouse steps watching one of the many demonstrations. Jensen, not knowing who she was, was standing near her, watching with an associate. She heard Jensen tell his friend that he meant to make me lose my temper before the jury. Then, he said, all the demonstrations on my behalf would be meaningless. So, when he approached me that afternoon, I knew what to expect: he wanted me to explode rather than engage in a good debating session. I felt that the whole exchange would be nothing more than another debate, only this time the stakes were high. I had spent too much time on corners, in bars, and in the classroom debating very complex subjects to get upset with Jensen's probing. He was a worthy opponent, but I knew that once he began to push me, he was going to be surprised at my responses. He had a false impression of me and expected me to respond in a way I was incapable of doing. Throughout almost two days of cross-examination, we struggled to see whose approach would prevail, mine or his, and I felt that during almost all of this time I controlled the situation. In responding to Jensen, just as I had responded to Garry, I did not pull any punches about criticizing the system or its agents. Though my life was at stake, I wanted to show my contempt. I sought to use their own apparatus to defy them, which was consistent with the revolutionary practices I have attempted to live by.

Jensen's entire cross-examination, nearly every incident he brought up, was intended to demonstrate that I loved violence and guns and that I was a personal threat and a menace to police officers merely trying to do their duty. He began by asking about our early patrols in the Oakland community, emphasizing for the benefit of the jury, in insidious ways, the fact that we had carried shotguns. He tried to imply that I would have preferred to carry a concealed pistol on these patrols but that the terms of my probation did not allow this. He reinforced this suggestion by having me read a poem, "Guns, Baby, Guns," I had once written for *The Black Panther* newspaper, which was filled with symbols and metaphors that have a particular meaning for Black people but are utterly lost on most whites. In the poem I had mentioned a P-38 revolver, and Jensen tried to suggest that this was the type of gun I had shot Frey with and that my poem suggested I liked this gun and would use it if the occasion demanded.

"What is a P-38?" he asked.

"It's an automatic pistol," I answered.

"Does it fire nine-millimeter Luger cartridges?" was his next question.

I explained to Jensen that I don't know much about hand guns. I always preferred a shotgun and would never touch hand guns while I was on probation. I explained to him that in this matter, as in all others, Black Panthers obey the law.

At that, he asked me if I remembered an incident in Richmond in 1967 when I *had not* obeyed the law, when, as he put it, I "got into a combat with Richmond police"? He was referring to the time the police had lain in wait for us until 5:00 A.M. outside a house where we were partying. I had taken an arrest that time in order to *avoid* combat after one young police officer had stepped on all the brothers' feet and another got me in a choke hold against a police car. I carefully explained the details to Jensen and the jury and told how an all-white conservative jury at my trial in Richmond had believed the police version of what had taken place, as they always do, and sentenced me to sixty days on the county farm. I made sure the jury learned about the policeman's remark after viciously beating the brother: "I have to go now because I promised to take my wife and kids to church at nine."

Then Jensen brought up the time the Black Panthers had responded to the little boy who ran into headquarters asking for help. The police had burst into his house when his father was away and were tearing up the place on some phony pretext of looking for a shotgun. We asked the police to leave because they had no search warrant, and in their rage they had arrested me for wearing a dagger in a holster, accusing me of "displaying a weapon in a rude and threatening fashion."

While describing this incident, I really got the best of Jensen. He had been on my right when he first asked the question, and the jury on my left. He wanted me to speak toward him, but I turned my back and began giving details of the incident to the jury, which took a while. Since he had asked the question about the incident, he could not interrupt my answer without looking stupid, so I seized the time and took the play away from him.

The jury seemed fascinated with my description of the affair and was with me all the way. Jensen obviously got so disgusted with what was happening that he left his position near the clerk's desk and sat down looking very dejected—as I was later told. At any rate, I described the incident fully, leaned back, and turned to my right for Jensen's next question; he was no longer there. I was surprised at not seeing him where he had last been standing, so I said, "Where is he?" Then I saw him seated at the table, and I smiled at him and said, "Oh, there you are. I thought you had gone home." The courtroom broke up at this, and the judge admonished me.

Much of Jensen's cross-examination had continual reference to official reports and documents, which he kept consulting while I was on the stand. Reading a report that is filed in some record system and stamped with an official seal of approval can be very impressive: the printed page somehow suggests that whatever is described represents the truth, that it faithfully describes what took place. And so, when Jensen brought up official police testimony of what had happened to me in the past—in arrests, in courts, in various trials—he thought he was offering the jury proof of my violent and crime-filled past. But,

far from distressing or embarrassing me, every one of his challenges presented a chance to tell the jury what had really taken
place and to describe them in the larger context of what life is
like for Black people in this country. In this way, I was able to
demonstrate how the police had harassed the Black Panthers
and looked for every opportunity they could to arrest us and
destroy our organization.

To give Jensen credit, he did not miss very much. But I countered every piece of "official" evidence with an explanation
that went beyond words on a page. And I think the jury came
to understand that no official document ever contains the whole
truth. Events are dictated by a number of mitigating circumstances and a whole system of values and customs that can
never be conveyed in print.

Jensen made another mistake by examining some of my
speeches and writings and reading into them exhortations to
violence. On this tack he quickly got out of his depth; he did
not understand the way language is used among Blacks and often took literally what was meant symbolically. Every time he
brought up something I had written or said that he thought
sounded dangerous, I patiently explained what it meant in
terms of organizing the Black community. In this way, I was
able to describe to the jury the goals the Party had for Black
people. I had hoped to do this—to take the initiative from Jensen and develop certain political points in the courtroom. It
was surprising how often I succeeded.

Finally, Jensen got around to the morning of October 28. He
came meticulously prepared, armed with photographs and
maps, to present his version of what had happened. Leading
me carefully through the whole incident, he had me describe
my every move and gesture. At one point I was even asked to
demonstrate with him how Frey had "smeared" me. He also
chose to bring up an encounter that Bobby Seale and I had had
with two policemen in 1966, because he believed the event related to the shooting of Officer Frey. As Jensen described this
incident, I had gotten into a fight with a policeman and had
tried to take his gun away from him. If Jensen had been able to
prove this, he could have used it as a foreshadowing of what

had happened in 1967 and as evidence that I had done the same thing with Frey. I do not know where he got his information, but I pointed out to the court that it was on record that one of the policemen who was hassling us in 1966 had admitted in court that he was drunk when he met Bobby and me. Jensen said, "Mr. Newton, isn't it a fact that you entered a plea of guilty to battery upon that police officer, the man in uniform?" I answered, "I accepted the deal that the district attorney's department offered."

"I see. And you pled guilty to a battery on a policeman?"

"I think it was simple assault."

(Sarcastically) "Is that right? Mr. Newton, did you see anyone shoot John Frey?"

"No."

"Did you see anyone shoot Officer Heanes?"

"No. I did not."

"You have no explanation at all of how John Frey was killed?"

"None whatsoever."

"I have no further questions."

With that, Jensen's cross-examination was completed. It had not gone according to his plan. I had never lost my cool. It was Jensen, in fact, who lost his.

Garry was masterful in his closing arguments. A defense lawyer has to be good at that point, because the prosecution gives the closing argument first, and then has the last word after the defense has spoken. Garry reviewed the evidence, showing the holes and the discrepancies in the prosecution testimony. He had brought a number of large posters into court with Grier's conflicting testimony lined up side by side, and with a pointer he painstakingly indicated all the contradictions in Grier's two sworn statements. The whole thrust of Garry's summing up was to illustrate how much of a "reasonable doubt" there was in the evidence presented by the prosecution.

But Garry did more than this. In a moving and heartfelt closing speech he addressed himself to the conscience of the jury and to their understanding of social conditions that had led to the death of Officer Frey:

"The Black community today, the Black ghetto, is fighting for the right of survival. The white community is sitting smug and saying, Let's have more police! Let's have more guns! Let's arm ourselves against the Blacks!

"That is not the answer. If you think that is the answer, we are all destroyed. If you think that Mayor Daley has the answer, we are all destroyed. If you think that this nation with all of its power and all of its strength can eliminate violence on the street with more violence, they have another thought coming.

"My client and his party are not for destruction; they want to build. They want a better America for Black people. They want the police out of their neighborhoods. They want them off their streets. Every one of you here possibly knows a policeman in your neighborhood. I know several men in police departments. I think they are wonderful people. I live in Daly City; I have a beautiful relationship with them. Those police live in my neighborhood, within three or four blocks. I know where one of them lives. I can call on him if I need him. But no police officer lives in the ghetto. Why don't they live in the ghetto? Because a man that is making eight or nine or ten thousand dollars isn't going to live in the kind of hovel that the ghetto is.

"Has anybody thought of uplifting the ghetto? So that it doesn't exist in the manner that it has? These are the things that Huey Newton and the Black Panthers and other people are trying to do. . . .

"White America, listen! White America, listen! The answer is not to put Huey Newton in the gas chamber. It is not the answer to put Huey Newton and his organization into jail. The answer is to wipe out the ghetto, the conditions of the ghetto, so that Black brothers and sisters can live with dignity, so that they can walk down the street with dignity."

The fire and eloquence of Charles Garry's final argument are difficult to describe; he was pleading for the principles and beliefs he feels most deeply about and to which he has dedicated his entire life. When he stood and spoke out for justice and truth and tolerance, he was not simply defending a man whose life was in jeopardy; he was speaking for all the downtrodden and oppressed in the world, and he was asking the jury to think about them also. Few people in the courtroom that day were unaffected by what he said.

In contrast, Jensen devoted most of his closing arguments to the particulars of the trial. He asked the jury to find me guilty of murdering John Frey and defended in detail the testimony of Grier and Heanes. Yet at a point in Jensen's summation in which he discussed the meaning of law and the process of justice the words could very well have been spoken by Garry. It was what my lawyers and I had been fighting for. But I feel sure Jensen had no idea of the irony in his remarks:

"We put together in the courtroom the notion that every right that goes to every citizen is implemented in our courts. I think that is so. And I think you should reflect on this: the notion that society accords a right to an individual has something that goes along with it, and that is that there is no such thing as a right without a duty that goes along with it. That is, if the law says a man has a right, the law also says that every other person must honor that right. He has a duty to honor that right.

"What is more fundamental, ladies and gentlemen, than the right to life? What is more fundamental than the right to a peaceful occupation and life?

"What we do in a courtroom is to seek out and declare a truth. We must, as I say, declare those truths in a courtroom. If we cannot declare those truths in a courtroom we are lost.

"And in a courtroom, just as there must be a duty to implement a right, a courtroom must exist on the basis of the declaration of truth."

With Jensen's final declaration that I was a murderer, the arguments were finished. The struggle between defense and prosecution was over, and the judge began to instruct the jury about what they must do to reach a verdict. "The function of the jury," said Judge Friedman, "is to determine the issues of fact that are presented by the allegations of the indictment filed in this court and the defendant's plea of not guilty. This duty you should perform uninfluenced by pity for a defendant or by passion or prejudice against him. You must not suffer yourselves to be biased against a defendant because of the fact that he had been arrested for these offenses, or because an indictment has been filed against him, or because he has been brought before this court to stand trial. None of these facts is evidence of his guilt, and you are not permitted to infer or speculate from any or all of them that he is more likely to be guilty than innocent."

As the jury filed out, led by David Harper, I felt everything was over for me. Some jurors had been impressed with my testimony and believed in me. I had watched them throughout the trial and felt they were sympathetic to the defense, but I had no hope of their steadfastness under the pressure of jury deliberations. Often, in such circumstances, people will appear to lean one way but change their minds when conflicting opinions bear down on them. So I went back to my cell prepared for a decision that would send me to the gas chamber. My work had prepared me well; organizing defense groups in the community had continually made me aware that I could be killed at any time, and I knew that when serious actions begin to go down against you, you must be ready. If you wait to prepare for death when the gas chamber is facing you, it is too late. It is the difference between having your raft ready when high tide comes or trying to make it after the waves are there. When death is staring you in the face, the heavy things take over.

The jury deliberated for four days—from September 5 until September 8—and despite the fact that my lawyers were with me constantly, the time passed very slowly. Nonetheless, I was in good spirits. My thoughts kept me occupied. I re-examined everything that I had done before and during the trial and found nothing to regret, nothing I had to square myself with. Our activities as Black Panthers had been worth all the trouble and pain we had seen, and there was no reason to feel we were losing everything. If I had had a chance to start again, nothing would have been any different.

I contemplated the gas chamber. Only two thoughts concerned me: how the last minute would be and how it would affect my family. First of all, I resolved to face it with dignity right to the end. Second, I worried about my family having to live through yet another ordeal. The whole experience had been terrible for them. Yet I knew that if necessary I would do it again, even though it meant more suffering for them. I felt great love for them and valued their support. If I had caused them anguish, I was sustained by the knowledge that one day the people would have the victory, and that this would bring some measure of satisfaction to those I loved.

Many people wondered what the Black Panthers would do when the verdict came down. The brothers had repeatedly said that the sky was the limit if the oppressor did not free me. At the time that was said, we meant that an unfavorable decision would be taken to the highest judicial level. But the statement was intentionally ambiguous and open to interpretation in order to put the whole Oakland power structure up tight. That plan certainly worked. An open interpretation not only attracted considerable publicity but also left us free to make specific decisions about action after the verdict was in, rather than before.

It was in the early evening of September 5, the first day of the jury's deliberations, that we were notified that the jury was returning to the courtroom. At first we thought they had reached a verdict, but no, they wanted to have Grier's statement to McConnell read to them again, and they also asked if they could see my bullet wound. When everyone was assembled, I went over to the jury box, lifted up my sweater to show the scar in my abdomen, and then turned around to show the exit wound. (Later, we found out that a disagreement had arisen among the jury members over the location of the wound. If Heanes's testimony were true [he testified that he was in a kneeling position and I was in a standing position], the wound near my navel would be lower than the exit wound in my back. But, if Frey had stood and shot me while I was in a kneeling position, the navel wound would be higher than the rear exit wound. I had testified that Frey had shot me as I fell to my knees. My demonstration supported my testimony.)

It was also during the jury's first day of deliberation that Garry found the mistake in Grier's testimony left uncorrected by Jensen. The jury had asked to see the transcript again, but when Garry discovered the error, he refused to allow the uncorrected copy to be sent in. Judge Friedman commented that he did not think the error made much difference. But Garry knew better. It was a vital correction as far as the defense was concerned, a mistake so serious that it could mean a new trial. Garry insisted that he and Jensen listen to the original tape, find out whether the word really was "didn't"—and send the correction in to the jury. Jensen at first claimed that his office did not have the proper machine to play the original tape. That evening one of my lawyers listened to a dub of the original on his own machine and swore the word was "didn't." Jensen did not listen to the tape until the next morning. It was a tense period for all of us, since the jury could have come in with a verdict at any moment. On Friday, September 5, my attorneys played the original tape in the press room for reporters and representatives of the media. Most of them thought the word was "didn't," and the news on television, radio, and in the press that day carried stories about this new discovery. Meanwhile, my attorneys went to an audio engineer who worked for a radio station in Oakland. He agreed to transfer the crucial part of Grier's testimony to another tape and then blow it up on his own hi-fi equipment so that they could hear the correct word distinctly, and once and for all. When this was done, the word Grier actually had said—"didn't"—came through loud and clear.

Meanwhile, the defense was working frantically against time, preparing a motion to reopen the case and trying to get the proper equipment into court to play the blown-up tape for Judge Friedman and Jensen. It was a real hassle, but in the end, over the vigorous objections of Jensen, who claimed it was too late and that Garry should have done this during the trial, the judge did listen to the blown-up tape and had to recognize that the word was "didn't." A corrected statement was sent in to the jury late Saturday afternoon, but Friedman would not allow any mention of the original error to accompany the transcript. We never learned whether the jury even noticed it, let alone understood how important and significant a correction it was.

Finally, on the fourth day of deliberations, September 8, around ten o'clock in the evening, the jury reached a verdict. I came back into the courtroom with my lawyers to hear it read by the clerk:

"Verdict of the jury. We, the jury in the above entitled cause, find the above named defendant Huey P. Newton guilty of a felony, to wit, voluntary manslaughter, a violation of Section 192, Subdivision 1 of the Penal Code of the State of California, a lesser and included offense within the offense charged in the first count of the Indictment. David B. Harper, Foreman.

"The next verdict, with the title of the Court and cause the same: We, the jury in the above entitled cause, find the above named defendant Huey P. Newton not guilty of a felony, to wit, assault with a deadly weapon upon a police officer, a violation of Section 245B of the Penal Code of the State of California as charged in the second count of the Indictment. David B. Harper, Foreman.

"The following verdict, with the title of Court and cause the same: We, the jury in the above entitled cause, find that the charge of previous conviction as set forth in the Indictment is true. David B. Harper, Foreman."

Manslaughter, not murder. *That* was a surprise. But Garry and I were unhappy with such an equivocal decision. It meant the jury believed I had killed Officer Frey, but only after severe provocation, and in a state of passion. It was absurd, however, that they did not think I had also shot Officer Heanes. Did the jury think someone else had shot him, and if so, who, and how did the two shootings connect? The verdict was a compromise that showed no justice at all, for there was clearly a reasonable doubt about my guilt in the minds of some jurors, although they failed to bring about my exoneration. All these questions began to surface when I realized that although I would have to go to jail, I had escaped the gas chamber. Some people thought the verdict was better than a hung jury and a mistrial; the state could not try me again for first-degree murder. But I disagreed with them.

The verdict caused a lot of dissatisfaction in the Black community. Some people were particularly angry at David Harper, the jury foreman, who, to them, had sold out in typical Uncle Tom fashion. I did not think so. To counteract this opinion, I sent out a message to the community shortly after I had a chance to analyze the verdict. This, in part, was my statement:

> The question has been asked: What do I think of the verdict of the jury? I think the verdict reflected the racism that exists here in America, and that all Black people are subjected to. Some specific things I would like to say about certain people on the jury: first, Brother Harper and other members of the jury who believed in my innocence owed an obligation to me and the Black community to adhere to their convictions that I was not guilty. I am sure that they, the people on the jury who agreed with Brother Harper (a strong man and also jury foreman), were in the minority. I believe that Brother Harper was interested in doing the best thing for my welfare. I think that the verdict was a compromise verdict; a compromise between a first-degree murder and an acquittal or not guilty. Why did Brother Harper compromise? He compromised because he truly believed that it was in my best interest. Mr. Harper made his decision based on the assumption that if a hung jury resulted, I would be tried in the next trial by an all-white jury and possibly convicted of first-degree murder. I believe that he based his action or his decision upon the fact that he saw how racist the majority of the jury was acting, and their whole attitude toward the case. I believe that there were few people joining Brother Harper and his just conclusion that I was innocent, and that I am innocent, but he did compromise. Because Harper failed to persuade the jury, or he felt that he could not persuade them or show them the truth or the fact that I was innocent, he thought that he would then give the lowest possible sentence. He might have considered that I had been in jail for the last ten months and that I might be in jail for another ten months awaiting a new trial and then stand the possibility of having the first-degree conviction stand, simply because of the racism that exists here in America. These are all my speculations, and I will tell you why I speculate on these things later on while I have this conversation with you.
>
> Brother Harper, like many people, believes that on a manslaughter charge, you would spend maybe two years or three years at the most in the state penitentiary, and further, that due

to the fact that I have already been in jail for one year, that while waiting trial another year as a result of a hung jury, I would already serve that time and even more. So, therefore, because he couldn't get an acquittal, he then chose to compromise and get the lowest sentence. The only problem with that, though, is that in a political case, the defendant is subject to do the maximum length of time. The sentence on a manslaughter charge with a prior felony conviction is from two to fifteen years. But I don't believe that Brother Harper had any idea of what he was doing, so, therefore, I want to ask the Black community sincerely and Brother Harper's son to forgive not only him, but also the other people who believed in my innocence, and who were compromising because they did not know what they were doing. I believe that they thought they were doing the best thing in my interest, and the best thing in the interest of the Black community, under the racist circumstances wherein which they had to operate. . . .

Even though he was unknowingly operating against it, he felt that he was acting in the capacity of one who loves the community. Therefore, I am asking the community that in the event that he teaches at Oakland City College next semester, that he be given all respect due to a Black man because he did not know what he was compromising to. . . .

I am very sure . . . that we will get a new trial not because of the kindness that the appellate courts will show us, but because of the political pressure that we have applied to the establishment, and we will do this by organizing the community so that they can display their will. The will of the Black people must be done, and I would like to compliment the people on the revolutionary fervor that they have shown thus far. They have been very beautiful, and they have exceeded my expectations. Let us go on outdoing ourselves; a revolutionary man always transcends himself or otherwise he is not a revolutionary man, so we always do what we ask of ourselves or more than what we know we can do. . . . At this time I would like to admonish my revolutionary brothers and sisters to use restraint and that we would not show violent eruption at this time for the reason that the establishment would like to see violence occur in the community in order to have an excuse to send in 2,000 or 8,000 troops. The mayor has already stated that he would be very happy if something were to happen in the community while the establishment is in a favorable situation. They would like to wipe the community out. . . . It is up to the VANGUARD PARTY to protect the community and teach the community to protect itself, and therefore at this time we should admonish the community to use restraint and not to open ourselves for destruction.

I cautioned restraint to the people because I knew the police were eager for a chance to kill Black people indiscriminately. They had been waiting a long time for this day, and an angry eruption by the community would have given them the excuse they needed. The community responded to my request and stayed cool. Any spontaneous and unorganized outburst would have caused great suffering. With everything quiet the night after the decision came down, the police felt cheated; they wanted some action, and that meant killing Blacks.

Unable to find any provocation, two drunken colleagues of Frey created one. They drove in their police cars to our office on Grove Street and fired a shattering volley of bullets into the front window. Then they went to the corner, turned around, and came back, shooting into the office again. By this time, some citizens had called police headquarters, and the two policemen were apprehended.

Fortunately for us, the office was purposely empty, and no one in the streets or the buildings nearby was hit by the bullets. But if Black Panthers had been in the office, the police probably would have claimed that we had fired on them first, and then tried to wipe us out. This time, however, they could not hide their treachery behind their usual lie—"justifiable homicide." The true nature of their crime—an unprovoked and unjustified attack on our office—had been exposed before the community. The two policemen were eventually dismissed from the force, but they were never brought to trial for breaking the law.

But the incident should also help make it clear to doubters that I was in fact innocent. Just as Frey's two colleagues felt free to go in search of Black people to kill, so, too, did Frey in the early morning hours of October 28, 1967. There are many who do not believe that a police officer, without provocation or danger, would draw his service revolver and fire upon a citizen. But that morning Frey had murder on his mind.

Charles Garry summed it all up when he told the jury that the Black community is in constant danger from the violence of the police:

"I wonder how many people are going to die before we recognize the brotherhood of man. I wonder how many more people are going to die before the police departments of our nation, the mayors of our nation, the leaders of our nation recognize that you can't have a society that is 66 per cent white racist ignoring the role of the Black man, the brown man, the red man, and the yellow man. . . .

"Officer Frey bothers me. His death bothers me, and the things that caused his death bother me. I can see this young man going through high school, varsity football, basketball, and all the other things that young men do, in good physical condition. Joining the police department and without proper orientation, without proper attitudes and without proper psychological training and all the other training which is necessary to being a policeman. Being thrown into the ghetto. In a year's time he becomes a rank and outright racist to such a point that when he comes to class to talk about his success as a police officer, the schoolteacher has to cringe and grimace to let him know that the use of the word 'nigger' was not appropriate.

"I just wonder how many more Officer Freys there are. His death bothers me, but Huey Newton is not responsible for his death."

27

In my case I worked hard from sunup until sundown trying to make a living for my family an it ended up to mean death for me. . . . You take big people as the president governors judge their children will never have to suffer. . . . The penitentiary all over the United States are full of people ho was pore tried to work and have something couldnt dos that maid them steel and rob. They were looking for money they were. While they are in prison for life thats what happens to the poor people.

From the dying statement of Odell Waller, a laborer,
written before his execution in Virginia, 1940

The Penal Colony

After my conviction and sentencing I was sent once more to the Alameda County Jail until a hearing could be held to decide my fate—I would either be released on bail pending an appeal to the higher courts or sent away to serve the two-to-fifteen-year sentence. The hearing was held early in October and bail was denied. Immediately after, I was ordered into the custody of the California Correctional Authority for confinement. At this point I became aware of a curious power I held over the prison authorities. They were worried about the role I might play as a political prisoner, and orders had come down for special treatment.

After a hearing, a prisoner is usually taken back to his cell, where he changes from civilian clothes to prison dress before a bus trip to the prison of his confinement. But when my bail hearing ended, I was hustled to the elevator in my civilian clothes and then downstairs to a car waiting in the basement. It was as if they had known all along that my bail request would be denied. In the basement I found all my property from the cell packed and ready to go. Then handcuffs went on, and a chain around my waist attached to the shackles around my ankles, and I was considered secure enough to make the trip. The sheriff's car, escorted by six others, sped through a tunnel to the exit. Only then did a deputy turn back toward me, speaking through the grille, to say where we were going—Vacaville Medical Facility, a detention center, where prisoners spend sixty to ninety days being tested, classified, and assigned to various penitentiaries. The ride took about forty-five minutes, and when we got to Vacaville, officials were waiting for us outside the building; the whole place was surrounded by guards holding shotguns.

At Vacaville I went through a ritual familiar to every inmate—the skin search. From that time forward, through my years in jail, I was never allowed to go from one building to another without this demeaning exercise. I took off all my clothes. Then they looked into my ears and nose, rubbed their hands through my hair, made me cough to prove there was nothing in my mouth; then I spread the cheeks of my buttocks while they searched my anus. After that, I was fingerprinted, given prison clothes, and assigned a number that I was to keep for the duration of my time in the penitentiary system. Giving a prisoner a number is another way of undermining his identity, one more step in the dehumanization process. Of course, it has historical roots: the SS assigned numbers to prisoners in Nazi concentration camps during World War II.

All my civilian clothes except socks and underwear were sent home to my family. Socks and underwear are habitually thrown away in prisons. I was curious about this and asked them why, particularly since my shorts were new and had been worn only once; I pointed out to them that they were in better shape than the rest of my clothing. No one knew why; it was simply the rule, the tradition, that a prisoner could send all clothing home except socks and underwear. "We just follow the rules." I did not mind their throwing the shorts away, but I did resent not being given an explanation. This is a small point, but it demonstrates the mentality that exists on every level of prison administration. The administrators and guards who run prisons are like George Orwell's brutes in *1984* who are chosen as policemen on the basis of ignorance, physical strength, and their predisposition to follow orders without question, however stupid or brutal.

Next, I was assigned to an isolation cell, but before the lockup I went to see the warden. This is another special privilege. I always have a chat with the warden right away. He lectured me against any attempt to organize; if that happened, he said, I would be placed in an isolation cell. It struck me as ironic that even as he spoke an isolation cell stood waiting to receive me. Tactics like this add to the nightmarish unreality of prison. Then the warden began dangling the carrot: if I co-operated, I could be like any other prisoner, not locked up all the time. They were going to treat me tight at first, he said, to educate and orient the other prisoners to my presence, but if all went well, they would let me out into the general prison population—the "main line," it's called. I sat silent, listening; I would never taste that carrot.

Prison systems are fond of tests, all kinds, psychological, I.Q., aptitude. During my stay at Vacaville I was interviewed several times by two or three psychiatrists who ran a battery of aptitude and I.Q. tests on me. I scored low on the I.Q. tests, about the third or fourth grade; I don't know about scores on the others. Puzzled over these low scores in view of my good grades in college, the psychiatrists asked me about it. I explained to them that I refused to relate to these tests because they are routinely used as weapons against Black people in particular and minority groups and poor people generally. The tests are based on white middle-class standards, and when we score low on them, the results are used to justify the prejudice that we are inferior and unintelligent. Since we are taught to believe that the tests are infallible, they have become a self-fulfilling prophecy that cuts off our initiative and brainwashes us.

I told the psychiatrists that if they really wanted to know my I.Q. they ought to examine my background and the work I had done in many areas, including creative disciplines like music. This seemed perfectly logical and obvious to me, but the psychiatrists either could not understand or preferred to remain ignorant. Their approach was so mechanical, so lacking insight, that *they* appeared unintelligent to *me;* they refused to see that it is more important to judge a person by his accomplishments than by some abstract tests that may or may not correlate to the facts of his life. It has been my experience in prison that psychiatrists are among the most rigid and inflexible members of the staff. They are programmed and computerized like robots and cannot approach inmates as human beings. With their tests and questionnaires they seem to have a preconceived idea of what an "adjusted" human being is. Any deviation from this mold is a threat to them.

During this testing, the authorities puzzled over where to put me. There was much speculation in the prison about that, and through the grapevine I heard that they had some trouble deciding. They wanted, above all, an isolated prison, but because of the public attention my case had received, they also wanted one that would be viewed in a favorable light, a kind of showplace for visitors. That way they could keep up the charade that penitentiaries are rehabilitation centers rather than concentration camps.

The administration at Vacaville even went through the motions of asking my preference, although they had not the slightest intention of allowing me to choose. I gave San Quentin as my first preference, with Folsom and Soledad next in order. These three afforded relatively easy communication with the outside. As far as I am concerned, all prisons are concentration camps. One is little better or worse than another. My preferences were strictly based on the possibility of contact. San Quentin is close to home, only a thirty-minute drive from Oakland, and even less from San Francisco; there my family and attorneys would be able to visit me fairly easily. I also had friends in San Quentin who could keep me in touch with my attorneys, my family, and with the media. Folsom came second for pretty much the same reasons: it was only about eighty miles from the Bay Area, I knew some people there, and the commuting would not be too bad for my family. Soledad was the farthest away of the three prisons—approximately 165 miles south of Oakland on Highway 101—and therefore the least desirable.

As it turned out, I did not go to any of them. I was taken by surprise when, after only twenty-five days at Vacaville—I was expecting to stay the usual sixty—I received a slip saying I would be leaving within twenty-four hours for the California Men's Colony, East Facility, in San Luis Obispo. This time I traveled on a bus with other prisoners. Not that the prison officials had stopped treating me in a special way. For every prison bus a list is prepared of the prisoners who will be taking it and where they will be going. The bus I rode had everybody's name on the transportation list but mine. It came from Folsom, picked us up, and went on to San Quentin and then to another jail in San Jose. From San Jose we went to Soledad, where I spent the night in isolation. Brother George Jackson was near, but I never saw him. The friendly inmates on the bus gave me a rundown on the situation at the Penal Colony, so I was somewhat prepared when we arrived.

Although called a Men's Colony by the authorities, San Luis Obispo inmates know it as the California Penal Colony, which sums up what it is all about—a penal institution and a colonized situation. The state believes in the power of euphemism, that by putting a pleasant name on a concentration camp they can change its objective characteristics. Prisons are referred to as "correctional facilities" or "men's colonies," and so forth; to the name givers, prisoners become "clients," as if the state of California were some vast advertising agency. But we who are prisoners know the truth; we call them penitentiaries and jails and refer to ourselves as convicts and inmates. This does not mean that we accept these labels as bad, only that we refuse to be deceived by the state's duplicity.

The California Penal Colony stands approximately halfway between Oakland and Los Angeles, about 250 miles from each, and getting there involves a major trip from both cities. In addition to its remoteness, it is not typical of California prisons. Fewer than 10 per cent of the inmates are Black or Chicano, even though those two groups make up more than 50 per cent of the prison population in California. Since there have been no riots, the institution has a reputation as a model prison. The authorities like to claim a happy inmate population. Yet, once inside it, the reasons for its calm reputation are easy to understand. The Penal Colony is divided into four self-contained quadrants, each with approximately six hundred inmates. Its layout and organization make it almost impossible for an inmate in one section to meet the three-quarters of the population in other quadrants. In addition, and very important, 80 per cent of the prisoners were homosexual, and homosexuals are docile and subservient; they tend to obey prison regulations.

I did not know one person at the Penal Colony when I arrived. Eventually, I met other prisoners and tried to reach them, but I found it hard to politicize men who lived largely for the next sexual encounter. To them, sex was all.

These men were exploited and controlled by the guards and the system. Their sexuality was perverted into a pseudosexuality that was used to control and undermine their normal yearnings for dignity and freedom. The system was the pusher in this case, and the prisoners were forced to become addicted to sex. Love and vulnerability and tenderness were distorted into functions of power, competition, and control.

Homosexual love at the Penal Colony was routinely simple. Each inmate, except me, had a key to let himself in and out of his cell during the day. A date would be made at mealtime or in the shower and a "point man" stationed outside in the hall to warn of approaching guards. This last step was unnecessary. The guards were content to look the other way as long as things stayed cool. Only political action brought quick, repressive steps. The guards would simply threaten to put the political offender on a bus and send him away from his lover. These threats always worked. As a matter of fact, many guards were themselves homosexuals. Often, as I showered, a guard would stand in the doorway, talking, looking not at my face but at my penis, and say, "Hey, Newton, how you doin' there, Newton? Wanna have some fun, Newton?" I laughed at them.

The reign of homosexual life in prison has changed somewhat with the introduction of conjugal visits. Liberals see this as a step forward, but it is not. The same coercion and control are there, even more so, because guards can deny a man his woman just as they denied a man his man; but the inmate cannot easily find another woman. This is prison, where every desire is used against you.

Procedurally, the Penal Colony was Vacaville all over again. First I was taken to the warden, who told me that they would allow me to stay on the main line if I went along with all the rules and did not attempt to organize. He was also against complaints; if I wanted to complain, I ought to wait until I got out of prison. Again, I said nothing. I expected to be there for fifteen years. That is enough time to achieve a purpose.

After my meeting with the warden I was assigned to a counselor, who proposed that I go through a "rehabilitation program" to prepare me to return to society. I felt no need to be rehabilitated; my only crime was to speak in defense of the people. But the counselor went on describing the program. As the first step in my rehabilitation, he explained, I was to work in the prison dining hall at no salary. Eventually I would be able to move into a job in one of the various prison industries, where the salaries ranged from a minimum of three cents an hour to a maximum of ten cents an hour.

I absolutely refused to engage in such exploitation, working at first for no salary and then for wages so low they could not be considered as salary at all. Instead, I offered a counterproposal. I would work willingly but only for a just compensation—union-scale wages. If they paid me union wages, and paid the same wages to all inmates, I would then be willing to work in any kind of job they chose. Further, I would also pay the cost of my room and board so that I would not be an expense to the state, even though it had put me there illegitimately. The staff, predictably, refused to consider this proposal.

I then offered another alternative—that my rehabilitation program consist of attending school in the prison. Even though I had completed an education beyond the level offered there, I knew that an educational program would permit me free use of the library to go on developing my knowledge. They refused this, too, on the ground that the education programs were a privilege and that I had to earn them by first working in prison industry for an unspecified period of time. In other words, first the stick—a dehumanization that satisfied them—and then the

carrot—pursuit of my own interests. I refused again. Their demands were rooted in a lie anyway. I knew that other prisoners
had been permitted to start out with educational programs,
and I also knew they would not allow me to do so because they
wanted to break me. But I was not going to be broken.

So they placed me on lock-up. This means that I remained in
my cell for most of the day and received no canteen privileges.
The cells at the California Penal Colony each have three locks.
One is centrally controlled and is in operation only at night. It
goes on after the general lock-up with a loud clack that can be
heard all over the prison. We call it "dropping the bar." The
second lock is opened only by the guard's key, and the third
lock by a key that the inmate possesses. Each morning, after
"raising the bar" (taking off the centrally controlled lock), the
guard went by and unlocked each cell; the inmate was then free
for the rest of the day to leave or enter his cell with his own key.
Because I was on lock-up, the guard passed my cell by when he
came down the row in the morning. I was permitted out of my
cell only for meals, for visitors, or for official prison business
such as going before the disciplinary board. So I got out each
day only from seven to eight for breakfast, twelve to one for
lunch, and five to six-thirty for supper. During those times I
also had to change my clothes, take a shower, and do any other
necessary tasks.

In lock-up one is denied all privileges. I could make no pur-
chases from the canteen, no cigarettes, soap, deodorant, tooth
paste, and mouthwash. I had only a state toothbrush and institutional tooth powder. Each week I received six pieces of paper
on which to write letters to any of the ten people on my visiting
list. Although I received the San Francisco *Chronicle* in the
mail, always one day late, even this was refused from time to
time. At first I was permitted to have no other reading material
or to do any other writing, but eventually my attorneys ob-
tained a court order entitling me to a typewriter as well as
books and writing material related to my case. I continued to
exercise and practice control of my thoughts, which I had per-
fected by then.

Lock-up was their way of "punishing" me for refusing to accept slavery. The shops at the Penal Colony make shoes and license plates, and do the laundry of other institutions; for these services the Penal Colony is paid good rates. It follows that by paying almost no salary to inmates, the system is little more than slavery. Prison is one of the most outrageous forms of economic exploitation in existence, although prison authorities see the system in a different light. I looked upon lock-up not as punishment but as liberation from servitude. Once a month I was called before the disciplinary board and asked if I was ready to co-operate with them and come off lock-up. Every month I refused.

The guards thought I was fighting a losing battle, that I would not be able to stand it for long. I would eventually break, they said, so why waste away in solitary? Moreover, by resisting prison rules and regulations, I was simply extending my time to the full fifteen years.

The isolation of lock-up was bearable, really more than that. My brain was active; there were many things to think about, and I filled the days working out ideas I had begun to develop back in Oakland City College. Furthermore, my family was able to visit me often, despite the long drive. Rules allowed visitors every day of the week except Tuesday and Wednesday, which were designated as nonvisiting days. If my attorneys wanted to see me, they deliberately came on a nonvisiting day, and my family worked out a schedule whereby I had a visit on three or four other days; so between family, lawyers, and friends I was quite often in the visiting area from nine in the morning until four in the afternoon.

My family sustained me. I needed their warmth and the news they brought from the outside. Except for mealtimes, I was not permitted to talk with other prisoners, and the San Francisco *Chronicle* is a limited source of information. Rehabilitation never offered mental health, just the reverse. It involved communication only with the staff, who are not worth any contact at all. To listen to their philosophy or accept their outlook will destroy you.

One piece of tragic news reached me in bits and pieces. Early in 1969—January—when I had been in prison for about four months, two worthy Los Angeles comrades, John Huggins and Alprentice "Bunchy" Carter, were assassinated on the UCLA campus by members of Ron Karenga's organization, US. I had first met Karenga when I was involved in the Afro-American Association at Oakland City College. He later went to Los Angeles to establish his own cultural nationalist group, which was, for a while, quite successful, largely because the Los Angeles Police Department supported him in many of his ventures. Mayor Yorty even used the group as a show of progressivism. US was in fact an agency to keep the Black community under control; courses in Swahili and a kind of cultist philosophy were offered. Advertised as a program to free Blacks, Karenga's US in fact exploited them.

The Black Panthers were a real threat to Karenga's game. Karenga was afraid of the Party because we were not cultists but grass-roots organizers, and we had begun to attract people that he wanted in his organization. However, he had the support of Los Angeles' power structure, which he supported, even to the extent of all but endorsing Mayor Samuel Yorty over his Black opponent, William Bradley, in the 1969 primary for mayor.

Our serious problems with Karenga had begun in February, 1968, while I was in the Alameda County Jail awaiting trial and the Party was organizing rallies in Oakland and Los Angeles to raise funds for my legal defense. In an effort to unite with as many groups as possible and create a solid front, we had organized the Los Angeles rally through the Black Congress, a coalition of Black groups in the area. Karenga's group was a part of the Black Congress.

The Oakland rally took place on February 17, my birthday. Stokely Carmichael, H. Rap Brown, City Councilman Ron Dellums, Charles Garry, Bobby Seale, Eldridge Cleaver, and others participated. It was a successful event. The Los Angeles rally was scheduled for the Sports Arena the next day, with many of the same people on the platform plus several leaders of organizations in the Black Congress. When the planning party for the Black Panthers arrived shortly before the rally, they found that Karenga had co-opted the event, particularly by having the Los Angeles Police Department provide security. Cops were everywhere, inside and out. The Central Committee called Karenga immediately and told him that the Black Panthers were not coming into that auditorium unless the police left. A lot of Black people had come down from the Bay Area, and if something went wrong and they found out why the Black Panthers refused to show up, Karenga would have lost even more of his credibility. So he persuaded the police to leave the building, and the rally came off successfully.

We had agreed that a portion of the money contributed would go to members of the Black Congress to cover their expenses, and the rest to my defense fund, but when it was all over, despite several calls to Karenga to discuss the funds, the Black Panthers never got anything in Los Angeles for my defense—the reason people had come in the first place—and the Black Congress was jived, too.

Less than a year later, Bunchy and John were killed at a meeting of the UCLA Black Students Union on the Los Angeles campus. The meeting was held to discuss the appointment of a director for the Black Studies program at UCLA. Karenga had been trying to run the whole show, and a number of Black Panthers, including Bunchy and John—who were in the program—went to the meeting to offer some opposition. A group of Karenga's followers were there. When the Black Panthers were having lunch in the student cafeteria, Karenga's men sneaked up on Bunchy and John and assassinated them.

When news of this reached me in prison, I realized that all Black Panthers were marked men. The assassinations had started with the murder of Little Bobby Hutton by the Oakland police. When the Chicago police killed Fred Hampton and Mark Clark, many people throughout the country began to suspect that there was a national police conspiracy to wipe us out, and each new attack on the brothers confirmed this suspicion. This homicidal campaign caused my spirits to sink. It is very difficult to take the loss of valuable comrades and personal friends, even though we recognize death as a price we have to pay in a revolutionary struggle. You never get used to it.

Some of the comrades in the Party sent messages asking me to let them go after Karenga, but I refused to do this. Open warfare between us would only harm the community, whose needs came before our desire for revenge. In time I knew the community would deal with Karenga, and eventually it did: a community tribunal was held in Los Angeles, and it found him guilty of deceiving the people. He had to leave Los Angeles and move his operation to San Diego. Now his group has faded from the scene. Two of his followers were sentenced to life imprisonment for the murder of Bunchy and John.

Soon after this, a man named Robert Hall came from Los Angeles to see me. I do not know how he got in; only ten people were permitted to visit me, and Hall was not on my list. Neither was he one of my attorneys. Furthermore, he came on a nonvisiting day. After the guard came to my cell and told me I had a visitor, I tried to figure out all the way to the visiting room who would be coming to see me on a day when visitors were not allowed. I was not expecting any of my lawyers. When I got there, I was surprised to see a complete stranger. He told me he had come to see if there was anything he could do to end the friction between Karenga and the Black Panthers. He wanted to bring about a truce, he said. I did not trust him—he must have had official approval to be there—and I told him that if Karenga wanted a truce all he had to do was stop killing Black Panthers; we had never attacked any of his men. It was a short visit because I had nothing more to say, and I have never seen Hall again.

After I had been on lock-up for six months, the guards began to look for cracks, signs of submission; bets were made about when it would happen. I ignored the probing, which puzzled them even more. A guard approached me one day and said, "Most guys go nuts after a few weeks in solitary, and you've already gone six months. What is it? Don't you feel any sort of tension?" Others began to show concern for my mental and physical health. When this started, I knew I had mastered them the way I had mastered the soul breaker.

To express my contempt for their system I wrote an article called "Prison Where Is Thy Victory?," smuggled it out with visitors, and had it printed in the Black Panther newspaper. At the time, I still was not permitted writing material—this was before the court order—but I managed to write the essay and see that it reached the Party. In the article I taunted the guards for thinking that because a man's body is in prison they have won a victory over the ideas that inspired his actions. My purpose was to show contempt for my captors and also to encourage the courageous comrades who were continuing the struggle. I was very pleased when the article was published and the guards got the message.

Now, the prison administration changed tactics. Convinced at last that I would not bow down, they began to tell the other prisoners that the only reason for my perseverance was a mistaken belief that my conviction would be reversed by a higher court. In other words, they said only hope sustained me, and without this hope to cling to, I would collapse. But I had no more faith in the higher courts than I had in the lower courts, and I was prepared to stay in isolation for the entire fifteen years. This was something they consistently failed to understand.

Very few people in America have any deep perception of conditions and treatment in prisons for an obvious reason: the authorities, who have total control of the situation, see to it that the public is not told the truth. Prisoners cannot communicate freely and privately with the outside. Therefore, what most people know about prisons is what the authorities want them to hear. Millions of people were surprised and shocked by the assassination of Comrade George Jackson and the massacre at Attica because they do not understand how oppressive even the best prisons are.

I have often pondered the similarity between prison experience and the slave experience of Black people. Both systems involve exploitation: the slave received no compensation for the wealth he produced, and the prisoner is expected to produce marketable goods for what amounts to no compensation. Slavery and prison life share a complete lack of freedom of movement. The power of those in authority is total, and they expect deference from those under their domination. Just as in the days of slavery, constant surveillance and observation are part of

prison experience, and if inmates develop meaningful and revolutionary friendships among themselves, these ties are broken
by institutional transfers, just as the slavemaster broke up families. In my own experience, a number of inmates who refused
to follow orders and stay away from me during mealtimes were
transferred for "institutional convenience." It is generally recognized that a system of slavery is degrading for the master and
slave alike. This applies to prison, too. The atmosphere of fear
has a distorting effect on the lives of everyone there—from
commissioners and superintendents to prisoners in solitary
confinement. Nowhere is this more evident than among "correctional officers," as the guards are euphemistically called.

Prison guards are pathetic figures. I had very little contact
with them because I stayed in my cell so much, but they harassed me every chance they got. When I went out to see visitors, they searched my cell, sometimes senselessly tearing it up,
throwing my washcloth on the floor, dumping my toothbrush
in the toilet, and creating a general disorder. If they ever found
items from the canteen, such as deodorant or hair oil, they
would write me up for having "contraband" in my cell, a violation of prison regulations. They took great pleasure in these
petty harassments, and after a time I developed a wry attitude,
seeing it for what it was—the childish behavior of small men.

Once I got a "beef" and went to the hole. I went without a
struggle. Since I was already in isolation, being in the hole
meant only that I ate my meals in my cell instead of the prison
dining room. It was the easiest solitary confinement I ever
pulled because I was allowed to have reading material there.
Most of the books were old and juvenile—Rin-Tin-Tin, Hop-
along Cassidy, and the like—but I also got hold of the Bible,
which I love, and which I read through again, for the third
time. Unlike the soul breaker, my cell contained a bunk, toilet,
washbasin, chair, and tin desk.

The guards never gave up their effort to keep me in a constant state of rage, but I recognized their limitations and avoided
their assaults, either by refusing to communicate with them or
not doing what they wanted.

Obviously the guards are victims, too, but the fact that they have a limited and very crude kind of power tends to corrupt and brutalize them. Some of them perceive dimly how blighted their lives are and try to compensate in pathetic ways. For instance, when the student disturbances broke out at the University of California at Santa Barbara in the spring of 1970, the Penal Colony dispatched members of the "goon squad" to assist in putting down the rebellion. When the guards returned, they were full of tales about how they had jailed professors and smart rich kids. This made them feel important, bigger than real life, and when they were not talking about revolutionaries as if they were dogs, they boasted about the fine motels they had stayed in while beating up members of the university community and the opulent meals they had eaten in "Sambo's" restaurant. In lives so empty and bereft of meaning, events like this were highlights.

One of the evils the guards were guilty of was promoting racial animosity in prison, using it to divide us. Many white inmates are not outright racists when they get to prison, but the staff soon turns them in that direction. While the guards do not want racial hostility to erupt into violence between inmates, they do want hostility kept high enough to prevent any unity. This is something like the strategy used by southern politicians to pit poor whites against poor Blacks. Unfortunately, many Black inmates, caught up in this madness for reasons of sheer survival, are goaded by the guards into turning against the white inmates, or the "Nazis," as they call themselves. In this situation the guards are the oppressors, and the "Nazis" are the tools of that oppression. Most degrading, the whites are not only duped and used by the prison staff, but come to love their oppressors. Their dehumanization is so thorough that they admire and identify with those who deprive them of their humanity. This kind of psychological aberration was so frequent in Nazi concentration camps that its rationale has been a major intellectual question for thirty years. One theory is that the prisoners were reduced to such a state of infantile dependence upon their keepers that they were acting out a kind of grotesque child-parent situation with them, believing that identification with their oppressors was their only hope of survival. A prison situation of this sort is both tragic and explosive.

Racial hostility, however, is only one reason for inmate resentment and rebellion. Most Blacks are now more aware of the political than the criminal nature of their incarceration. They have learned to see themselves as political prisoners in the classic, colonial sense: they were not tried before juries of their peers or a cross-section of the community, but by juries wholly unfamiliar with any aspect of their lives. Many activities defined by the ruling class as criminal are the acts of poor and exploited people, desperate people, who have no access to the channels of opportunity. And the juries deciding their fate are made up of privileged middle- and upper-class citizens who are threatened by the fact that a man who is shut out of the privileged structure can create his own opportunities. The jury is incompetent to judge the accused; it does not understand the circumstances that brought on his actions. Jurors in America are not peers; they are a part of the system of oppression. As a result, the poor end up in penitentiaries as political prisoners. They have every reason to feel bitter, especially when it is plain to see how leniently these juries handle accused persons of their own class, if indeed they are ever brought to trial.

There is a process of self-enlightenment that operates among inmates, a process that moves far beyond the level desired by the authorities. A "rehabilitated" prisoner may see the "incorrect" nature of his past actions. He may even see that the assault or robbery, or whatever, was a "mistake." But he comes to see that "mistake" in a particular light. Many prisoners reach this point and fly past it to a deeper and broader assessment. They begin to assess society and see that their "crimes" were in part a result of a capitalist and exploitative society. Frequently, they become socialists, recognizing that capitalism has given birth to the murderous twins: imperialism and racism. These enlightened and politically conscious prisoners arrive at convictions that the authorities find unacceptable and threatening. Even though inmates at this point may have no intention of ever committing crimes again, they are held in prison for a longer time because of their new opinions rather than because of their prior activities. When they appear before parole boards, they are questioned not about the past but about their views of contemporary social issues. If they are honest and tell the truth, they are denied parole. They were sent to prison for what they did, but they are kept in prison for what they believe. These are political prisoners. George Jackson and Booker T. Lewis are two well-known examples, among thousands less visible.

Another type of political prisoner is the one who has committed no crime at all, but who holds political attitudes and beliefs that threaten the privileged status of the ruling circle in the United States. Among them are many gallant warriors of the Black Panther Party who want justice for all men and an end to the oppression of the lumpenproletariat. They are given long sentences on flimsy charges. Such injustices are clearly deliberate attempts to strangle the freedom struggles of peace-loving people.

I was such a political prisoner, but this did not discourage me during my twenty-two months in the Penal Colony; I knew that a political consciousness was growing among people both in and out of prison. I could see it when I talked with other inmates at mealtimes; we got into heavy raps about the situation in this country. It was obvious in the growing movement outside the prison—among students, welfare recipients, hospital employees, and community workers, to name only a few. This confidence lay behind my ability to withstand the oppression. They could lock up my body but not my spirit; that was with the people. The spirit of revolution will continue to grow within the prisons. I look forward to the time when all inmates will offer greater resistance by refusing to work as I did. Such a simple move would bring the machinery of the penal system to a halt.

Though the guards eventually realized that I would never break under their harassment, other members of the prison staff could not accept my resistance. They kept probing for weaknesses. In the spring of 1970, prior to my first parole hearing, I was summoned to the prison psychiatrist for an evaluation. From the minute I entered his office I made my position clear. I told him that I had no faith or confidence in psychiatric tests because they were not designed to relate to the culture of poor and oppressed people. I was willing to talk with him, I said, but I would not submit to any testing. As we talked, he started running games on me. For instance, in the midst of our conversation he would try to sneak in psychological questions such as "Do you feel people are persecuting you?" Each time he did this I told him I would not submit to any sort of testing, and if he persisted I was going to leave the room. The psychiatrist insisted that I had a bias against psychological testing. He was correct. In response to this I showed him flaws in the psychological systems of Freud, Jung, Skinner, and others that made these systems inapplicable to Black people. When he asked me whether there was any psychological system that I could trust, I told him I accepted the theories of Frantz Fanon. He had never heard of him, so I suggested some books by Fanon that he could read, and left.

Their psychological warfare got them nowhere. My counselor, a man named Topper, held a preboard hearing with me and tried to get me to come off lock-up; I refused. Topper had told me earlier that he was glad I was on lock-up and he wanted me to stay there, but in the preboard hearing he switched his tactics and strongly hinted that if I came off lock-up I would almost certainly be given a parole date by the board. I knew this was not true. He probably reasoned that if I came off lock-up and the board did not give me a parole date then I would lose status in the eyes of the other inmates. This was very important to the prison, because it would undermine my position. On the other hand, they could work out their strategy from another angle. I could have been given a date if I remained on lock-up. Then they could say that a date for my release had been established but they would not be able to honor it because I refused to co-operate with them. This would make the public think that I was blocking my own release. They were trying to steal my only weapon against them—my dignity.

I knew from other sources that Deputy Superintendent McCarthy had told people that he thought my demand for a minimum wage in prison was reasonable. Yet neither he nor

Topper had the courage to state their feelings publicly. Like so many other administrators they went along with the system. It just took too much courage to take a stand for prisoners' rights. They were unimaginative, mediocre, and fearful men. It was no coincidence that they had chosen to work in prisons; they blended right in with the grey dullness and impersonality of institutional life.

I finally went before the parole board in April, 1970, and even though I did not expect anything from them I looked forward to the chance for debate and the opportunity to show my contempt for their system. Seven or eight board members sat with me around a table, talking casually and drinking coffee. One of the first things they asked me about were the violation reports in my folder, which said I had contraband in my cell. I asked them if they knew what the nature of the contraband was, and it turned out they had not looked closely enough to see. When they read the violation reports in full, they were surprised to find that the so-called contraband was soap, deodorant, and toilet articles from the canteen, which had been passed on to me by other inmates. I told them I refused to do without certain basic amenities and that I would continue to obtain them. They ordered the guards to allow toilet articles in my cell. This was a small but sweet victory.

Then we got into the heavy things—the reasons for my refusal to work, et cetera. I was ready for them. But when I gave my explanation, they replied that I wanted to pick and choose the rules I would obey and that this was a very arbitrary attitude. I responded by expressing a total lack of faith in the penal system and the parole board and let them know that I did not expect parole then or any other time. I told them I was willing to obey rules I disagreed with, but I would never obey rules that denied my dignity as a human being. Furthermore, I urged them to disobey those rules that violated *their* integrity and dignity. One of the board members, a Negro, was so shocked that he expressed doubt about my sanity. This is a good example of the mentality controlling prisons across the land, one so narrow that it regards human dignity and strength of character as abnormal.

After that hearing I resolved never to go before a parole hearing again, even though my attorneys advised against this decision.

The prisons definitely need to be transformed, but this cannot be accomplished in a vacuum or by random incidents. Prisons are an integral part of a complex whole that can be defined as the American institutional superstructure of the world. I say the world because the United States is an empire, not a nation, and the way prisoners and minorities are treated here has a definite relation to the way the American power structure treats people around the world. The world must become a place in which poor and oppressed people can live in peace and with dignity. If we still need prisons after that transformation, they must be true rehabilitation centers rather than concentration camps. In the new society the centers would not be called prisons or penal institutions and they would not be ancient rock fortresses in inaccessible areas. They would be an important part of the community, in which people who are not well or who are unhappy would still be made to feel that they are part of humanity. Most of the men in prison have been made to feel superfluous from birth. James Baldwin has pointed out that the United States does not know what to do with its Black population now that they "are no longer a source of wealth, are no longer to be bought and sold and bred, like cattle." This country especially does not know what to do with its young Black men. "It is not at all accidental," he says, "that the jails and the army and the needle claim so many. . . ."

Many now recognize that most of the people in prisons do not belong there. When they can be motivated to believe that they have something to offer society, something desperately needed, which only they can contribute, then there will be no need for prisons. But each man must first be convinced of his own value and uniqueness, and that this uniqueness is his, and his only, to give to others. That is what true rehabilitation means.

All the time I was at San Luis Obispo, Charles Garry and his staff were working to appeal my conviction before the California Court of Appeals. Their proceeding was based on a num-

ber of improper maneuvers that had been used by the prosecution
in their determination to convict me. Among them were: the
grand jury, as well as the trial jury, was illegally tainted with racism; my previous conviction of felony should have been struck;
the evidence for a first-degree murder conviction was not sufficient; the prosecution suppressed material evidence, and the
trial judge failed to reopen the trial when it was discovered; the
trial judge contributed to the highly charged atmosphere and
made many prejudicial rulings; the judge had failed to give the
jury an important instruction. My attorneys followed the appeal process closely and kept me advised of every step, but I
took little notice, having no faith in the court system. They had
kept me in jail without bail for almost a year while awaiting
trial. Then, after the conviction, they denied me bail pending
an appeal. Even when we appealed the decision denying bail,
we were given no consideration. I could find no reason to hope
that the state would reverse my conviction. As far as I was concerned, I would pull fifteen years in the penitentiary, and pull it
in isolation.

Fay Stender, who had worked with Charles Garry on my defense, sent word in May of 1970 that a decision would be issued shortly; she did not know what it would be, of course, but
apparently the court had written a very long opinion. Usually,
in the case of a public figure, a long opinion means a denial because the court wants to show the public that they have given
careful consideration to every point of view. So Fay sent word
to expect a denial. Another attorney, Alex Hoffmann, held the
opposite view. He argued with Fay that a long opinion could
mean a reversal; the court might want to show very carefully
that the reversal was based on legal technicalities rather than
upon the weight of public opinion—which in my case was felt
by the courts and the correctional system. I sided with Fay and
gave the appeal no more attention. I had other things to con-
centrate on.

And so, when the reversal of my conviction by the California
Appellate Court was announced on Friday, May 29, it came as
a complete surprise. I had spent the day in the visiting room,
hearing nothing, and about four-thirty I was on my way back

to my cell when a prisoner stopped me and said that he had heard on his radio that my conviction had been reversed. I did not believe him, and he could scarcely believe it himself, so I asked him to recheck. When I got back to the quad, the guard in charge of my tier got red-faced when he saw me. He said nothing, just turned the color of fresh-cooked lobster and fumbled with his key while locking me in my cell. Only then did I begin to suspect that something good had happened.

Outside in the yard, beneath my window, I heard a great commotion; a group of prisoners were gathered there, throwing up rocks and clapping hands. They were so happy and excited that I began to feel optimistic, too. Prisoners are not allowed to congregate in groups of more than two in the prison yard, but these men were defying the rule. When the guards approached them, the inmates took their identification cards and threw them on the ground in violation of a regulation that requires inmates to surrender their identification cards to guards on demand. After they had thrown them in the dirt, they stood their ground without moving; the guards kept at a distance and did not advance.

The prison officials were upset by the reversal and angry at the inmates for demonstrating in my support. They tried everything they could think of to dampen the enthusiasm that spread throughout the jail, but their efforts were unsuccessful. The only mention of my reversal ever made to me by prison officials was the question of how I could possibly be released before the new trial since bail was rumored to be set at $200,000.

The reversal by the Appellate Court was based on Judge Friedman's incomplete instructions to the jury. He had told the jury that I could be found guilty of murder in the first degree, murder in the second degree, manslaughter, or I could be found not guilty. But he neglected to tell the jury that there were two possibilities within the manslaughter category: voluntary or involuntary. Voluntary would mean that the jury felt I had acted in the heat of passion and after severe provocation, but that I had killed the policeman. This was the verdict that the jury did return. There was also a possibility of involuntary manslaughter, which would mean I had been unconscious at the time as a result of shock and loss of blood, but that I acted without being aware of what I was doing. The judge did not give this instruction to the jury, even though we had introduced expert testimony showing that the wound I received and the subsequent loss of blood—verified by hospital records—was consistent with the possibility of neurogenic shock. Therefore, the Appellate Court ruled that since the jury had not been given all the possibilities for reaching a verdict, my conviction was to be reversed and I would have to stand trial once more. But I could not be tried for murder again, only manslaughter. If the jury had found me guilty of involuntary manslaughter, the court could not have imposed a jail sentence on me.

Even though I had to wait ninety days for the decision to become final, I began immediately to make plans for my departure. Needless to say, I was eager to get out, but also apprehensive about what my life would be like when I returned to Oakland. I felt I would not be ready to plunge back into things until I had a chance to look around and get a picture of the entire situation. I had been off the block for almost three years.

My departure from the California Penal Colony seems like a dream now. Psychologically I had prepared myself for a longer stay, and my freedom seemed a lucky extension of life, a chance to accomplish more than I had expected. I wanted to get the Black Panthers back on the right track, taking action that could be done only in conjunction with my comrades and the Central Committee.

Early in August word came from my attorneys that I would be getting out soon, since I had a bail hearing coming up on August 5, a Wednesday. The Friday before, I spent packing my things in case they decided to move me over the weekend, but nothing happened. Then, on Monday, I went through the whole release process, but I did not leave that day either. No one, including the warden, seemed to know exactly what was going on; he asked me to tell him what time I was leaving and on what date. I guess he thought I had some special word from my attorney, because, according to him, the Alameda County sheriff's department would not tell him how I was going to be transported, or when. There was some legal entanglement; even though my conviction had been reversed, the California Appellate Court had given the state attorney general a thirty-day extension to appeal their decision. So technically my fate was still in the California Appellate Court's hands, and I could not be removed until those thirty days were up. However, Charles Garry worked out an arrangement with the attorney general to get me released. The attorney general did not want too much of a fight because public opinion was in my favor, and people would want to know why I had to sit there for another thirty days after all their legal maneuvers had been exhausted. I was in limbo.

That Monday, August 3, I was all checked out and ready to go. I had been having interviews constantly with a number of television and newspaper reporters who had come to see me. All day long I walked around the joint, going from the yard up to the visiting room for interviews and then back to my cell. A rumor circulated that I was supposed to leave at twelve noon. The inmates were very excited. Every time I went for an interview they would say, "Well, he's gone; I saw him get into a car." Then I would show up again in the yard, and they would be let down because I was spoiling the rumors. Then they would ask me again, "When are you leaving? Why do you keep starting to leave?" Finally, just to stop the questions, I told them I was not leaving until the end of the week.

Privately, I was pretty sure that the Alameda County sheriff's department would want me to leave in secret and therefore would probably come to get me very late at night. That was why they had not given the warden any definite time; they did not want to wade through the thirty or forty reporters standing outside the gate. I told only a few friends that I might leave late that night. I was particularly close with one inmate at San Luis Obispo. He was happy that I was getting out, but he was also depressed because another friend had just left a few days before. Now I was leaving, and he would be pretty much alone. He had done a long time in prison and had no definite idea of when he would be getting out. Most inmates who pull a long time become somewhat introverted and stay in their cells most of the time.

On that final day I went back to the visiting room after dinner and was interviewed until about 9:30; then I returned to
the yard for the general lock-up at 10:00 P.M. While I stood
outside talking to several inmates, a guard came out and saw
me. He knew I was supposed to be back in my cell, but he just
said, "Well, you don't have to lock up." I had never been given
a break before, and I thought that was pretty strange, but since
only about thirty minutes remained before general lock-up, I
decided that they were overlooking an infraction this once, and
I went on talking with my friends. About ten minutes later, five
or six guards, the "Red Squad"—a roving group of guards assigned to watch subversives—appeared in the yard and came
over to me, saying, "You know we have to lock you up." It was
an obvious setup. They were resentful because I was leaving
and were looking for trouble at the last minute. My friends encouraged me to resist them by refusing to go to my cell, but I
knew if I started a fight, they would be involved, too. I did not
mind a fight—I was leaving—but my friends had to stay. I did
not want them to be subjected to further prison discipline,
maybe a delay in their parole dates, or even a new beef against
them. Besides, general lock-up time was near, so we had little to
gain from a fight. I went to my cell after saying a few more
words to them. The guards were true to form right up to the
end. They could not get in the last blow—that would be mine
when I walked through those gates—but they got in as many
licks as they could.

The day had been extremely tiring, so sleep came quickly. It
seemed as if I had been sleeping only a few minutes, although
it was actually 2:30 A.M., when the guards opened the door
and told me to "roll it up." I had turned in all my prison clothes
except underwear, pants, shirt, and my own shoes. I put them
on. The cop asked me if I had a jacket—it was pretty chilly
out—but I had turned it in. When I came out of the cell block
into the yard, it felt cold, but nonetheless refreshing, a kind of
misty chill. As I walked out into the cool night air, I realized
that never again, or at least not for a long time, would I take
that walk from my cell to the central area where processing is
done. I went through the strip search again, taking everything

off, and having my mouth, ears, nose, and anus probed. They searched my pockets. There was little I wanted to take out of that prison, but the ritual proceeded as usual. Then I was given release clothes—a pair of khaki pants and a khaki shirt—but they kept my jail underwear and socks. I signed my release papers, and next I was taken to another room to await the arrival of the men from the sheriff's department. One guard was stationed in the room with me, and he tried to start a conversation. He told me about his record collection and his elaborate stereo component and multiplex system. Then he talked about how he had been a brawler when he was young and how his nose had been broken over and over again. When he had first started work at the penitentiary, he said, he used to get into a lot of fights with inmates, but he found out later that it was better to call other cops before the convicts got out of line and jumped him. Why he attempted this conversation is hard to figure out, but I guess he was trying to let me know that he realized he could no longer consider me his inferior. Since our convict-guard relationship had changed, he wanted me to know that he was a human being with certain thoughts and feelings. He even offered me a cigarette, but I told him I did not smoke. Then he went into a long monologue about how he almost got cancer from smoking, that he had had pleurisy and had caught it just in time. He went on and on, mostly talking to himself.

Guards are odd people. It is incomprehensible to me how a person can endure such a meaningless life day after day, year after year, and seem to be satisfied with it. Their main concerns are dull and petty, centered around retirement, lawns, fishing, hi-fi sets. This guard was near retirement. People like him are really lost, as so many people are, without a purpose in life or the ability to relate to others.

Finally, at 3:30, I was told the sheriff's men had arrived. I took my two boxes of legal material—they were all I could carry—and started down the hallway, the guard following resentfully with my typewriter and another small box. When I got a short distance from the room, the warden and his assistant met me and wished me luck on my release. It was like a scene from Kafka or Genêt's *The Balcony*—normal and logical on the surface but nightmarish and phantasmagorical in essence. It had the quality of a symbolic ritual; no one was truly involved or affected. We simply went through the motions.

I walked through the visiting room and out the open gates, the first time I had gone through them; I had arrived by bus the back way. Then we walked down the stairs and toward the main gate of the prison—the last barrier. As we approached, the electric gate buzzed and ground open. This made the whole scene even more unreal because no one could be seen opening the gates; they simply parted when we stepped toward them. Two deputy sheriffs in plain clothes were waiting beside two uniformed guards from the Penal Colony. The cops greeted one another; they were old buddies. I signed some final papers confirming that I had all my property, and once more I was in the control of the Alameda County sheriff's department.

PART SIX

There is an old African saying, "I am we." If you met an African in ancient times and asked him who he was, he would reply, "I am we." This is revolutionary suicide: I, we, all of us are the one and the multitude.

28

What turns me cold in all this experience is the certainty that thousands of innocent victims are in jail today because they had neither money, experience nor friends to help them. The eyes of the world were on our trial despite the desperate effort of press and radio to suppress the facts and cloud the real issues; the courage and money of friends and of strangers who dared stand for a principle freed me; but God only knows how many who were as innocent as I and my colleagues are today in hell. They daily stagger out of prison doors, embittered, vengeful, hopeless, ruined. And of this army of the wronged, the proportion of Negroes is frightful. We protect and defend sensational cases where Negroes are involved. But the great mass of arrested or accused black folk have no defense. There is desperate need of nationwide organizations to oppose this national racket of railroading to jails and chain gangs the poor, friendless and black.

The Autobiography of W. E. B. Du Bois

Release

There was no time to feel relief, let alone an illusion of freedom once I had come through the gates. Before I got my bearings, one of the deputy sheriffs came over to me. "We're going to have to shackle you," he said. I did not reply. They put chains around my waist and under my crotch; two chains went from my waist to each wrist and another from one hand to the other. Then they shackled my ankles and ran a chain from my crotch to the chains on my ankles. Finally, they put a six-inch chain from one ankle to the other, so that I had to shuffle when I walked. I could barely move my arms. The police carried my boxes, while I shuffled about twenty-five yards to an unmarked car. I got in and tried to find a comfortable position. It was not easy.

The two deputies got in front. While one of them was start-ing the engine, the other one said, "Wait a minute, I have to get my equalizer out of the trunk." I glanced back as he was com-ing around the car and saw him putting what looked like a snub-nosed .38 revolver in his belt. With his gun and me in chains, I guess we were equal.

I had not been in an automobile for twenty-two months, and it felt strange to be speeding down the highway at eighty miles an hour. We passed a large sign saying "Huey Road," which pointed off to the right. I had seen it on the bus coming to the Penal Colony, and I remember telling the other inmates, "The last time they saw Huey he was tearing up Huey Road at high speed." This time I passed it without imagining myself taking off up that little dirt road.

The deputies talked to each other about how stupid it was of President Nixon to make the statement about Charles Manson the day before.* I agreed with them about Nixon's stupidity. It did not surprise me to learn that he had made a remark that vi-olated the ethics and principles of the legal profession. Nixon is a man who should never stray from his speech writer's notes, because every time he does, he sticks his foot in his mouth. Now there was the possibility that Manson would have to be given a new trial.

The deputies asked me what I thought my bail would be. I told them I had no idea. They guessed somewhere between

---

*On August 3, President Nixon, speaking in Denver, Colorado, on the theme of law and order, mentioned the trial of Charles Manson and three women co-defendants in Los Angeles, that was then under way. They were being tried for the August 7, 1969, murders of Sharon Tate, a film actress, and six friends who were visiting her at her home in Benedict Canyon, Los Angeles. President Nixon said that Manson "was guilty directly or indirectly of eight or nine murders without reason." Because of the nationwide consternation over his remark, President Nixon, a lawyer, immediately issued a statement saying that "he did not intend to speculate as to whether the Tate defendants are guilty, in fact, or not. . . . Defendants should be presumed to be innocent."

$100,000 and $200,000 and went on speculating about the amount and whether I would get out or not. I assured them that I would be released immediately, even with a bail of a million dollars, because the people would not stand for my remaining in jail. They agreed that I probably would be released. I was always arrogant with policemen. If you take any other attitude with them, they interpret it as weakness, because they assume an innate superiority over you. When they stopped at a little truck café in King City to get coffee and doughnuts, they asked me if I wanted any, and I said no. Later they asked me where H. Rap Brown was; again, I had no idea. I cannot imagine why they asked me since I certainly would not have told them even if I had known.

Coming up on Salinas we passed Soledad State Prison, eerie in the early morning light. They grey walls loomed up—silent and ominous—in the half light. I thought of all my brothers in there, and George Jackson. It was weird and unsettling to be such a short distance from them—without their having the slightest awareness of it. But they were probably asleep at that hour. The deputies said they were glad they did not work at Soledad because of the militancy of the prisoners and the constant trouble and upheaval. They talked about different prisons in the state and asked me about the Penal Colony. I described the layout and physical facilities, which are probably better than any other penitentiary in the state, with the exception of Chino. Chino has far better facilities—a swimming pool and golf course—and prisoners are allowed to wear their own clothes. Also, security is less strict. The Penal Colony is only about ten years old, so it is also cleaner than most. But all prisons are the same; an inmate has to live in a space ten by seven and a half feet, with a toilet, washbasin, desk, chair, bunk, and concrete floor, no matter where he is. When you are locked in a room like that day after day, it does not matter where you are. The deputies admitted that there seemed to be no answer to the problems of prisons, that they just do not work. Conjugal visits for prisoners would help, they seemed to think, the way it worked in Mexico, despite the poor physical facilities

and conditions. I pointed out that since 80 per cent of the inmates in the Penal Colony were homosexuals, it probably
would not make much difference there.

They talked for a while about Mexico, how nice it is there in
the summer and how beautiful the parks and buildings are,
particularly in Mexico City. But one of them said that every
time he goes to a Latin country, even Mexico, he is afraid a guy
like Castro will take over and kidnap all the Americans and not
let them return to the United States. I assured him that even if
someone like Castro came to power, he would probably pay
the cop's trip back on the fastest plane. This is what is done in
Cuba: flights for counterrevolutionaries leave frequently. Fidel's
policy is that anyone who wants to should get out immediately.
Even Cuban nationals—members of the bourgeoisie—are allowed to leave, and most of them now live in Miami, so many,
in fact, that it is called Little Havana. Cops are generally unin-
formed and politically naïve, but on the subject of socialism, they
are especially ignorant.

It was beginning to get light as we drove through Gilroy,
thirty-three miles south of San Jose, about 5:30 A.M. All the
way back to Oakland, I could not take my eyes off the passing
landscape, yet my impressions were hazy, partly because we
drove so fast, but mainly because it was just too much for me
to take in. It was the sensation of being heavily bombarded
with a variety of stimuli. Most people take these stimuli for
granted, but after two years in a restricted and monotonous
environment, it is impossible to absorb what you see. We passed
houses, fields, farm laborers, animals, and all sorts of sights
grown dim in my memory. The mountains in the distance, the
sky, the movements of life—I wanted them all at once, but I
could not handle it. It disturbed me.

Shortly after Gilroy, we stopped at a gas station to fill up,
and the driver asked me if I wanted to go to the bathroom; I
said no, and he ambled around the side of the station while the
other cop stayed with me. The attendant was a young kid who
did not seem to know his way around cars. After he started the
gas, he opened the front door of the car with the comment that
the lights were on. When he hit the button to cut them, the cop

became very tense, but the boy did not notice anything inside. Then he went to the front to check the water and oil. He opened the hood about the same time the other cop came out of the bathroom, and, turning to the cop, he said, "What's this?," indicating something under the hood. When the cop told him it was a siren, the boy turned bright red, quickly closed the hood, and went around to finish the gas. Then he kind of peeked in the car, and when he saw my chains, he got even more flustered. When we pulled off, I watched him out of the rear window, standing there in amazement.

We ran into some commuter traffic around San Jose, nothing too bad, and finally, about 7:00 A.M., arrived in Oakland. The streets were still deserted. I noticed immediately how many things had changed; there were buildings I had never seen before. We went by the construction site of the new Bay Area Rapid Transit building and the new museum that had been going up while I awaited trial. During those eleven months I used to watch its day-to-day progress from the county jail. The deputies named the new buildings, telling me about them and trying to be friendly in their own way. When they indulged in small talk of a pleasant kind and asked me questions, I did not hesitate to answer them. Not that it brought us closer—nothing so superficial will do that—but it is the easiest way to keep the situation cool. As a matter of fact, I recommend this kind of behavior; no matter what is going through a person's mind, it is always to his advantage to keep the enemy off balance.

As we drove through the Oakland streets, the deputies talked to the police at the county jail and told them we were coming into the courthouse through the tunnel. The answer was to use the front entrance because the elevator was tied up. We swung around to the front of the building, right across from the Lake Merritt Park, where Little Bobby Hutton's rally was held after his funeral in 1968. It brought back memories—for the better part of a year, from the window of the county jail, I had watched the park and the people walking in it.

Now, a few people were on the street. How colorful their clothes seemed. This is what I mean by being bombarded with an overwhelming amount of stimuli all at once. I could not get a clear impression of any one thing; everything tended to blur and become indistinct. The whole experience was devastating. Where I had been for thirty-three months everyone wore the same clothes, did the same things, and went to the same place every day. You never wondered where people were going or what they were doing. On any day all you expected to happen was what had happened the day before, and the day before that. In my first few days outside jail I had to make an attempt to remain calm, to keep the action and unpredictability from exciting my nervous system. Even the sight of ordinary activities, such as cars stopping for traffic lights, some going in one direction, some in another, people in the street, was too much.

When we stopped in front of the jail, the shackles were removed from my legs, although the chains on my waist and arms were left on. The people carried my baggage while I walked through the front door. A cop had come down to meet us from the jail on the tenth floor. His face was familiar. Unless we had a run-in, the cops do not make much of an impression on me; they just come and go, locking me up or letting me out, and that is all there is to it. But this cop's face was too familiar to pass off; I tried to recall what kind of run-in I had had with him.

When we got on the elevator, this one had a kind of chicken smile on his face. "Well, are you going to get your old suite back?" he asked. "I don't know," I answered, "but I can do time any place in this jail. That's what I did before, and I can do it now, particularly since I will probably be out in a few hours." "Yeah, I guess so," he replied. "You think you'll make bail? How much do you think it will be? A couple of hundred thousand, maybe five hundred thousand?" The same old question. "I'll be out in two hours," I said. "Well, it really helps to be rich, eh, Newton?" "Maybe it does," I shot back, "but I'm not rich. The people will sacrifice whatever is necessary and get me out." He changed the subject then. "You've gotten big; you must be working out."

My mind was not on the conversation. I was still trying to place him, but I said, "Yeah, I worked out every day." He said, "Yeah, that's what I should have been doing." He had trouble saying that. Suddenly, I remembered him. He had gotten pretty fat, but he was the same policeman I had had a run-in with in solitary. One night during my trial, about 1:00 A.M., this fellow came around to take the count with a Black policeman. I was half asleep. He opened my door quickly, then, starting to close it, he asked, "Did I wake you up, you asshole?" I jumped up. The door was locked, but I guess I woke up half the jail shouting at him, calling him everything except a child of God and inviting him back to open the door so he could show what kind of a man he was.

While I was yelling, the Black policeman with him started to laugh as they walked down the hall. I do not know whether he was laughing at me or at his partner. Some of the other inmates who were awake thought he was laughing out of desperation. The other policeman would not come back; he was much too cowardly. The next day, when I went to court, the Black cop was still on duty—he must have been pulling two shifts that day—and I asked him the white cop's name. He said that he thought we knew each other and were just kidding. I told him that he knew very well I did not kid around with any of them, including himself. The only relationship we had was that of prisoner-guard—nothing else. I did not appreciate the other guard's remarks, I said, and I was definitely going to bring it up in court. The Black cop said that if I brought it up in court, he would feel compelled to testify on my behalf and say that I was right and the cop was wrong. He had not said anything at the time, he repeated, because he thought we played together all the time. He promised to tell the other cop about my reaction, and after I reminded him that I did not play with any of them, he said no more about it. It did not come up in court, and I never learned whether the Black cop would have testified for me.

All this was racing through my mind as we rode up in the elevator. Once off the elevator, we walked into the bullpen, the waiting area of the jail. The shackles were taken off my hands and waist, and I was stripped and searched again. After I put my clothes back on, we went through the long booking and processing procedure. Then I was assigned to a cell in B tank, which is the receiving and reception tank.

Right around the corner, about fifteen feet away, was the

hospital tank, where inmates are kept in semi-isolation. It holds only about five guys, and inmates who have minor illnesses are kept there, but never for very long. Most of the men who come there are either from Death Row at San Quentin or on their way to Death Row and awaiting sentence after conviction of first-degree murder. The regular tanks in the county jail all adjoin a dayroom outside the cells. Inmates are taken out of their cells at seven in the morning and locked up again at seven at night, spending the entire twelve hours in between in the dayroom. They have no access to their bunks during the day. But in the hospital tank the inmates can go back and forth to their cells whenever they please. The men on their way to Death Row are put in this tank because many of them need ready access to the legal material in their cells. They can also keep typewriters in the hospital tank, another taboo in the regular tanks. The hospital tank is called "Little Death Row" by the inmates, because prisoners there are either from Death Row, fighting some part of their case, or they are on reversal prior to retrial. Most of the inmates from Alameda County on Death Row at Quentin went through this hospital tank at some point. I had been there on Little Death Row myself, for four months, while I was in the county jail serving time for the Odell Lee assault case. I had gotten to know a number of guys there then.

Within an hour, I was back in touch with inmates I had met there thirty-three months before. During the interval, some had gone away and come back again to jail on new beefs. One of them was a young guy called "Nice Man." Nice Man had gained weight, too, since I had last seen him. He was a big one—six feet, three inches and 230 pounds—very articulate and bright but not well educated because he had spent most of his young life inside jails. But nobody was better at survival on the block. This time he was in for bank robbery or kidnaping—I'm not sure which. Of his twenty-two years, eleven had been spent in various juvenile halls—Tracy and Soledad.

I asked the inmates about another friend, McPherson. He was a white guy I became pretty close to when we did time together in Little Death Row before he had been sent on to Death Row at Quentin; I had heard something about a reversal, and it turned out to be true. McPherson was in the hospital tank, right around the corner, so I yelled out to him. He was happy to hear my voice, and we cut up about old times for a while. When I asked him about his case, he told me he expected to draw another death penalty. He had been convicted again of first-degree murder, and he was going through his penalty phase* starting the next week.

McPherson has only one eye. He lost the other one at Santa Rita prison before he was charged with murder. In isolation, where no one was allowed to talk to him, McPherson went out of his mind and stuck a pencil in his eye. The guard said that when McPherson put this pencil in his eye, he fell out, shouting, "I killed Goscher." Goscher was a German engineer whom McPherson was accused and convicted of killing. But McPherson got a reversal because the Appellate Court ruled him insane at the time of the statement. They ruled that even if he had made the statement, it could not be used against him as a confession. At the new trial they convicted him all over again when his cousin, who at first had been charged with the murder, took on a wheeler-dealer attorney for himself, got immunity from the prosecution, and then testified against McPherson. The cousin admitted participating in the murder but testified that McPherson did the killing, and no amount of denial could save McPherson. His cousin never did any time.

About 10:00 A.M. two of my attorneys came to discuss bail, which they thought would probably be about $100,000. They were trying to get me released on my own recognizance, but the outcome was uncertain. The district attorney seemed very indulgent and co-operative, which would have been surprising under any circumstances but was particularly unexpected now, because the district attorney was Lowell Jensen the prosecutor in my trial; he had succeeded Frank Coakley as district attorney of Alameda County. We puzzled over this new attitude and decided that Jensen knew bail in my case was inevitable; there-

---

*In California, defendants facing the death penalty are given two trials. The first trial is to determine guilt. If found guilty of first-degree murder, they must stand trial again, with the same jury, to decide what sentence will be given. The penalty phase is the time between the two trials.

fore, he was being co-operative to show his "fairness." Defeat would have been a strike against him, and bail was mandatory anyway, since I could no longer be tried for a capital offense. But how much would it cost? My attorneys had gone first to court, and the judge had sent them to the district attorney. When they tried that, Jensen had told them to see the judge; they were just passing the buck back and forth. But, finally, when the district attorney was notified that the buck stopped with him, he resigned himself to it.

My lawyers pointed out that I had never jumped bail and had always appeared in court on time. Jensen said he believed that I would show up in court, so there was no question of not granting bail. While he did not want to upset the Black community by setting bail too high, he also did not want to make his friends angry by setting it too low. As far as Jensen was concerned, justice had nothing to do with the procedure, only politics. My attorneys reminded him that in cases like mine, where a person has a reputation for showing up in court, bail is usually never higher than $5,000. Although Jensen agreed, he said he would have to set a higher bail because I had already been convicted, because of the seriousness of the matter, and because Eldridge Cleaver had jumped bail.* My lawyers said we would agree to something like $10,000, although they felt that amount was too high. These negotiations took place in the district attorney's office on Tuesday morning, August 4, and I

---

*After the April 6, 1968, ambush of the Black Panthers by the police, in which Bobby Hutton died, Eldridge Cleaver was sent to Vacaville prison by the California Adult Authority for parole violation and other charges. He remained there for two months. Charles Garry petitioned for a writ of habeas corpus in the court of Solano County Superior Court Judge Raymond Sherwin, who reversed the Adult Authority order on September 27, 1968. Judge Sherwin noted that Cleaver's parole had been revoked without hearing and that no proof had been supplied to support the charges brought against him. Cleaver was released on $50,000 bail, and the Adult Authority immediately began moves to have Judge Sherwin's ruling reversed by the California Appellate Court. Both the Appellate Court and the State Superior Court agreed with the Adult Authority's decision to revoke parole, and Cleaver was ordered returned to jail on November 27, 1968. He failed to appear and fled first to Cuba, and later to Algeria.

was scheduled to appear in court the next day, Wednesday. While they talked, I waited in jail, and my attorneys reported from time to time.

Meanwhile, nothing much had changed at Alameda County Jail. Poor food, dirty cells, harassment by guards, and a hundred other human indignities were routine. Nice Man and I had a good discussion about the Black Panther Party. He was a tank trusty with more freedom than the rest.

One of Nice Man's duties was to pass out food to the rest of the prisoners at mealtimes; for this he got an extra sandwich and coffee. Every day around 6:00 P.M. the police escorted the trusties bringing the food from the kitchen to the tank, and Nice Man passed it out in the dayroom. That Tuesday, just twelve hours after I arrived, a number of the inmates were inside their cells; I do not know why, maybe they were not feeling well. This meant that the cop was supposed to open the gate to each cell so the trusty could give the prisoner his food. Otherwise, the trusty would have to slide the tray under the door. There is an excellent reason not to slide the trays. The bars of the cells are filthy, and if a tray of food is slid under, crud is likely to fall into it. More than two years before this, when I was first in the Alameda County Jail, a grand jury had toured the jail, and one of their recommendations had been that no food was to pass underneath the door. When Nice Man asked the guard to open up, the cop refused and told Nice Man to slide the tray underneath. Nice Man refused, explaining why.

At this point, the cop went into an irrelevant diatribe, telling Nice Man if he acted like a man he would treat him like a man. Nice Man said that he did not want to be treated like a man; he wanted to be treated like a convict, and in turn he would treat the cop like a policeman. Nice Man is an interesting person to watch in tense situations because he moves when he means things, and now he was making little movements with his arms and legs. The argument went back and forth for some time. Finally, Nice Man slid the food underneath the door, but the argument continued. I tried to get Nice Man to cool it. I know what happens in situations like that; when you are locked down, there is no win. And while you have to defend some principles all the way, others do not infringe upon basic rights, and it is best to go along until conditions are more favorable. In other words, it is hard to win, and most of the time you lose. Before going too far, you should be sure that the principle is worth your life.

Now it escalated. Every time the cop said something, Nice Man replied. Sliding the food under the door was no longer the subject; it was just an angry argument heavy with insults. I tried again to get Nice Man to stop arguing, but he would not. He just stood there at the door to the tank, going back and forth with the cop, moving and twitching. Everyone else was eating quietly and watching.

Abruptly, the cop left; I told Nice Man about the grand jury finding years before. He was absolutely right, I said, but he ought either to do something or not do it, but not argue about it. He should just let the chips fall where they may, because arguing would not get anything down.

Ten minutes later, when all was cool again, the cop came back and ordered Nice Man to "roll it up"—he was going to the hole. Nice Man flew into a rage; he was not going, and the cop went away for reinforcements. In the county jail every prisoner has a wooden box where he keeps his possessions. As soon as the cop left, Nice Man got his box out, jumped on it, and broke off a piece of wood about four feet long and two inches thick; then he stood there waiting for the onslaught.

The cop who had provoked this incident was Black, and now he came striding back with six of his white colleagues. The seven of them opened the gates, ordered everybody else to roll into the cells, and told Nice Man to come with them to the hole. Nice Man stood silently, clutching his club. Impasse. Had we rolled into our cells, Nice Man would have been left alone in the dayroom with them. Everyone looked at me. I did not move; nobody else did either. If I had moved, it would have been to go down with Nice Man, since he was a friend of mine and 100 per cent right. In wondering why the other inmates did not roll in, it finally dawned on me that I was the reason. So we stood frozen, the cops with their long clubs and their Mace, the inmates watching, and Nice Man with his broken box.

This kind of unified action is unusual among inmates in jail. I have been in a number of uprisings at the Alameda County Jail, and each time there was always a split between the guys who would ease back into their cells and those who were willing to defy the guards. This time the prisoners were solid—white, Black, and Chicano. Finally, two cops convinced Nice Man to come out, and I went over to the bars to intervene and asked the policeman if I could speak with him. He said no, and another cop shouted out, "If no one will roll in, do you guys know what this means? This is a riot—an insurrection—disobeying orders. You have one last chance." Still no one moved. Then the other cop turned to me and said, "Newton, did you have something to say to me?" I went back to the bars and spoke to him in a low voice, telling him that he was wrong because he had provoked the whole thing. It was a matter of saving face now, I said, and Nice Man also had to save face and not be intimidated. They could both save face by a compromise: I would try to convince Nice Man to move to another tank with the same facilities as B tank. In this way, they would still be in authority, but Nice Man would not be punished, which was best, because he had been right all along. If they would not accept this plan, trouble was certain. Since I was going to court to be released the next day, I really did not want a battle, but I had made up my mind to be involved if it was forced on me. I was not going to let them take Nice Man to the hole without a fight.

While I talked, the police gathered around and listened. Finally, they accepted the plan and promised they would not jump Nice Man once he came out of his cell and that they would not put him in the hole. Then I went over to Nice Man and explained the plan to him. At first he refused, then reluctantly agreed to go out, dropping his weapon inside his cell and walking down the hall with the guards close behind. We listened for scuffling but heard nothing.

About fifteen minutes after the incident, this same Black cop came back and ordered everyone to roll in. Then, after the inmates were locked up, he called me to the bars and informed me that I would be isolated the next day. When I asked him why, he cited the incident. Was he saying that I was responsible for the incident, I asked. No, he said; my presence was the reason the prisoners would not roll in when ordered and the reason they resisted as one group. I told him that I doubted that I was the cause of their united action. The prisoners showed their solidarity because they were tired of being mistreated and pushed around. As for me, I went on to say, I could do time anywhere, including the hole, because I did not have long to stay. "So move me wherever you want to," I told him. "There is no argument whatsoever." Then I added that he did not have to wait until the next day; I could go right away because I wanted to get situated at once and be comfortable. I do not like to move once I get settled in a cell. He began to excuse himself, saying, "It's not my fault; it's already on the movement sheet that you have to be isolated anyway. You can wait for the next shift to isolate you in the morning." But I told him no explanation was necessary; they could move me right away.

Actually, the hole was a bluff. They had me scheduled to go to Little Death Row, around the corner, and took me there that night. When I arrived, I found my friend McPherson and two other guys, one of them a brother with a murder beef on him, who was a real psych case. He should not have been in a jail but in a hospital, or, rather, in good hands, because the hospitals are no good. He was obsessed with his earlier time in a hospital, where they filled him with poison and gave him shock treatments. Back in a hospital he felt sure he would die.

He had earlier killed a guy on the street who approached him the wrong way and put his hands on him, a violation of the code on the block. For people like that he explained that he kept a sharp knife, sitting on his porch, sharpening his knife with a stone all day long, watching to make sure that no pervert messed with the little girls in his neighborhood. The new murder beef went like this: one day as he sat in a restaurant talking to a lady friend, some guy rushed up and poked his finger on his chest saying, "Don't talk to my woman." When the guy did that, the brother slit his throat. He did not want to be in jail, and he feared returning to the hospital. As far as the hospital was concerned, he was right to be fearful, but he did need help; he should not have been in jail.

The other white guy had been on Death Row in Quentin for a few years before his reversal. He was preparing to go to trial again. McPherson, the fourth guy, was my old friend, convicted again, and waiting for sentencing. He thought he had little chance of escaping Big Death Row.

Little Death Row was a depressing experience. When I had been there before, I was facing the gas chamber, too, and felt more a part of it. We were all in the same thing, McPherson, myself, and another guy who is now on Big Death Row. Back then, I had accepted Little Death Row as a thing to be dealt with. But now I would be on the streets in a few hours while the others might never walk out. Knowing I could do little for them left me feeling like an outsider, and also privileged, and I never like to feel privileged. But they all wished me luck. I bedded down for the night with these things going around in my mind, knowing that it was the last night I would spend in jail for some time. It had been a long day, and I rested well.

The next morning I had to be in court at 9:15. My attorneys came early, and we talked for a short time until I was herded into an elevator with so many other inmates we could hardly breathe. They were all interested in my case, and knowing that I would be out soon, asked me questions and tried to find out if I would do errands for them and other favors. On the fifth floor we were placed in holding cells while we waited for the court session to begin. My name was called first. As I entered the packed courtroom, the first people I saw were Charles Garry, Fay Stender, and Barney Dreyfus at the attorneys' table. Behind them were my family and friends and quite a few reporters I had come to know over the past two years.

Going into the packed courtroom and seeing the reporters on one side, my family, friends, and spectators on the other was like a flashback to the same scene two years before. The whole thing seemed to be starting over again. It reminded me of a line from Kafka's *The Trial* that I think of when events seem to be repeating themselves. When K., the hero of the novel, is about to be executed, he says ". . . at the beginning of my case I wanted it to finish, and at the end of it [I] wanted it to begin again." At first K. is bothered by the confusion of going through the court system—the slow wheels of justice or injustice, the questioning, the stifling routine. It is a slow, draining process, which K. equates with the absurd toil and the endless striving of life. I felt the same emotions—wanting the absurdities and the eternal toil to end. Then, at the end, I was not quite ready for it to be over, and felt a vague desire for it to start all over again. Two years were obliterated. The judge sat in the same seat as if he had never moved from it; the attorneys stood at the same table. Perhaps the two years had only been a nightmare between days in court, and now I had awakened, to go through the trial again and again, in a vicious circle.

Then, with a surge of happiness at seeing my old friends in the spectator section, I realized that it was really over. It had been worth it—the perseverance, the hanging on, the not ever giving up. Now I could return to them with my head high because I had not let them down. And they, on their part, had not let me down; together we had endured and prevailed over the ordeal without letting it change us in essential ways. That was my feeling. Suddenly, the bad dream of thirty-three months seemed insignificant.

The district attorney had promised to come up with a "happy medium" regarding bail. His happy medium turned out to be $50,000, and when he recommended this amount to the judge, it was accepted. This was a high and unjust sum. Who has that kind of money? I knew it would be a hardship for the people to raise that much cash. The judge did not show any courage, either, by lowering the bail—or even raising it. He went right along with the recommendation, so it was really the district attorney who set bail. This is the kind of "justice" dealt out to the people. The defense attorney is also an officer of the court and is supposedly on the same footing as the district attorney. But the district attorney has many more privileges because he represents the established order—the powerful and the rich—who see to it that he is backed up and supported. The defense attorney merely represents the people.

After my bail was set, I returned to the holding cell. The inmates waiting to go to court offered congratulations all around,

happy that I would soon be free. Then I was taken back upstairs, where I sat with my attorneys in the lawyers' room and
discussed the bail situation. We had raised some money, but
not enough, and they were in favor of getting it from a bail
bondsman, but I was against this idea. Rather than come out
right away, I wanted to stay in jail until all the bail had been
raised. This was important. A bail bondsman fee was about
$5,000, and I felt that if all the money could be raised without
him, that $5,000 was better spent for community programs.

Argument was intense. The attorneys and all my brothers
said it was more important that I hit the street right away, to
give the movement a positive jolt. I argued that the Party has
always discouraged putting up 10 per cent bond for other comrades. Policy has been to stay in jail until the whole amount
was raised, so that the Party recovered the whole amount. In
the first four years of the Party we had been forced to raise several million dollars in bail around the country; if the 10 per
cent that had gone to pay bail bondsman fees had been chan-
neled into community programs, we would have been better
off. To me it was a matter of principle to stay in jail, but I was
overruled. In the end, it all came to nothing anyway. No bail
bondsman had an insurance company that would let him put
up the money. We had to raise it all.

I did not return to my cell, but remained in the attorneys'
room. I was hungry now. On leaving the Penal Colony, I had
resolved not to eat until I was free. I simply fasted. In some respects Alameda County Jail had changed. It did not seem as
dirty as it once had been, but the food was still unacceptable.
Also, everyone washes his own tray in a five-gallon bucket of
water, and with thirty guys washing in one bucket, the water
gets really slimy. Part of my resolution to fast had to do with the
lack of sanitary methods of cleaning the utensils. It is a miracle
that everyone does not come down with dysentery—or worse.

While we were waiting, my lawyer noticed a group of police
leaving the building with boxes of clubs. "They must be about
to release you," he said. "They're going out with clubs." After
this, some prisoners passed through the room, a couple of

brothers out of the tank. I gave them the power sign, and they returned it.

A few moments later, one of the sheriff's deputies came in to ask me to go directly across the street upon my release in order to avoid a confrontation with the police. A crowd had gathered outside in anticipation of a rally to be held at Lake Merritt Park as soon as I got out. The people were blocking the street, he said, and in the interest of the court they would have to clear it. He had a big, sneaky smile on his face. I looked into his cold blue eyes and told him I would leave the jail, and that was it. Then my attorneys signed some papers, and I went back to my cell to pick up my paraphernalia and bid all the inmates good-bye. I had to do this quickly, because again I felt guilty over my good fortune while so many of them would have to go without freedom for a long time—perhaps even until the climax of the revolution. My only consoling thought was that perhaps after my release I could do something to hasten that event.

My lawyers took my boxes, and I went to the gate and walked out of the jail on the tenth floor. Ahead, along the hall, was a solid wall of newspapermen and TV reporters, cameras and lights. Everyone was yelling, asking questions, demanding answers. I tried to make my way to the elevator with my brothers Walter, Jr., Melvin, David Hilliard, and a couple of Black Panthers clearing the way. We managed to get in the elevator, but at the last minute, with a desperate lunge, reporters crowded in with us. We started down, but the overloaded elevator stopped cold, just below the fourth floor. We walked the rest of the way down the stairs.

On the first floor we made our way out to the main entrance on Lake Merritt Park. It was a bright, blue-sky day, just the kind of day I had wanted. Looking ahead, I could see thousands of beautiful people and a sea of hands, all of them waving. When I gave them the power sign, the hands shot up in reply and everyone started to cheer. God, it was good. I felt this tremendous sense of release, of liberation, like taking off your shirt on a hot day and feeling free, unbound by anything. Later, I did take my shirt off, but it was obvious now that we would not be able to get out the front door. A mass of cheering supporters stretched from the steps all the way across the street into the park. I had to fight back the tears. It was wonderful to be out, but even more exhilarating to see the concern and emotion of the people. The crush was so overwhelming that we turned back and went to the other exit. But the people quickly ran around to the other side, and as we went down the stairs and into the street they surged around us, shouting joyfully, carrying us along.

My sisters Leola, Doris, and Myrtle ran up to me, and we embraced. Fay Stender, Alex Hoffman, and Edward Keating were in front of me, while Charles Garry was swamped by newsmen. My brothers Melvin and Walter were there, David and Pat Hilliard, Masai Hewitt, the Minister of Education, and many Black Panther comrades. It was almost a stampede. I could not walk; I felt I was suffocating, but it did not matter. In the euphoria I just held on to my relatives, friends, and comrades, and was dragged along, my feet hardly touching the ground. It was a beautiful day.

When we finally got to the car, we could not move it because of the crush. The only way to clear the area was to climb up on top of the car. First I asked them to clear the street, but they demanded that I say something. I was going to make a speech and hold an impromptu rally right then and there, but from my vantage point I could see the police edging toward the crowd with their clubs, shields, and helmets. They were itching to move in. Since it is against Party principles to encourage mass confrontations with the police if it can be avoided, I just said a few words and asked them to clear the street. They still would not leave, but demanded more, so I told them to go to Bobby Hutton Memorial Park, where we would hold a rally. At that, the people broke for their cars, which was fortunate, since it slowed the cops down. Now we had to do something. I had lied to get the people out of there and away from the police. No rally was scheduled for Bobby Hutton Memorial Park, and I sent a brother to the park to tell them we could not come there that day for security reasons. Everyone—my lawyers included—

advised me not to show up unprotected at big gatherings like
this. It was just an open invitation for some maniac to take a
shot at me. There was still so much feeling about the case in
Oakland that we decided to wait for cooler times before I appeared at mass gatherings.

I wanted to go directly home, but my brothers and sisters
thought it would be too much of a shock for my father, who was
not well and unable to sustain high emotion. My mother was
in the hospital. She knew nothing of my release, but Melvin
and the others figured she could handle it better than my father.
Before I saw her, however, I went to a friend's house, got out of
my prison clothes, and went to a news conference at Charles
Garry's office. The news conference was unusual. Because it included a lot of movement people I had come to like over the
months in jail, it was anything but the kind of cool encounter I
usually have with the regular news media. A question would
come at me, and when I started to answer I would suddenly realize that this was a person I wanted to rap with personally.
This happened over and over again with people there that day.
Some of the Establishment press came, but it was 90 per cent
underground press. At this press conference I offered Black Panther troops to the National Liberation Front of the People's Republic of Vietnam.

When we left the news conference, I went to the hospital to
see my mother. It was a joyous reunion. Later, when my father
and I met, he was deeply moved, and wept. He told me he had
not expected to live long enough to see me freed from prison.

During the first few days out of jail, I wondered when reality
would come again—in relation to myself, to the world around
me, to all that was happening to me. I had literally forgotten
how to live outside.

I had to develop all over again my old reflex actions to avoid
being startled or puzzled by certain phenomena. People who
have never served time in prison do not realize that a large percentage of their behavior is a conditioned response involving
no reasoning process. They instinctively react in the right way
because they are used to the familiar patterns in their lives. Social stimuli and social forces do not baffle them.

Cut off from all of this for a few years, life around me at first seemed jerky and out of synchronization. All the sounds, movements, and colors coming on simultaneously—television, telephone, radio, people talking, coming and going, doorbells and phones, ringing—were dizzying at first. Ordinary life seemed hectic and chaotic, and quite overwhelming. I even had to figure out what to eat and what time I was going to bed. In prison, all this had been decided for me.

Walking through the streets was an indescribable experience, the closest I have ever felt to being truly free, with people walking by, recognizing me, and waving. I went everywhere, visiting people in the community, to the surprise of many who never expected to see me on the street, only on television or maybe in Hollywood after I was released. But I was determined to get back among them. I walked in Oakland, Berkeley, Richmond, and San Francisco. I went to Seventh Street, Sacramento Avenue, Potrero Hill, Hunter's Point, Richmond, North Richmond, West Oakland, Peralta Street, Cypress Street, East Oakland, and Parchester Village. I visited several bars, where I had done a lot of recruiting. And everywhere I got the same reaction: people wondered why I had come back to them. I explained that neither news reporters nor television cameras had got me out of prison; the people had freed me, and I had come back to thank them and be with them.

At Father Earl Neil's church, St. Augustine's, I talked to members of his congregation. That, too, was a warm experience. Father Neil is a young Black Episcopal priest who has worked with the Black community and the Party since coming to Oakland. We consider him our chaplain. He was involved in civil rights in Mississippi in the early 1960's, and he knows all about brutality and violence. During my trial he came often to the courtroom to lend his support.

Although people received me warmly, I was at first a symbol. Our relationship had changed. There was now an element of hero worship that had not existed before I got busted. But I wanted our rapport to get back to where it was before I went to jail, that is, a relationship based on face-to-face communication between people working together for survival. I think their

faith and trust in me was restored, although perhaps it will
never be the same again: the earlier close family tie has been
enlarged by an image of me created through publicity and the
media. So much had been written, so much said, that I was dis-
tanced from them; there was a slight estrangement. It would be
overcome.

All this time I was under immense pressure to give interviews, to fill speaking engagements, to appear on talk shows
and television programs, but I accepted none of these for about
six months. I even received a brochure from some Hollywood
outfit. It contained newspaper clippings about me and a letter
saying. "You're star quality," or something like that, which
would have been amusing had it not been such an overt capitalist attempt to co-opt the revolution. Too many so-called leaders
of the movement have been made into celebrities and their revolutionary fervor destroyed by mass media. They become Hollywood objects and lose identification with the real issues. The
task is to transform society; only the people can do that—not
heroes, not celebrities, not stars. A star's place is in Hollywood;
the revolutionary's place is in the community with the people.
A studio is a place where fiction is made, but the Black Panther
Party is out to create nonfiction. We are making revolution.

29

People who come out of prison can build up the country.
Misfortune is a test of people's fidelity.
Those who protest at injustice are people of true merit.
When the prison-doors are opened, the real dragon will fly out.

HO CHI MINH, "Word-Play II," *Prison Diary*

Rebuilding

Back on the street, I quickly became involved again in the life-and-death issues that govern existence in the Black community. The most important task before us was to free Bobby Seale and Ericka Huggins, who were in jail in Connecticut awaiting trial on first-degree murder charges.* Bobby and Ericka should never have spent one day in jail for the ridiculous charges concerning Alex Rackley. It was all part of an Establishment plot to push Bobby into a death sentence or a jail cell, which they had been trying to do ever since the Party was formed. After failing in Sacramento and Chicago, the Establishment made its most serious attempt with the murder charge in Connecticut. Strong and effective counteractions were needed to defeat it.

---

*Ericka Huggins (the widow of Black Panther John Huggins), along with eight other Black Panthers, including Bobby Seale, George Sams, Warren Kimbro, and Lonnie McLucas, was charged with murder and conspiracy to commit murder in the killing of a New York Black Panther, Alex Rackley, on May 21, 1969. Sams and Kimbro pleaded guilty to murder in the second degree of Rackley and were sentenced to life imprisonment; McLucas was found guilty of conspiracy to commit murder and was given a prison term of twelve to fifteen years. The trial of Ericka Huggins and Bobby Seale, which was held separately, ended in a hung jury, and the state declined to try them again, dismissing all charges.

Then there were the Soledad Brothers—Comrades George Jackson, Fleeta Drumgo, and John Cluchette—who were nearing trial for their lives on a trumped-up charge of murdering a prison guard. The Party had provided the initial funds and support to get their defense committee in operation, and we were working hard to give them greater support. We were also helping the defense of Los Siete de la Raza, the seven Chicanos who were awaiting trial in San Francisco on charges of killing a police officer. My own pending case seemed insignificant compared with the pressures the Establishment was bringing to bear on our noble warriors. I was facing only thirteen more years in jail, but my comrades, every one of them, faced death.

A number of other Party matters also required action. When I got out of prison in August, 1970, it was less than a month before the preliminary session of the Revolutionary Constitutional Convention to be held in Philadelphia over the Labor Day weekend. The second session was scheduled for Thanksgiving weekend in Washington, D.C. It had been Eldridge Cleaver's idea to hold these conventions. I was never enthusiastic about them, but because the Central Committee of the Party went along with Eldridge, I followed their direction. The purpose of the conventions was to discuss the plight of Black people and to write a new Constitution for the United States. I could not see much point in spending time and effort writing a Constitution when we had no power to implement it. Eldridge was then in Algeria, and we spoke by telephone about this on several occasions; I pushed the point of view that our most urgent commitment was to build a strong base of community support behind Bobby and Ericka, as well as the Soledad Brothers. Eldridge expressed some agreement with me, and toward this goal we arranged for Kathleen Cleaver, who had great drawing power, to return and speak at the Washington session. My address at the Philadelphia rally would be my first major public appearance since being released. People were expecting a lot of me, and I worked hard on the speech.

In the meantime, the Philadelphia police were determined to prevent the conference from taking place. A few days before it was scheduled to begin, they raided the Black Panther Party headquarters and arrested most of the comrades. In a strong show of unity, the community came together within hours, reopened the offices, handled the telephones, and went ahead with arrangements for the conference. This community support was living proof that we can never bring about the revolution without the people.

On the other hand, I was disturbed by much of what I saw at the Philadelphia session. I tried in my speech to make some contribution to the people's understanding and the advancement of their consciousness. What I wanted to show was that Black people and other minorities in this country had been betrayed by the American Constitution, the legal foundation of government. I stressed that the United States of America came into being at a time when the nation comprised a narrow strip of land on the eastern seaboard and whose population was small and homogeneous both racially and culturally. The economic system then was different, too—essentially agricultural. A small population and fertile land meant that people were able to advance according to their motivation and ability. In this way, democratic capitalism flourished in the new nation. Then I went on to say:

> The following years were to see this new nation rapidly develop into a multilimbed giant. The new nation acquired land and spread from a narrow strip on the eastern seaboard to cover almost the entire continent. The new nation acquired a population to fill this newly acquired land. This population was drawn from the continents of Africa, Asia, Europe, and South America. Thus a nation conceived by homogeneous people of a small number and in a small area grew into a nation of a heterogeneous people, comprising a large number and spread across an entire continent. This change in the fundamental characteristics of the nation and its people substantially changed the nature of American society. Furthermore, the social changes were marked by economic changes. A rural and agricultural economy became an urban and industrialized economy, as farming was replaced by manufacturing. The democratic capitalism of our early days became caught up in a relentless drive to obtain profits until the

selfish motivation for profit eclipsed the unselfish principles of democracy. Thus 200 years later we have an overdeveloped economy which is so infused with the need for profit that we have replaced *democratic capitalism with bureaucratic capitalism.* The free opportunity of all men to pursue their economic ends has been replaced by constraints (confinement) placed upon Americans by the large corporations which control and direct our economy. They have sought to increase their profits at the expense of the people, and particularly at the expense of the racial and ethnic minorities. . . .

We find evidence for majority freedom and minority oppression in the fact that even while the early settlers were proclaiming their freedom, they were deliberately and systematically depriving Africans of their freedom. . . .

Generation after generation of the majority group have been born, they have worked, and they have seen the fruits of their labors in the life, liberty, and happiness of their children and grandchildren. Generation after generation of Black people in America have been born, they have worked, and they have seen the fruits of their labors in the life, liberty, and happiness of the children and grandchildren of their oppressors, while their own descendants wallow in the mire of poverty and deprivation, holding only to the hope of change in the future. This hope has sustained us for many years and has led us to suffer the administrations of a corrupt government. At the dawn of the twentieth century this hope led us to formulate a civil rights movement in the belief that this government would eventually fulfill its promise to Black people. We did not recognize, however, that any attempt to complete the promise of an eighteenth-century revolution in the framework of a twentieth-century government was doomed to failure. The descendants of that small company of original settlers of this land are not among the common people of today, they have become a small ruling class in control of a worldwide economic system. The Constitution set up by their ancestors to serve the people no longer does so, for the people have changed. The people of the eighteenth century have become the ruling class of the twentieth century, and the people of the twentieth century are the descendants of the slaves and dispossessed of the eighteenth century. The Constitution set up to serve the people of the eighteenth century now serves the ruling class of the twentieth century, and the people of today stand waiting for a foundation of their own life, liberty, and pursuit of happiness.

As I talked, it seemed to me that the people were not really listening or even interested in what I had to say. Almost every sentence was greeted with loud applause, but the audience was more concerned with phrasemongering than with ideological development. I am not a good public speaker—I tend to lecture and teach in a rather dull fashion—but the people were not responding to my ideas, only to an image, and although I was very excited by all the energy and enthusiasm I saw there, I was also disturbed by the lack of serious analytical thought.

After Philadelphia, we tried to organize rallies across the country in preparation for the Washington convention. We had been counting on Kathleen Cleaver's return to organize these rallies in support of Bobby and Ericka, since we knew that Kathleen could draw in people, speak effectively, and give us the boost we needed. Then, for reasons unfathomable to us at the time, Eldridge changed his mind and refused to let her come. This was a real setback. We had announced that Kathleen would be at the convention, but when Eldridge would not allow that, I tried to change the direction of the Washington meeting. In an important way, the convention marked a turning point in the Party's development. Instead of focusing on a new Constitution, we concentrated on plans for building community-organizing programs. I sent out a directive to all chapters and branches telling them to come prepared to set up displays explaining community programs and to urge people to sign up for them. Then, when the comrades returned home, they would have a list of names of committed people who could be organized.

For me, the theme of the convention in Washington was not a new Constitution but organization for survival, and from that time on, we began to refer to the Party community programs as survival programs. The whole idea of the community programs had been developed by Bobby Seale while I was in prison, and his brilliant organizing methods had helped to establish them. The Breakfast for Children program was set up first. Other programs—clothing distribution centers, liberation schools, housing, prison projects, and medical centers—soon followed. We called them "survival programs pending revolution," since we needed long-term programs and a disciplined organization to carry them out. They were designed to help the people survive until their consciousness is raised, which is only the first step in the revolution to produce a new America. I frequently use the metaphor of the raft to describe the survival programs. A raft put into service during a disaster is not meant to change conditions but to help one get through a difficult time. During a flood the raft is a life-saving device, but it is only a means of getting to higher and safer ground. So, too, with survival programs, which are emergency services. In themselves they do not change social conditions, but they are life-saving vehicles until conditions change.

The Washington convention could have been a great leap forward, but nothing worked out well. Howard University had agreed to host the convention, but at the last minute the university withdrew its facilities, and the comrades had to find another hall. Some churches made space available, so we were able to hold our workshops and meetings in them. But there was poor planning, poor co-ordination, and a deficiency in skills needed to organize and execute such a gigantic undertaking.

Another weakness was the diffuseness of goals among those who came to the convention, especially among the whites. My goals were different from theirs. They had been drawn to the Party by Eldridge's rhetoric, and their views had come to influence too many of our activities. I made up my mind that we could not let white radicals define the struggle for us; they knew too little about the Black experience and life in Black communities. Deep into the violence of the revolution, they wanted the Black Panthers to write a new Constitution, overthrow the government by force, and implement it. When this did not come about in Washington, we got critical letters claiming we were no longer the vanguard of the movement. I paid no attention. In fact, we were glad to be rid of the radicals because all they did was talk. Those who understood the true nature of revolution stood with us.

The defection of both Eldridge Cleaver and the Party were summed up in the shambles of the Washington convention. Cleaver was demanding that we act out his fantasies of instant power. In Philadelphia, the crowds had been overwhelmingly Black—they kept us down to earth—but in Washington the white radicals' fantasies and those of Cleaver merged, and we, the all-too-human Black Panthers, could not gratify them. In metaphysical streets, Cleaver and the infantile leftists were waiting on corners for the revolution to come to *them*. We were not able to hand down a manifesto like Moses on Sinai. Our grievous error had been that for a moment in time we, too, had joined the suicidal dance around the golden calf. The bad news from Washington, D.C., the city of lies, was that the American Revolution had only reached the end of the beginning, not the beginning of the end.

In the months after my release I traveled from city to city, meeting comrades and doing what I could to organize committees for Ericka and Bobby. In my travels I observed the work being done in dozens of communities and saw evidence that the Black Panthers had built a strong organization. But we needed to do more—much more. We had the base now on which to construct a potent social force in the country. But some of our leading comrades lacked the comprehensive ideology needed to analyze events and phenomena in a creative, dynamic way. We had tried to develop their understanding in political-education classes. Now we needed a structure, and after discussion in the Central Committee, we organized the Ideological Institute in Oakland in December, 1970. It was formed to train our more advanced comrades to observe and define phenomena along lines set down by the Black Panther Party. I had thought a good bit since my release about new ideas and concepts, but I did not want to be, could not be, the only one developing ideas and programs. Given the opportunity, other comrades would be able to come up with imaginative programs and fresh solutions as they encountered changing conditions. This is essential for the advance of revolutionary thought. The Ideological Institute has succeeded in providing the comrades with an understanding of dialectical materialism. About three hundred brothers and sisters attend classes to study in depth the works of great Marxist thinkers and philosophers.

Meanwhile, our efforts on behalf of Bobby and Ericka continued. On one of my trips to New Haven to prepare for the trial, I met Erik Erikson, the renowned author and professor of developmental psychology at Harvard. His son, Kai, a sociologist and master of Trumball College at Yale, thought it would be interesting for us to hold a series of discussions. I agreed, and he arranged a three-day seminar in early February of 1971 at Yale University, in which two faculty members and fourteen Yale students—eight white and six Black—also took part. The discussions were held in the library of Yale University Press.

I liked Erikson very much, and we got along well despite some trouble communicating during the first two days of the seminar. At first we repeatedly talked past each other, and the students talked such madness that they impeded our conversation. They had come to hear revolutionary slogans and violent rhetoric and were not satisfied with anything less than absolute solutions to the problems besetting society. The talks centered on Black Panther ideology, and Erikson saw the validity of the Black Panther approach. He pointed out that two people can love each other only when both have dignity. If one person is without dignity, then the relationship is something else. Erikson noted that it is necessary to understand the complexity of all issues and all relationships. He brought many insights to our talks, drawing on his early days as a student of Freud and his studies of Gandhi and Martin Luther. Although there were moments of frustration, I think we both learned much from each other.

At the time of the Yale meeting with Erikson, my secretary was a Party member named Connie Matthews. Connie was from the West Indies, but she had migrated to Europe and lived for a time in one of the Scandinavian countries. She claimed to speak several languages fluently. Connie had joined the Party after hearing Bobby Seale speak on one of his European trips, while I was still in prison. At first she stayed in Europe to orga-

nize groups there but later moved to our Algerian embassy under the direction of Eldridge Cleaver. Less than two months
after my release from prison, Eldridge sent her to Oakland to
work out of Central Headquarters, where she was assigned to
handle the details of my travel, speaking engagements, and the
like. I found her somewhat unreliable and several times considered sending her back to Algiers, but Eldridge insisted she remain in Oakland.

In late 1970 she had married Michael "Cetawayo" Tabor, a
Black Panther from New York and one of the twenty-one defendants in that circus the state called a conspiracy trial.* Cetawayo was an effective organizer and a good speaker, but he
had suffered through some heavy drug and prison scenes. He
fell completely under Connie's spell.

When the meetings with Erikson came to an end, Connie and
Cetawayo disappeared, taking many of my personal papers
with them. Of course, when Tabor jumped bail, this placed the
other New York 21 in jeopardy, but more than that, I was puzzled about where they might have gone. Connie was not a citizen and would have trouble staying in the United States;
Cetawayo was a fugitive who could not travel easily outside
the country unless he went to Cuba or Algiers. I did not think
they would go to Cuba—they were not hard workers—and if
they went to Algiers they would be right in our hands. But the
Algerian possibility started me thinking. After considering the
alternatives, I began to suspect that something was wrong between Eldridge Cleaver in Algiers and the Central Committee
of the Party in Oakland. But I said nothing; without enough
evidence to be certain, I decided to wait and see.

In the meantime, a big rally was planned for Oakland on
March 5, 1971, to kick off a large-scale effort in support of all

---

*On April 2, 1969, twenty-one New York Black Panthers were arrested and
charged with conspiring to bomb several New York police stations and department stores, the New York Botanical Gardens, and the New Haven Railroad.
Bail was set at $100,000 each, and the defendants spent ten months in jail
awaiting trial. On May 13, 1971, after a trial that lasted eight months, the
thirteen defendants who stood trial, including two who fled to Algeria, were
unanimously acquitted of all twelve counts of the indictment.

political prisoners, with the main focus on the trial of Bobby and Ericka in New Haven. The rally, called the Intercommunal Day of Solidarity, was scheduled for the Oakland auditorium. Its keynote speaker would be Kathleen Cleaver, with musical entertainment provided by The Grateful Dead and The Lumpen, a Black Panther group whose primary purpose was not entertainment but political education through music and song. We wanted to attract a broad cross-section of the Bay Area community.

While we made preparations, I talked a number of times with Eldridge by telephone, and although we had some disagreement about strategy and tactics, we did agree that the rally should come off as planned. However, doubt grew in our minds whether Kathleen would show up. We had good reason for uncertainty; at the Revolutionary Constitutional Convention in Washington the previous November, she had failed to appear. But when I expressed these doubts to Eldridge, he assured me that Kathleen would be there.

In addition to the Oakland rally, we were planning a series of meetings across the country featuring Kathleen and local speakers. These rallies were meant to attract people whom we could organize into groups to work for the various trials as well as participate in the survival programs the Party was developing.

In order to publicize the Intercommunal Day of Solidarity, I had agreed to appear on a local TV talk show. My appearance would be a means of using the oppressor's media to carry our message to the people. About three hours before the show, I had an idea and called Eldridge to discuss it with him. The TV show was one on which people called in to ask questions, but I suggested a reversal of this procedure. The show's host would call Eldridge in Algeria, talk about the rally on the air, and announce that Kathleen was coming to speak. I knew this would arouse interest and increase attendance. Best of all, it would be done at the expense of the media. The station was enthusiastic. When I told Eldridge of the plan, he liked it, too, and said he would be prepared for the call. When I arrived at the station that morning, I felt optimistic. We were getting the best local publicity; a large crowd would attend the rally; we had begun to build a strong base for our work to free political prisoners.

Then the call to Eldridge went through, and the world turned upside down. At first I could not believe what he was doing. He launched into Party business—and not only Party business but Central Committee business, beginning with the Central Committee's expulsion of Connie Matthews Tabor, Cetawayo Tabor, the New York 21, and Elmer "Geronimo" Pratt, a Black Panther from Los Angeles. All these Black Panthers were guilty of serious offenses—actions that had jeopardized other comrades and the Party. The New York 21 had written an open letter to the Weathermen saying that they felt the leadership of the Party had lost its revolutionary fervor and that the Weathermen were the true vanguard of the revolution. That was all right with us if they wanted to take that position, but the Central Committee decided that with that statement the New York 21 had resigned from the Party. Expulsion was simply a Party recognition of that fact. In the other cases, there was also ample evidence to justify the actions of the Central Committee.

Now, in this public setting, before thousands of viewers, Eldridge chose to disagree with the actions of the Central Committee. However, he did not attack me; he attacked David Hilliard, the Chief of Staff. Eldridge accused David of having allowed the Party to fall apart and said that we had expelled many loyal comrades without sufficient cause. I disagreed with him and defended David. David had done a good job of sustaining the Party while I was in jail, often working with scant support, yet keeping things together from coast to coast. In my opinion, if anyone was at fault, it was me. Whatever wrongs there were in the Party, I said, I took full responsibility.

Very angry about Eldridge's stunt, I nevertheless kept calm, and after Eldridge and I finished talking, I answered questions from listeners. But my mind was no longer on the show. I was trying to figure out why Eldridge had pulled this act in public, particularly when just three hours earlier he had agreed to participate. What was going on? Even as I began to understand, as details fell into place in my mind, I still believed it was a contradiction that could be handled within the Party structure. It had not occurred to me that Eldridge might want to undermine the Party.

On leaving the TV studio, I went straight to a pay phone and placed a call to Eldridge. I had been cool in public, but I was seething inside, and I wanted him to know my real feelings. When we were connected, I let him have it: he had shown no concern for the political prisoners, and on this occasion, when we had an unusual opportunity to make a major move to organize behind them, he had gone on an individualistic trip, talking madness. Bobby's New Haven trial was just beginning; we had no idea what the outcome would be, yet Eldridge had shown complete disregard for him and all the others facing trial. When I finished, I flew to Boston, and there I called Eldridge again. What I did not know when I made those two calls was that I was not talking to a man but to a tape recorder. Eldridge taped my calls and then released them to NBC in New York, which played my "private, privileged" remonstrance over the American network. The Minister of Information had set me up. He was committing reactionary suicide and trying to take me down with him.

It soon became clear that Eldridge had organized a plot to subvert the work of the Party and sacrifice Bobby and Ericka to the Establishment. He had done this by questioning Party ideology and by attempting to turn a number of Black Panthers against the Party and the Central Committee. Immediately after these public charges against Hilliard, the key members in four Black Panther branches in New York and one in New Jersey publicly announced that they supported Eldridge and thereby resigned from the Party. Obviously this campaign had been planned well in advance. The perpetrators were only waiting for a propitious time to carry it out. The final evidence of the plot came when Connie Matthews Tabor and Michael Cetawayo Tabor turned up in Algiers. Everything pointed to the fact that Eldridge had sent Connie here in October of 1970 with subversion in mind, and it finally came to pass in February, 1971. Eldridge's defection was now out in the open.

The next few weeks were tense, but we went ahead with our preparations for the Intercommunal Day of Solidarity on March 5. I was now to be the keynote speaker. I knew that everybody at the rally would expect me to say something about

Cleaver in answer to all the charges he was making against us through transatlantic interviews. But when the night of the rally arrived, I decided against mentioning him and gave a brief address with no direct reference. The rally was a great success. It raised people's awareness of the survival programs and brought increased support for political prisoners. More and more people from the Black community were joining us in our determination that political oppression, imprisonment, and even death would not deter us from our efforts to free our imprisoned brothers and sisters.

The spring and summer following the rally brought increased momentum into my life. The survival programs, the Ideological Institute, the reorganization of the Party required my full attention. And events—both tragic and joyful—rushed in on one another during those months. At the end of May, Bobby and Ericka, who had been defended by Charles Garry, were acquitted of the false charges brought against them by the state of Connecticut. After a brief delay, Bobby was released, and he and Ericka returned to Oakland to resume their work in the community. Seeing Bobby again was a moving experience. We had not been together on the streets of Oakland since August, 1967, in the early, uncertain days of the Black Panther Party. Now, almost four years later, we were once again on the block with our comrades. We had gone through a great deal of danger and pain during those years, but we had survived, stronger and more committed than ever. Everything we had suffered had been worth the price. And during that time the Party had grown from a local group to a network of branches and chapters in North America and abroad. Many of our noble warriors had been cut down, and other early members had shown themselves unable to withstand the pressures of a protracted revolutionary struggle, but we were happy to be together again, united in our goals for our people.

The Establishment, however, was determined to keep us on the defensive. The district attorney of Alameda County began his moves to have me tried a second time. Even more serious were his efforts to railroad Chief of Staff David Hilliard into prison on the trumped-up charges that had come from the shoot-out on April 6, 1968, when Bobby Hutton had been murdered. The charge: assault with a deadly weapon against a police officer "known to be in pursuit of his duty." David had been arrested that night, although there was no evidence that he had a weapon or even that he was at the scene of the shoot-out. Yet the district attorney who conducted his prosecution got the kind of jury he wanted (as they usually do) and was able to lead them into convicting David on these charges, even though the district attorney himself could not prove that David had a weapon. Once again the Black Panther Party got the kind of "justice" we had come to expect. In July David was sentenced to serve one to ten years in the state prison and was quickly whisked off to Vacaville, as I had been three years earlier.

During the five years since the Party had been formed, it always seemed that time was measured not in days or months or hours but by the movements of comrades and brothers in and out of prison and by the dates of hearings, releases, and trials. Our lives were regulated not by the ordinary tempo of daily events but by the forced clockwork of the judicial process. No sooner had David begun serving his term than we turned our attention to the upcoming trial of George Jackson, who had been falsely charged with killing a prison guard at San Quentin. His trial was scheduled for August 23. Two days before it was to begin, on August 21, while attempting to save his brothers in a San Quentin cell block from being massacred by guards, he was shot and killed by his enemies. He had fulfilled his own prophecy: "I know that they will not be satisfied until they've pushed me out of this existence altogether."

30

The Black Panther is our brother and son, the one who wasn't afraid.

GEORGE JACKSON, *Soledad Brother*

Fallen Comrade

George Jackson had genius. Genius is rare enough and should be treasured, but when genius is combined in a Black man with revolutionary passion and vision, the Establishment will cut him down. Comrade Jackson understood this. He knew his days were numbered and was prepared to die as a true believer in revolutionary suicide. For eleven years he insisted on remaining free in a brutal prison system. All along he resisted the authorities and encouraged his brothers in prison to join him. The state retaliated: parole was continually refused; solitary confinement was imposed on him for seven years; threats on his life were frequent—from guards, from inmates who called themselves "Hitler's Helpers," from "knife thrusts and pick handles of faceless sadistic pigs." And finally they murdered him.

In the months before his death everything began to close in. He was one of the few prisoners who was shackled and heavily guarded for his infrequent trips to the visitors' room. Attempts on his life became almost daily occurrences. But he never gave in or retreated. Prison was the crucible that shaped his spirit, and George often used the words of Ho Chi Minh to describe his resistance: "Calamity has hardened me and turned my mind to steel."

I knew him like a brother. At first, I knew him only spiritually, through his writing and his legend in the prison system, when I was at the Penal Colony and he was at Soledad. Then, not long after my arrival, I received through the prison grapevine a request from George to join the Black Panther Party. It was readily granted. George was made a member of the People's Revolutionary Army, with the rank of General and Field Marshal. For the next three years we were in constant communication by means of messages carried by friends and lawyers and inmates transferred from one prison to another. Despite the restrictions of the prison system, we managed to transmit our messages on paper and on tapes. Among George's contributions to the Party were articles he wrote for *The Black Panther* newspaper, which furthered our revolutionary theory and provided inspiration for all the brothers. In February, 1971, I received this letter from him:

2/21/71

Comrade Huey,

Things are quiet here now, tonight we have discipline and accord, tomorrow all may fly apart again—but that's us.

I have two articles that I would like to be put in the paper, one following the other by a week. The one on Angela first. Then if you approve, I would like to contribute something to the paper every week or whenever you have space for me.

If yes, let me know if there is any area in particular you would like me to cover (comment on).

Then do I comment as observer or participant?

One favor—please don't let anyone delete the things I say or change them around, I don't need an editor, unless what I say is not representative of the Party Line, don't let anyone change a word. When I make an ideological error of course correct it to fit the party's position. And don't let them shorten or condense; if something is too long, part one–part two it.

If you want to use me to say nasty things about those who deserve it, it may be best for me to comment as an observer, that way less contradictions between yourself and people you may have to work with.

You told —— that you and I had a "misunderstanding" once

but that it was cleared up. When was it that we misunderstood each other?

Be very careful of messages or any word that has supposed to have come from me. I really don't recall any misunderstanding.

People lie for many reasons.

Try to memorize my handwriting, that is how all messages will come in the future (if we have a future).

Did you know that Angela and I were married a while back? And I had almost pulled her all the way into our camp, just before Eldridge made that statement?

I had done so well in fact that C.P. tried to cut our contacts, attack my sanity in little whispers and looks in conversing with her, and cut off my paid subscription to their two newspapers.

Strange, that they would be afraid of the F.B.I., and not afraid of the Cat. Perhaps they've reached an understanding. Some of them anyway.

Is ———— C.P.? Man, whats happening with her. She has no control at all of her mouth. Or ego.

Arrange for a good contact or write and seal messages with a thumbprint. I have ideas I'd like to leave with you all.

Thanks Brother for helping us. Beautiful, hard, disciplined brothers in here, I'd like to deliver them to you someday.

George

In the last three years of his life Comrade Jackson felt sustained and supported by the Black Panther Party. He had struggled alone for so long to raise the consciousness of Black inmates, and his example encouraged thousands who were weaker and less intrepid than he. But the price he paid in alienation and reprisals was fearsome. Within the Party he was no longer alone; he became part of the burgeoning and invincible revolutionary liberation movement. In his second book, *Blood in My Eye,* he expressed this faith: "The Black Panther Party is the largest and most powerful political force existing outside establishment politics. It draws this power from the people. It is the people's natural, political vanguard."

George asked the Party to publish his first book, *Soledad*

Brother, but in the difficult negotiations between go-betweens and without direct contact, the arrangements fell through. To make sure this mistake would never happen again, he left his estate and all his writings to the Party. More important, he bequeathed us his spirit and his love.

George's funeral was held in Oakland on August 28, 1971— exactly one week after his murder—at St. Augustine's Episcopal Church, pastored by Father Earl Neil. A crowd of about 7,000 friends gathered to pay their last respects to our fallen comrade, and the Black Panther Party had a large contingent of comrades on hand to handle the crowd and protect the Jackson family. I arrived at the church shortly before the funeral cortege. The second-floor sanctuary was empty, but from the window I could see the crowd stretching for more than a block in each direction, filling every available space and closing off the streets to motor traffic.

A number of Black Panthers sat talking quietly downstairs. Occasionally they relieved the comrades who were controlling the crowd and directing traffic outside. The children from the Intercommunal Youth Institute were there, and although they had been in the building since early morning, they did not complain of weariness. The children felt the loss of George deeply; when they had learned of his death the previous week, all of them had written messages of condolence to his mother. They loved George, and in their faces I could see their determination to grow up and fulfill his dreams of liberation.

Tensions were high. We had received many threats the previous week, from prison guards, from police, and from many others, stating that the funeral would not be held, and if it was, there would be cause for more funerals of Black Panthers. We were ready for anything. The comrades were angry about the threats, and they were righteously angry about the continued oppression of the poor and Black people who live in this land. You could see it in their faces, in their measured, firm strides, in their clenched fists, and in their voices as they greeted the hearse with shouts of "Power to the People" and "Long Live the Spirit of George Jackson."

When the funeral cortege arrived, Bobby and I prepared to

meet the people in it as they entered the door of the church. It was the first time Bobby and I had shared a public platform in over four years, but there was no cause for rejoicing. We said nothing to each other; we knew only too well what the other was thinking.

As the casket bearing the body of Comrade George was brought into the sanctuary, a song was playing—Nina Simone singing "I Wish I Knew How It Would Feel to Be Free." Inside the church the walls were ringed with Black Panthers carrying shotguns. George had said that he wanted no flowers at his funeral, only shotguns. In honoring his request we were also protecting his family and all those who were dedicated to carrying on in his spirit. Any person who entered that sanctuary with the purpose of starting some madness would know that he did not stand a chance of going very far. In death, even as in life, George thought about the best interests of his companions.

Father Neil made a short but powerful statement about the lesson of George Jackson's death, that Black people would have to get off their knees and take their destiny in their own hands. Bobby read some of the many messages from around the world, Elaine Brown sang "One time's too much to tell any man that he's not free," and I delivered the eulogy, which went in part:

> George Jackson was my hero. He set a standard for prisoners, political prisoners, for people. He showed the love, the strength, the revolutionary fervor characteristic of any soldier for the people. He inspired prisoners, whom I later encountered, to put his ideas into practice and so his spirit became a living thing. Today I say that although George's body has fallen, his spirit goes on, because his ideas live. And we will see that these ideas stay alive, because they'll be manifested in our bodies and in these young Panthers' bodies, who are our children. So it's a true saying that there will be revolution from one generation to the next. This was George's legacy, and he will go on, he will go on into immortality, because we believe that the people will win, we know the people will win, as they advance, generation upon generation.
>
> What kind of standard did George Jackson set? First, he was a strong man, without fear, determined, full of love, strength, and

dedication to the people's cause. He lived a life that we must praise. No matter how he was oppressed, no matter how wrongly he was done, he still kept the love for the people. And this is why he felt no pain in giving up his life for the people's cause. . . .

Even after his death, George Jackson is a legendary figure and a hero. Even the oppressor realizes this. To cover their murder they say that George Jackson killed five people, five oppressors, and wounded three in the space of thirty seconds. You know, sometimes I like to overlook the fact that this would be physically impossible. But after all George Jackson is my hero. And I would like to think that it was possible; I would be very happy thinking that George Jackson had the strength because that would have made him superman. (Of course, my hero would have to be a superman.) And we will raise our children to be like George Jackson, to live like George Jackson and to fight for freedom as George Jackson fought for freedom.

George's last statement, the example of his conduct at San Quentin on that terrible day, left a standard for political prisoners and for the prisoner society of racist, reactionary America. He left a standard for the liberation armies of the world. He showed us how to act. He demonstrated how the unjust would be criticized by the weapon. And this will certainly be true, because the people will take care of that. George also said once that the oppressor is very strong and he might beat him down, he might beat us down to our very knees, he might crush us to the ground, but it will be physically impossible for the oppressor to go on. At some point his legs will get tired, and when his legs get tired, then George Jackson and the people will tear his kneecaps off. . . .

So we will be very practical. We won't make statements and believe the things the prison officials say—their incredible stories about one man killing five people in thirty seconds. We will go on and live very realistically. There will be pain and much suffering in order for us to develop. But even in our suffering, I see a strength growing. I see the example that George set living on. We know that all of us will die someday. But we know that there are two kinds of death, the reactionary death and the revolutionary death. One death is significant and the other is not. George certainly died in a significant way, and his death will be very heavy,

while the deaths of the ones that fell that day in San Quentin will
be lighter than a feather. Even those who support them now will
not support them in the future, because we're determined to
change their minds. We'll change their minds or else in the
people's name we'll have to wipe them out thoroughly, wholly,
absolutely, and completely. ALL POWER TO THE PEOPLE.

All words are inadequate to express the pain one feels over a
fallen comrade. But in a poem my brother Melvin came closer
than anyone in voicing our feelings about the loss of George
Jackson:

WE CALLED HIM THE GENERAL

The sky is blue,
Today is clear and sunny.

The house that George once
lived in headed for the
grave,
While the Panther spoke
of the spirit.
I saw a man move catlike
across the rooftops,
Glide along the horizons,
Casting no shadow,
only chains into the sea,
using his calloused hands
and broken feet to
smash and kick down
barriers.
The angels say his name
is George Lester Jackson—

El General.

All the people went home to
their hovels,

He to the world of gods,
heroes, tall men, giants.
He went like the rushing
wind, the rolling tide;
The thunder's roar,
The lightning's flash;
Smashing all challengers
and devils in his path,
While caressing the leaves,
sand and sky.

Surviving

Shortly after David Hilliard was incarcerated, jury selection began for my second trial. The same problems in selecting an impartial and fair jury faced Charles Garry once again. One of the persons questioned for my panel had just served on David's jury. Under oath he stated that he knew nothing about the Black Panther Party and its leaders. When it was pointed out that he had just convicted David Hilliard, he said he did not know David was a Party leader. It was clear the prosecution was out to get a hanging jury.

Being tried a second time on the same charges was a strange experience, a combination of suspense and *déja vu;* most of the time I was bored by what seemed a stale rerun of a familiar and flawed drama. It was just another charade to justify their attempts to put me back in state prison for another thirteen years. The major difference between the two trials was that this time I was out on bail, which meant that during the evenings I could conduct Party business. Also, I could not be found guilty of a more serious offense than the one I had been convicted of the first time, voluntary manslaughter. Lowell Jensen, the first prosecutor in the first case, had become district attorney, and an assistant named Donald Whyte was arguing for the prosecution. He was no match for Charles Garry, but it did not matter, anyway, because all he had to do was follow the script from the first trial.

The trial opened and moved along, with most of the same set of witnesses testifying. Once again, the prosecution leaned

heavily on the testimony of Officer Heanes, and during Charles
Garry's cross-examination of him, the first major surprise of
the trial came, one that said a great deal about our opponents.
During his questioning of Heanes, Garry was making the basic
point that when I was ordered out of the car by Officer Frey, I
was carrying only my criminal evidence lawbook. The book
had my name written in it, in my own handwriting, and my
blood was all over its pages. It had been a very important piece
of evidence in the first trial, for it countered the prosecution
charge that I had carried a gun that night. Garry turned to the
court clerk and asked for the book, which had been entered
into evidence in the first trial. The clerk replied that it had been
"lost." For a moment I could not believe my ears, but I quickly
realized that they were serious. They actually did not have the
book. How could such a major piece of defense evidence disappear? Their explanation was that when the Appellate Court reviewed the trial and the evidence, they had taken everything
related to the case, and somewhere between the Appellate Court
and the Alameda County Court House the book had been lost,
although all the other exhibits were available. My second trial,
which had at first seemed just a charade, now appeared to be
turning into a circus.

Although he claimed to be "upset" by the "loss" of the book,
the prosecutor was not too convincing. He offered a photograph of it to be entered into evidence and generously stipu-
lated that the photograph was a facsimile of my book and had
indeed been a part of defense evidence in the first trial. But a
photograph is not a book. The prosecution had a witness on
the stand who said that I had turned and started firing at two
policemen on October 28, yet the piece of evidence that disproved this claim, the only object I was carrying that night, was
missing. And now they wanted to replace it with a facsimile.
The jury could not see my bloodstains on the pages; they could
not read my name on the flyleaf; and they could not see where
I had underlined the relevant portions of the criminal code
about reasonable cause for arrest, the section I always read to
police and citizens during our encounters. Charles Garry pro-

tested this loss of crucial defense evidence and asked for a mistrial. It was denied.

Then the trial went from charade to farce. The state had still another stunt to pull, and it came the next day when a squad of plain-clothes men escorted a timid and very frightened man into court—Dell Ross. It had not occurred to us that he would be called as a witness in the second trial, because his credibility had been so thoroughly destroyed in the first. But we should have known better. Dell Ross appeared out of nowhere, well, not exactly out of nowhere, since he related how the prosecution had sequestered him in another state and brought him in for this trial—just as they had done with Henry Grier. I suspect that Ross had been pushed around and threatened, because he was very fearful. The papers referred to him as an "ex-motorist," in reference to his explanation that he had "been traveling" since the first trial.

On the stand Ross said what was expected of him. He testified that he had lied in the first trial and then went on to give the testimony that he had offered before the grand jury. After listening to his admission that he had perjured himself in the first trial, the court was nonetheless agreeable to his placing his testimony in evidence. Yet anybody who saw that intimidated soul meekly agreeing to the questions of the prosecutor would have had trouble taking his testimony seriously. I marveled that they had the gall to put him on.

At first I felt sorry for him all over again, but I soon became angry with the prosecutor for staging such a ridiculous farce and calling it a trial. I was looking forward to the moment when Charles Garry would go to work on Ross in his cross-examination. But because the district attorney had not told us that Ross would be called to the stand, Garry was unprepared to question him. He asked for a recess to return to San Francisco and get the tape and transcript of the interview he had held with Ross before the first trial. This evidence was extremely important because it demonstrated what an unreliable witness Ross was and cast doubt on his testimony. But the judge denied this reasonable request and ordered him to proceed with his questioning of the witness.

At this point, I could hold back my anger no longer. I felt that a cruel injustice was being done to us, and the need to make my views known was too strong to be overcome by the protocol of the courtroom. I stood up and declared that the trial would not continue unless they gave us time to prepare a proper cross-examination of Dell Ross. The defense was justified in asking for time, I declared, particularly in light of the fact that the day before an important piece of defense evidence had been confiscated by the state. Now they refused us an hour's recess to secure critical information, although the prosecutor was routinely granted such delays. The courtroom was tense as I went on and told them that I had stood between "the ignorance of my own people and the violence of the state with a lawbook in my hand, and now you have 'lost' it." I told them to take me back to jail. Turning to the angry crowd, I urged them to be calm. "If they touch me, you know what to do," I said, "but be disciplined now." The people were beautiful and remained in place until I told them to leave the courtroom. Then they congregated in the hall outside and refused to clear the building, so I went out of the courtroom into the hall, where the police were beginning to gather their forces. It was obvious that they wanted a mass arrest so that we would be caught in a net of charges, bail, and trials. Realizing that they ought to clear the building, I told them to go, that I could deal with the state and serve time for this. They left quietly.

Then, amid the general confusion, I went back into the courtroom and approached Dell Ross on the witness stand. The poor brother's eyes were wild with fear. "Why are you sitting there, brother?" I asked him. "Are you afraid?" A detective interrupted and told him not to listen to me, but I continued. "Why do you obey him when he tells you not to speak? I don't hate you; I love you, brother." The police saw that my words were having an effect on him, so they took him away.

When the courtroom was cleared, Garry left for his office in San Francisco. My plan had worked. I had recessed the trial, and now Garry would have time to check his office. Everything was under control, even though there were police everywhere and the judge did not seem to know what was going on. I went upstairs to the jail and told the guards to open my cell, but they wanted me to sign papers admitting myself back into jail, thus revoking my bail. I refused to sign anything. "Just put me in jail," I said. They opened a cell for me and said they would wait a few hours while Garry looked for the transcript, but if, after that, I did not sign the papers, they would kick me out of the jail. I lay down in the cell and fell asleep.

Garry searched thoroughly for the tape and the transcript of his interview with Dell Ross in 1968, but he could not find them. The office had been burglarized a few weeks before, and the Ross evidence was among the items that had been stolen. So, empty-handed but not discouraged, he returned to Oakland, and the trial resumed with his cross-examination of Ross. We need not have worried. Even without the transcript, Ross was such a strange witness that his credibility was destroyed all over again. First, he admitted to the court that he had been lying in the testimony he had given only an hour before. He had been guilty of perjury not merely once or twice, but seventeen times. Second, he admitted that he was afraid of the district attorney and everyone else in the courtroom—the judge, the jurors, everybody. As if this were not enough, Ross then asked the judge's permission to address a question to the court, and the judge granted his request. There was a moment's silence. Then, looking out into the courtroom, Ross said, "Is there anybody here who believes in the truth? Would you raise your hand?" This was such a bizarre development that the entire courtroom sat stunned. No one moved or spoke except the district attorney, who raised his hand and said, "Mr. Ross, I believe in the truth." The judge leaned over and told Whyte to put his hand down. Then Dell Ross continued, "Because I don't know what the truth is myself."

With that, Ross's effectiveness as a witness was demolished. I was sorry to see him so dehumanized, for he seemed to me living proof of what American society can do to oppressed and poor people. A despicable abuse of power had intimidated a weak man, a man who had little to lose, but who was terrified to let go of that. The whole pattern of his life had taught him to fear and defer to those who control society's institutions. At last, faced with a crucial test that resembled all the earlier small, humiliating choices in his life, he had no resources to help him resist. He gave in again, and his defeat ended in misery and shame.

After this thunderbolt, everybody needed a respite, and the court recessed for the weekend. Later that day, thinking about what had happened to Ross and how the prosecution had manipulated him, I had an idea. What I planned to do would certainly end the trial and might even send me back to jail, but I felt it would be an important political statement. When the trial resumed the next Monday morning, I would stand up again and announce that I was making a citizen's arrest of the prosecutor for aiding and abetting a felony, to wit, the perjured testimony of Dell Ross. Then I would ask the judge to assist me in making this arrest of the prosecutor. Since the judge would undoubtedly refuse to do so, I would then turn to the jury and ask them to assist me in making a citizen's arrest of the prosecutor and judge. My action would demonstrate to the public that it is difficult for an ordinary citizen to get justice in the courts when those who are trying him break the law to get him convicted. There is no recourse but to appeal to the people's sense of justice. Such a political message would have a strong impact on the consciousness of the people.

My lawyers were skeptical, but they agreed to do the legal research on my plan, since I wanted a solid legal foundation for what I was about to do. However, after reading the law, they told me it was not possible to make a citizen's arrest of a district attorney or judge. They were officers of the court, and only a grand jury could indict them. I abandoned the ploy, although still convinced I had a good point. What other avenue was open when law enforcers could break the law with impunity while ordinary citizens have no defense against them? If it had been possible to arrest the district attorney and judge, I might have had to go back to jail, but a strong point about the need for revolutionary justice would have been made.

The remainder of the trial was uneventful. The same ballistics experts testified about the same things, and it became even more boring with repetition. This time our defense was much shorter than during the first trial. I took the stand first and told the truth about the incident. Prosecutor Whyte then cross-examined me, performing a lot of courtroom antics in the process, but he was not too successful in his attempts to undermine my testimony. I did not budge an inch. He lacked the polish and skill of Lowell Jensen, and, as a result, our exchange was neither challenging nor stimulating.

The jury deliberated for what seemed a long time in view of the fact that this was a second trial and there were fewer charges. The longer the deliberations dragged on the more confident I became that someone was holding out for acquittal. Finally, the jury filed back into court and told the judge that they were hopelessly deadlocked, eleven for conviction and one for acquittal. The judge declared a mistrial and dismissed them. I would have to face yet another trial.

During the third trial everything really went our way. It was the same tired old show all over again—Prosecutor Donald Whyte, Herbert Heanes, Henry Grier, and Dell Ross, and their supporting cast. However, the whole scene had become more and more Kafkaesque. The script did not run the same way, and the first evidence that the plot was changing in our favor came when Officer Heanes forgot his lines.

All through the first and second trials Heanes had said that Gene McKinney and I were the only ones at the scene of the incident besides himself and Frey. Then, in the third trial, he said that he remembered another person at the scene, a man who had on a light tan jacket but who was not the passenger. This third man came to light while he was being cross-examined by Garry, and when Heanes realized that he had forgotten his script, he became confused and dropped his head in shame. Shortly after that, when the court took a recess and the jury filed out, the district attorney grabbed Heanes by the collar and scolded him in the open courtroom. Heanes's memory slip had changed everything, and I knew then we would win this one in spite of the testimony of Henry Grier.

A third man. Had Heanes harbored the third man in his memory all this time? Had an amnestic curtain lifted for this policeman who had never been the same since that night? Was the third man the real killer of Frey whom Heanes had covered up for all these years? Had the state given up, and was the introduction of the third man their way out? The questions were academic now, the state's motives and conspiracies banal and irrelevant.

When it came time for the defense to present its case, Garry was ready with a special surprise for the prosecution: he was going to disprove the entire testimony of Henry Grier. One surprise had been carefully prepared during the first and second trials, and now we were ready to bring it out. *Henry Grier had never been at the scene of the October 28 shooting.*

During Garry's cross-examinations of the prosecution witnesses, especially the police who were there that morning, he had been careful always to ask about the location of and get a description of every person and every object within a radius of sixty yards from the scene of the shooting. He had asked each policeman to describe everything he had observed when he arrived. Not one policeman would say he saw a bus. Why? Because there was no bus. None of them was willing to perjure himself, even though all of them were willing to let the bus driver commit perjury.

Charles Garry called to the stand the one man who was able to verify Grier's route and time schedules the night of the incident—the supervisor for the bus company. We had wanted the supervisor to testify in the earlier trials, but we were also afraid that he might lie and support the perjury of Grier. Still, we wondered why the prosecution had not brought in the timer and supervisor to back up Grier's story. We were still cautious about using his testimony during the second trial, but we began to gather all the evidence to the effect that in the space of sixty yards in every direction no policeman had seen a bus. In the first trial we were even afraid to bring in these measurements because we thought they might spring the supervisor on us, so we waited and waited, making an airtight case against Grier before we finally discredited his testimony.

Grier had testified that he was within ten feet of the whole incident, that he had driven up in his bus and braked very near to the parked automobiles, and had seen the shooting clearly. With a sixty-foot bus so close to the scene, it would be difficult for a policeman to miss it, and yet not one of them testified to seeing it. When we became sure of our evidence, we called in the bus superintendent, and he testified that according to the company records of the route Grier followed and Grier's own time schedule, it was impossible for Grier to have been at his checkpoints and also at the scene of the shooting. According to the supervisor's records, Grier must have been at least one and a half to two miles away at the time of the incident. Thus the bus supervisor backed up the police who testified for the prosecution: there was no bus on the scene.

The prosecution's case was steadily growing weaker. First Ross, now Grier. This time the jury deadlocked 6–6, and the judge finally had to declare another mistrial. I was summoned to appear in court again on December 15 to have the date set for a fourth trial, but I felt sure the charges would be dropped because the prosecution's main witnesses were no longer credible. I was right.

At the hearing on December 15, Lowell Jensen appeared in court. I had not seen him since my bail hearing during the summer of 1970. After the judge opened the proceedings, Jensen rose to speak, saying that he had never thought he would see the day when he would be in court asking for a dismissal of my case. The judge looked at him. "Are you asking for a dismissal in the interest of justice?" he asked, using the proper legal terminology. Jensen replied, "No, it's not in the interest of justice, because it's not just. I didn't think I would ever have to say these words, but I think the case should be dismissed."

The dismissal was granted, bringing to an end the insane and unjust series of legal assaults that had started more than four years earlier. I had spent thirty-three months in prison; my family had suffered untold personal agony; the Party had spent many thousands of dollars in my defense, money that could have been used to help the community. Jensen was right, but not in the sense he intended. Justice had not been served.

32

The people who have triumphed in their own revolution should help those still struggling for liberation. This is our internationalist duty.

CHAIRMAN MAO, Little Red Book

China

Today, when I think of my experiences in the People's Republic of China—a country that overwhelmed me while I was there— they seem somehow distant and remote. Time erodes the immediacy of the trip; the memory begins to recede. But that is a common aftermath of travel, and not too alarming. What is important is the effect that China and its society had on me, and that impression is unforgettable. While there, I achieved a psychological liberation I had never experienced before. It was not simply that I felt at home in China; the reaction was deeper than that. What I experienced was the sensation of freedom—as if a great weight had been lifted from my soul and I was able to be myself, without defense or pretense or the need for explanation. I felt absolutely free for the first time in my life—completely free among my fellow men. This experience of freedom had a profound effect on me, because it confirmed my belief that an oppressed people can be liberated if their leaders persevere in raising their consciousness and in struggling relentlessly against the oppressor.

Because my trip was so brief and made under great pressure, there were many places I was unable to visit and many experiences I had to forgo. Yet there were lessons to be learned from even the most ordinary and commonplace encounters: a question asked by a worker, the response of a schoolchild, the attitude of a government official. These slight and seemingly unimportant moments were enlightening, and they taught me much. For instance, the behavior of the police in China was a revelation to me. They are there to protect and help the people, not to oppress them. Their courtesy was genuine; no division or suspicion exists between them and the citizens. This impressed me so much that when I returned to the United States and was met by the Tactical Squad at the San Francisco airport (they had been called out because nearly a thousand people came to the airport to welcome us back), it was brought home to me all over again that the police in our country are an occupying, repressive force. I pointed this out to a customs officer in San Francisco, a Black man, who was armed, explaining to him that I felt intimidated seeing all the guns around. I had just left a country, I told him, where the army and the police are not in opposition to the people but are their servants.

I received the invitation to visit China shortly after my release from the Penal Colony, in August, 1970. The Chinese were interested in the Party's Marxist analysis and wanted to discuss it with us as well as show us the concrete application of theory in their society. I was eager to go and applied for a passport in late 1970, which was finally approved a few months later. However, I did not make the trip at that time because of Bobby's and Ericka's trial in New Haven. Nonetheless, I wanted to see China very much, and when I learned that President Nixon was going to visit the People's Republic in February, 1972, I decided to beat him to it. My wish was to deliver a message to the government of the People's Republic and the Communist Party, which would be delivered to Nixon when he made his visit.

I made the trip in late September, 1971, between my second and third trials, going without announcement or publicity because I was under an indictment. I had only ten days to spend in China. Even though I had no travel restrictions and had been given a passport, the California courts could have tied me down at any time because I was under court bail, so I avoided the state's jurisdiction by going to New York instead of directly to

Canada from California. Because of my uncertainty about what the power structure might do, I continued to avoid publicity after reaching New York, since it was not implausible that the authorities might place a federal hold on me, claiming illegal flight. By flying from New York to Canada I was able to avoid federal jurisdiction, and once in Canada I caught a plane to Tokyo. Police agents knew of my intentions, and they followed me all the way—right to the Chinese border. Two comrades, Elaine Brown and Robert Bay, went with me. I have no doubt that we were allowed to go only because the police believed we were not coming back. If they had known I intended to return, they probably would have done everything possible to prevent the trip. The Chinese government understood this, and while I was in China, they offered me political asylum, but I told them I had to return, that my struggle is in the United States of America.

Going through the immigration and customs services of the imperialist nations was the same dehumanizing experience we had come to expect as part of our daily life in the United States. In Canada, Tokyo, and Hong Kong they took everything out of our bags and searched them completely. In Tokyo and Hong Kong we were even subjected to a skin search. I thought I had left that routine behind in the California Penal Colony, but I know that the penitentiary is only one kind of captivity within the larger prison of a racist society. When we arrived at the free territory, where security is supposed to be so tight and everyone suspect, the comrades with the red stars on their hats asked us for our passports. Seeing they were in order, they simply bowed and asked us if the luggage was ours. When we said yes, they replied, "You have just passed customs." They did not open our bags when we arrived or when we left.

As we crossed into China the border guards held their automatic rifles in the air as a signal of welcome and well-wishing. The Chinese truly live by the slogan "Political power grows out of the barrel of a gun," and their behavior constantly reminds you of that. For the first time I did not feel threatened by a uniformed person with a weapon; the soldiers were there to protect the citizenry.

The Chinese were disappointed that we had only ten days to spend with them and wanted us to stay longer, but I had to be back for the start of my third trial. Still, much was accomplished in that short time, traveling to various parts of the country, visiting factories, schools, and communes. Everywhere we went, large groups of people greeted us with applause, and we applauded them in return. It was beautiful. At every airport thousands of people welcomed us, applauding, waving their Little Red Books, and carrying signs that read WE SUPPORT THE BLACK PANTHER PARTY, DOWN WITH U.S. IMPERIALISM, or WE SUPPORT THE AMERICAN PEOPLE BUT THE NIXON IMPERIALIST REGIME MUST BE OVERTHROWN.

We also visited as many embassies as possible. Sightseeing took second place to Black Panther business and our desire to talk with revolutionary brothers, so the Chinese arranged for us to meet the ambassadors of various countries. The North Korean Ambassador gave us a sumptuous dinner and showed films of his country. We also met the Ambassador from Tanzania, a fine comrade, as well as delegations from North Vietnam and the Provisional Revolutionary Government of South Vietnam. We missed the Cuban and Albanian embassies because we were short of time.

When news of our trip reached the rest of the world, widespread attention focused on it, and the press was constantly after us to find out why we had come. They were wondering if we sought to spoil Nixon's visit since we were so strongly opposed to his reactionary regime. Much of the time we were harassed by reporters. One evening a Canadian reporter would not leave my table despite my asking him several times. He insisted on hanging around, questioning us, even though we had made it plain we had nothing to say to him. I finally became disgusted with his persistence and ordered him to leave. Seconds later, the Chinese comrades arrived with the police and asked if I wanted him arrested. I said no, I only wanted him to leave my table. After that we stayed in a protected villa with a Red Army honor guard outside. This was another strange sensation—to have the police on our side.

We had been promised an opportunity to meet Chairman Mao, but the Central Committee of the Chinese Communist Party felt this would not be appropriate since I was not a head of state. But we did have two meetings with Premier Chou En-lai. One of them lasted two hours and included a number of other foreign visitors; the other was a six-hour private meeting with Premier Chou and Comrade Chiang Ch'ing, the wife of Chairman Mao. We discussed world affairs, oppressed people in general, and Black people in particular.

On National Day, October 1, we attended a large reception in the Great Hall of the People with Premier Chou En-lai and comrades from Mozambique, North Korea, North Vietnam, and the Provisional Government of South Vietnam. Normally, Chairman Mao's appearance is the crowning event of the most important Chinese celebration, but this year the Chairman did not put in an appearance. When we entered the hall, a band was playing the *Internationale,* and we shared tables with the head of Peking University, the head of the North Korean Army, and Comrade Chiang Ch'ing, Mao's wife. We felt it was a great privilege.

Everything I saw in China demonstrated that the People's Republic is a free and liberated territory with a socialist government. The way is open for people to gain their freedom and determine their own destiny. It was an amazing experience to see in practice a revolution that is going forward at such a rapid rate. To see a classless society in operation is unforgettable. Here, Marx's dictum—from each according to his abilities, to each according to his needs—is in operation.

But I did not go to China just to admire. I went to learn and also to criticize, since no society is perfect. There was little, however, to find fault with. The Chinese *insist* that you find something to criticize. They believe strongly in the most searching self-examination, in criticism of others and, in turn, of self. As they say, without criticism the hinges on the door begin to squeak. It is very difficult to pay them compliments. Criticize us, they would say, because we are a backward country, and I always replied, "No, you are an underdeveloped country." I did have one criticism to make during a visit to a steel factory.

This factory had thick black smoke pouring into the air. I told the Chinese that in the United States there is pollution because factories are spoiling the air; in some places the people can hardly breathe. If the Chinese continue to develop their industry rapidly, I said, and without awareness of the consequences, they will also make the air unfit to breathe. I talked with the factory workers, saying that man is nature but also in contradiction to nature, because contradictions are the ruling principle of the universe. Therefore, although they were trying to raise their levels of living, they might also negate the progress if they failed to handle that contradiction in a rational way. I explained that man opposes nature, but man is also the internal contradiction in nature. Therefore, while he is trying to reverse the struggle of opposites based upon unity, he might also eliminate himself. They understood this and said they are seeking ways to remedy this problem.

My experiences in China reinforced my understanding of the revolutionary process and my belief in the necessity of making a concrete analysis of concrete conditions. The Chinese speak with great pride about their history and their revolution and mention often the invincible thoughts of Chairman Mao Tse-tung. But they also tell you, "This was *our* revolution based upon a concrete analysis of concrete conditions, and we cannot direct you, only give you the principles. It is up to you to make the correct creative application." It was a strange yet exhilarating experience to have traveled thousands of miles, across continents, to hear their words. For this is what Bobby Seale and I had concluded in our own discussions five years earlier in Oakland, as we explored ways to survive the abuses of the capitalist system in the Black communities of America. Theory was not enough, we had said. We knew we had to act to bring about change. Without fully realizing it then, we were following Mao's belief that "if you want to know the theory and methods of revolution, you must take part in revolution. All genuine knowledge originates in direct experience."

33

We must undoubtedly criticize wrong ideas of every description. It certainly would not be right to refrain from criticism, look on while wrong ideas spread unchecked and allow them to monopolize the field. Mistakes must be criticized and poisonous weeds fought wherever they crop up.

CHAIRMAN MAO, *Little Red Book*

The Defection of Eldridge and Reactionary Suicide

A revolutionary party is under continual stress from both internal and external forces. By its very nature a political organization dedicated to social change invites attack from the established order, constantly vigilant to destroy it. This danger is taken for granted by the committed revolutionary. Indeed, oppression first shaped the spirit of resistance within him, and so it can neither defeat nor destroy his resolve. But he has two far greater enemies—the failure of vision and the loss of the original revolutionary concept. Either of these can lead to alienation from those the revolutionary seeks to set free. Eldridge Cleaver was guilty of both.

When I came out of prison in August, 1970, the Party was in a shambles. This was understandable for a number of reasons: Bobby and I had been off the streets and in jail for a long time, and it had been difficult to direct the Party on a day-to-day basis from prison cells. Then, too, the Party was harassed and beleaguered. Intelligence organizations throughout the country had become obsessed with the desire to destroy the Black Panther Party. Many of the brothers had been hunted down, imprisoned, or killed.

These external assaults were formidable. But there was a far more serious reason for the Party's difficulties, one that threatened its very *raison d'être:* the Party was heading down the road to reactionary suicide. Under the influence of Eldridge Cleaver, it had lost sight of its initial purpose and become caught up in irrelevant causes. Estranged from Black people who could not relate to it, the Black Panther Party had defected from the community.

The Party was born in a particular time and place. It came into being with a call for self-defense against the police who patrolled our communities and brutalized us with impunity. Until then, there had been little resistance to the occupiers. We sought to provide a counterforce, a positive image of strong and unafraid Black men in the community. The emphasis on weapons was a necessary phase in our evolution, based on Frantz Fanon's contention that the people have to be shown that the colonizers and their agents—the police—are not bulletproof. We saw this action as a bold step in making our program known and raising the consciousness of the people.

But we soon discovered that weapons and uniforms set us apart from the community. We were looked upon as an ad hoc military group, acting outside the community fabric and too radical to be a part of it. Perhaps some of our tactics at the time were extreme; perhaps we placed too much emphasis on military action. We saw ourselves as the revolutionary "vanguard" and did not fully understand then that only the people can create the revolution. At any rate, for two or three years, our image in the community was intimidating. The people misunderstood us and did not follow our lead in picking up the gun. At the time, there was no clear solution to this dilemma. We were a young revolutionary group seeking answers and ways to alleviate racism. We had chosen to confront an evil head on and within the limits of the law. But perhaps our military strategy was too much of "a great leap forward."

Nonetheless, I believe that the Black Panther approach in 1966 and 1967 was basically a good and necessary phase. Our military actions called attention to our program and our plans for the people. Our strategy brought us dedicated members, and it gained the respect of the struggling peoples of the Third World. Most important, it raised the consciousness of Black and white citizens about the relationship between police and minorities in this country. It is difficult to realize now how much police relations with the Black community have changed in six short years. Our communities are still not free from brutal incidents and corruption, but it is nonetheless true that police departments have become more sensitive to the problems of urban minorities. Today, it is the rare police commissioner who has not tried to establish some form of public relations between police and Blacks. The average citizen, too, has a greater awareness of police abuses that once were systematically overlooked. This advance in consciousness is due in large part to our military phase. Ho Chi Minh said that military tactics made public for military reasons are unsound, while military tactics made public for political reasons are perfectly correct. We have done as he said. Our military strategies are now known for political reasons.

But revolution is not an action; it is a process. Times change, and policies of the past are not necessarily effective in the present. Our military strategies were not frozen. As conditions changed, so did our tactics. Patrolling the community was only one step in our ten-point program and had never been regarded as the sole community endeavor of the Black Panther Party. As a matter of fact, the right to bear arms for protection appeared near the end of our program, as Point 7, and came only after those demands we considered far more urgent—freedom, employment, education, and housing. Our community programs— now called survival programs—were of great importance from the beginning; we had always planned to become involved in Black people's daily struggle for survival and sought only the means to serve the community's needs.

But the Party was sabotaged from within and without. For years the Establishment media presented a sensational picture of us, emphasizing violence and weapons. Colossal events like Sacramento, the *Ramparts* confrontation with the police, the shoot-out of April 6, 1968, were distorted and their significance never understood or analyzed. Furthermore, our ten-point program was ignored and our plans for survival overlooked. The Black Panthers were identified with the gun.

Eldridge Cleaver identified with other negative aspects of the Party. It is not coincidence that he joined the Party only after the *Ramparts* confrontation. What appealed to him were force, firepower, and the intense moment when combatants stood at the brink of death. *For him this was the revolution.* Eldridge's ideology was based on the rhetoric of violence; his speeches abounded in either/or absolutes, like "Either pick up the gun or remain a sniveling coward." He would not support the survival programs, refusing to see that they were a necessary part of the revolutionary process, a means of bringing the people closer to the transformation of society. He believed this transformation could take place only through violence, by picking up the gun and storming the barricades, and his obsessive belief alienated him more and more from the community. By refusing to abandon the position of destruction and despair, he underestimated the enemy and took on the role of the reactionary suicide.

Long before Eldridge's actual defection from the Party he had taken the first steps of his journey into spiritual exile by failing to identify with the people. He shunned the political intimacy that human beings demand of their leaders. When he fled the country, his exile became a physical reality. Eldridge had cut himself off from the revolutionary's greatest source of strength—unity with the people, a shared sense of purpose and ideals. His flight was a suicidal gesture, and his continuing exile in Algeria is a symbol of his defection from the community on all levels—geographical, psychological, and spiritual.

From a dialectical point of view, something positive has arisen out of Eldridge's defection. While he and his followers still identify with aspects of the Party that once alienated us from the community, the Party has moved in a different direction. He has taken the media's image squarely upon his own shoulders. We are glad to be free of the burden. What little we lost in credibility we have gained in a wider acceptance of the Party by the community. We have reached a more advanced state. There has been a qualitative leap forward, a growth in consciousness.

Camus wrote that the revolutionary's "real generosity toward the future lies in giving all to the present." This, he says, grows out of an intense love for the earth, for our brothers, for justice. The Black Panther Party embraces this principle. By giving all to the present we reject fear, despair, and defeat. We work to repair the breaches of the past. We strive to carry out the revolutionary principle of transformation, and through long struggle, in Camus's words, "to remake the soul of our time."

EPILOGUE

I Am We

There is an old African saying, "I am we." If you met an African in ancient times and asked him who he was, he would reply, "I am we." This is revolutionary suicide: I, we, all of us are the one and the multitude.

So many of my comrades are gone now. Some tight partners, crime partners, and brothers off the block are begging on the street. Others are in asylum, penitentiary, or grave. They are all suicides of one kind or another who had the sensitivity and tragic imagination to see the oppression. Some overcame: they are the revolutionary suicides. Others were reactionary suicides who either overestimated or underestimated the enemy, but in any case were powerless to change their conception of the oppressor.

The difference lies in hope and desire. By hoping and desiring, the revolutionary suicide chooses life; he is, in the words of Nietszche, "an arrow of longing for another shore." Both suicides despise tyranny, but the revolutionary is both a great despiser and a great adorer who longs for another shore. The reactionary suicide must learn, as his brother the revolutionary has learned, that the desert is not a circle. It is a spiral. When we have passed through the desert, nothing will be the same.

You cannot bare your throat to the murderer. As George Jackson said, you must defend yourself and take the dragon position as in karate and make the front kick and the back kick when you are surrounded. You do not beg because your enemy comes with the butcher knife in one hand and the hatchet in the other. "He will not become a Buddhist overnight."

The Preacher said that the wise man and the fool have the same end; they go to the grave as a dog. Who sends us to the grave? The unknowable, the force that dictates to all classes, all territories, all ideologies; he is death, the Big Boss. An ambitious man seeks to dethrone the Big Boss, to free himself, to control when and how he will go to the grave.

There is another illuminating story of the wise man and the fool, found in Mao's *Little Red Book:* A foolish old man went to North Mountain and began to dig; a wise old man passed by and said, "Why do you dig, foolish old man? Do you not know that you cannot move the mountain with a little shovel?" But the foolish old man answered resolutely, "While the mountain cannot get any higher, it will get lower with each shovelful. When I pass on, my sons and his sons and his son's sons will go on making the mountain lower. Why can't we move the mountain?" And the foolish old man kept digging, and the generations that followed after him, and the wise old man looked on in disgust. But the resoluteness and the spirit of the generations that followed the foolish old man touched God's heart, and God sent two angels who put the mountain on their backs and moved the mountain.

This is the story Mao told. When he spoke of God he meant the six hundred million who had helped him to move imperialism and bourgeois thinking, the two great mountains.

The reactionary suicide is "wise," and the revolutionary suicide is a "fool," a fool for the revolution in the way that Paul meant when he spoke of being "a fool for Christ." That foolishness can move the mountain of oppression; it is our great leap and our commitment to the dead and the unborn.

We will touch God's heart; we will touch the people's heart, and together we will move the mountain.